MUST LOVE TREES

an unconventional guide

TOBIN MITNICK

ROCK
POINT

Brimming with creative inspiration, how-to projects, and useful information to enrich your everyday life, quarto.com is a favorite destination for those pursuing their interests and passions.

Inspiring | Educating | Creating | Entertaining

First published in 2023 by Rock Point,
an imprint of The Quarto Group,
142 West 36th Street, 4th Floor, New York, NY 10018, USA
T (212) 779-4972 F (212) 779-6058 www.Quarto.com

Rock Point titles are also available at discount for retail, wholesale, promotional, and bulk purchase. For details, contact the Special Sales Manager by email at specialsales@quarto.com or by mail at The Quarto Group, Attn: Special Sales Manager, 100 Cummings Center Suite 265D, Beverly, MA 01915 USA.

10 9 8 7 6 5 4 3 2 1

ISBN: 978-1-63106-924-6

Publisher: Rage Kindelsperger
Creative Director: Laura Drew
Editorial Director: Erin Canning
Managing Editor: Cara Donaldson
Editor: Keyla Pizarro-Hernández
Cover Design: Laura Drew
Cover and Interior Illustrations: Trey Conrad
Interior Design: Evelin Kasikov

Printed in China

Library of Congress Cataloging-in-Publication Data

Names Mitnick, Tobin, author.
Title Must love trees an unconventional guide Tobin Mitnick.
Description New York, NY Rock Point, 2023. Includes bibliographical references. Summary Must Love Trees is a blend of engaging stories and observations, beautiful drawings, and interesting scientific trivia, featuring 100 types of trees--Provided by publisher.
Identifiers LCCN 2022040603 (print) LCCN 2022040604 (ebook) ISBN 9781631069246 (hardcover) ISBN 9780760380314 (ebook)
Subjects LCSH Trees--North America--Popular works Trees--North America--Guidebooks Trees--Humor
Classification LCC QK475 .M58 2023 (print) LCC QK475 (ebook) DDC 582.16097--dc23eng20221018
LC record available at httpslccn.loc.gov2022040603
LC ebook record available at httpslccn.loc.gov2022040604

This book provides general information on various widely known and widely accepted self-help concepts that tend to evoke feelings of strength and confidence. However, it should not be relied upon as recommending or promoting any specific diagnosis or method of treatment for a particular condition, and it is not intended as a substitute for medical advice or for direct diagnosis and treatment of a medical condition by a qualified physician. Readers who have questions about a particular condition, possible treatments for that condition, or possible reactions from the condition or its treatment should consult a physician or other qualified healthcare professional.

MIX
Paper from responsible sources
FSC® C016973

FOR AMANDA, LUCY, AND SAPLING #2

"It's almost as if I were seeing these trees for the
first time in my life . . . What beautiful trees they are!
And how beautiful the life around them ought to be."

— Anton Chekhov, *Three Sisters* (1900)

Part III

Introduction

What You Can Expect from This Book

If I do believe in God or some kind of God, which seems to change on a whim these days, I'd imagine that the book I've written tells me the following: the Godhead spends as much time marveling in their creation as they do cracking jokes about it.

When I started writing this book in late 2021, I had to take a hard look at my strengths and weaknesses when it came to my favorite subject: trees.

My weaknesses: no degree in dendrology or a related field, no practical work experience with trees, no research experience, no science-writing background, no personal experience with environmentalist groups or climate change activism. Nothing, in fact, that could be considered expertise in the field of trees whatsoever.

My strengths: I loved trees, I thought about them all the time, and I had somewhat popular social media accounts.

I decided to lean into the latter; because if there's one thing I *am* an expert in, it is what I, Tobin Mitnick, think about trees. It also seemed like a good opportunity to expand my thoughts beyond 38-second pine cone reviews.

My social media presence @JewsLoveTrees comes from a lifelong fascination with the natural world, and trees in particular, combined with a dire need to focus my energy during the early days of the pandemic. It also made sense

to pair it with who I am as a Jew: an inheritor of a tradition famous for its shameless tree love.

Rather than seeing my lack of conventional qualifications as a liability, I decided to understand it as an asset. Sure, that sounds like the reasoning of a garden-variety con man, but hear me out . . . As an enthusiast writing about my subjective experience, I'm not necessarily bound to the same rules that a researcher or a committed nonfiction writer might be. So, while this book sacrifices microscopic leaf descriptions, painstakingly researched ideas, and helpful solutions for our collective future at the time when we need them most, it makes room for opinions, fancies, humor, tangents, dramatizations, anthropomorphoses, personal reflections, and a variety of other tree experiences. Nature writing is a big genre, after all.

That's why I refer to this guide as "unconventional"—not because it stands in opposition to works of research or science, but because it acts as a complement to them in the overarching human effort to catalog our interactions with the natural world.

This guide is divided into three parts: Part one discusses my personal interactions with trees and my thoughts about them. This is where I place no limits on my wonder and whimsy. Part two describes the botany, biology, and ecology of trees. This is where I abide by the rules of science. But the gloves come off again in part three, where I ask and answer an important question about one hundred of the most treasured North American trees: Who would they be if they all attended high school together? You'll also find a slightly cheeky glossary at the end of this book (pages 210 to 212), so you can reference any scientific terms used throughout it.

Lastly, whenever I mention a tree, I will also note its scientific name in parentheses. If things still seem unclear, I've provided a chart below of what you can expect in a conventional tree guide in contrast with this unconventional one.

WILL I FIND . . .	A CONVENTIONAL TREE GUIDE	THIS UNCONVENTIONAL TREE GUIDE
Tree IDs using disciplined scientific taxonomy?	Yes	I certainly tried
Trees as characters in a high school?	No	Yes
Phrases like "celestial sentinels in a dance of sublime kinship"?	Yes, used earnestly	Yes, used facetiously
A history of my personal relationship with trees?	No	Oh yes
My personal opinions and grievances?	No	Yes, in spades
Advice on applying tree metaphors in your own life?	Probably not	Yes
Dispatches from a universe where trees are at the center of pop culture?	No	Yes
A complete examination of the Chris Pine (*Pinus crisus*)?	No	Yes, get excited
Botanical terms that give you nightmarish flashbacks to seventh-grade science?	Yes	Only when necessary
A bonsai section?	Maybe?	Of course!
Profanity?	No	Eight or ten "s-words," four or five "a-words," some "damns" and "craps"
Essays about tiny people who live in pine cones?	No	Great idea—adding that now

An Imagined Dialogue with Methuselah, the Oldest (?) Tree in the World

Tobin Mitnick treks the bare, rocky soils of the Methuselah Grove in the White Mountains of California. He suddenly stops, releasing a deep breath, spying a twisted, begnarled ancient Great Basin bristlecone pine. He walks up to it.

‹‹‹

 TOBIN: Hey, legend.

No response.

 TOBIN: Wanted to see how you were holding up since the news broke.

No response.

 TOBIN: Oof, that bad, huh?

He lays a hand on the bristlecone. Suddenly, the tree seems to shake and convulse, and a river of old needles and spiky pine cones fall from its spare crown like tears.

 METHUSELAH: (*sobbing*) You know, a lot of people—a lot—wish they knew exactly where I'm located so that they could come up here and point me out and say that I'm the oldest tree in the world in the hopes that it'll get them laid—

 TOBIN: Shh, I know . . . I know . . .

 METHUSELAH: That's why my location is a secret! Because I don't exactly feel like having my hard-earned, hard-wrought growth rings—all five thousand of them—

 TOBIN: Shh, Methuselah, shh . . .

METHUSELAH: —massaged by a bunch of clowns that just *like old stuff!* Do they know about my ability to compartmentalize poor tissue? My symbiotic relationship with Clark's nutcracker? My secret to keeping needles fresh and flirty even after forty years of gale-force winds? God, I'm so much more than just the world's oldest tree! And now I'm not even that, because a Fitzroya tree—*a friggin' Fitzroya*—has been found to be five hundred years older than I am!

 TOBIN: Come on, that finding's not yet peer-reviewed—

 METHUSELAH: Oh, shut up. You know it's true. I had one thing going for me: age. Now I don't even have that. I'm done. Obsolete. Now they'll just tell everyone where I am willy-nilly because protecting me doesn't matter anymore. And people will come and stomp all over my roots and carve their stupid initials into my trunk, and laugh and say things like, "Yup, that's Methuselah, who used to be the oldest tree in the world."

Methuselah breaks down into hysterical sobbing.

 TOBIN: Hey, hey, come on . . . people don't love you because you are the oldest tree in the world—

 METHUSELAH: *Were . . .*

 TOBIN: Were, whatever. I'm pretty sure everyone knows that there's always going to be an older tree out there somewhere. Older than that knucklehead Fitzroya, even. Some people never even believed *you* were the oldest.

 METHUSELAH: (*hurt*) . . . what?

 TOBIN: Oh, sure . . . some people think that it's Old Tjikko, a Norway spruce in Sweden, whose root system has been carbon-dated to nearly ten thousand years, but it keeps regenerating trunks every five hundred years or so, clonally. Or Pando, a glorious quaking aspen colony in Utah whose marvelous golds and greens have been sharing and suckering off the same root system for perhaps fifty thousand years—

METHUSELAH: (*blubbering*) Friggin' Pando.

 TOBIN: Do you see what I mean? People don't love you simply because you're the "world's oldest tree." They love you because you're *proof*.

The tears stop.

 METHUSELAH: . . . proof?

 TOBIN: Yes, my old friend. They drive four hours up here, they look for that one park ranger with a glint in her eye, and they work up the courage to ask, "Um, excuse me, but is there any way you could point me towards, uh, Methuselah?" All this in the hopes that they won't be scolded for asking the general location of a secret, sacred old tree so that they can feel the presence of an unfailing history, where a single life has continued unabated despite the war and disease and heartache among mankind. *Proof* that hoping for tomorrow is not a fool's errand.

A beat.

 METHUSELAH: What are you smokin', dude?

 TOBIN: Don't make jokes. Look at me, *I'm* not making jokes right now. Listen, I want you to know one thing: you're a good tree. One day, I will be old, like you are now. Well, not quite like you. But when I feel my time coming to a close, there's nowhere I'd rather be than under a very old, very good tree like you.

‹‹‹

Tobin embraces Methuselah. Methuselah recoils slightly, surprised.
Lights down.

Part I

MY PERSONAL EXPERIENCE WITH TREES AND THOUGHTS DERIVED THEREOF

I grew up in rural Pennsylvania, where I couldn't have been less interested in the Norway spruce and eastern hemlock trees out my window or the magnolia and apple trees that bisected my view of our ancient barn. But our farmhouse kitchen, which had a bay window overlooking our yard, was always filled with the oversized cones of the California pines—the lengthy sugar pine cone, the dangerous coulter pine cone, the gentle Jeffrey pine cone, all mementos from my father's trips out west. The progenitors of these strange objects captivated my imagination far more than the ones directly outside.

So I grew up like so many people do, believing California to be the land of all the cool stuff that I didn't have on the East Coast. But by the time I actually moved there in 2015, I was far more concerned with trying to get my failing acting career off the ground than seeking out the great wonders of the arboreal world.

Then, years ago, following a low point in my life, I began running. That forced me to go outside a lot more, and I found that all my old fascinations were popping up in ways that sparked my curiosity and—dare I say it—*joy*.

Since then, time has been a blur. A blur of books and bonsai and giant sequoias and mulberry leaves and finding that there are a great many people in the world who are strongly attracted to the presence of trees for reasons that they can't decipher. This ineffable bewitchery, I think, is the most joyous thing about loving trees: every explanation for it, from woo-woo to woodwork, always fails to grasp the charming enormity of it.

For myself, I don't have a good "why" to offer. But if I had to give an answer, it would be that, as I get older, trees make me feel younger. Not only because of their comparatively superior lifespans, but also because of their bottomless resources of wonder. I didn't enjoy feeling like a child when I was a child, but now that I'm an adult, I'm quite into it.

I often wonder what I was doing many years ago, when I would walk down the same city blocks or country paths that I walk down now. Is it possible that I was *not* looking at the trees?

I certainly do now.

Chapter 1

My Everyday Tree-Sperience

Here I invite you into the recesses of my mind. For most people, this is the home of the dirtiest, most depraved aspects of their hidden desires. But for me, this is where you will find trees.

I am going to put on my Serious Cap for a moment.

(*A note about the Serious Cap: it's fashioned from birch bark. Trés chic.*)

Real talk: I am barely qualified enough to talk about trees, and I am certainly not qualified enough to talk about mental health or the lack thereof. And I say this having watched nearly half of *Monk*'s eight brilliant seasons.

But I do have these things called "personal anecdotes" that I'm going to draw upon presently. Perhaps you will be able to relate. Perhaps you won't. In that case, you have my permission to skip ahead.

Here goes:

Like our brilliant TV detective friend Adrian Monk, I deal with an adorable little thing called obsessive-compulsive disorder (OCD). But unlike his majesty Monk, I don't have an obsession with cleanliness,

or phobias of heights and ladybugs, which lead to particular rituals meant to dispel the anxiety associated with the obsession.

My obsessions are far more embarrassing, and they generally revolve around paranoia concerning neurodegenerative disorders. Way less sexy than ladybugs, I know. When I was in my darkest place in March, April, and May of 2019, I filled up journals with my delusional thoughts and my vital statistics, believing them to be crucial records of my body's decline. When I read the journals now, it's clear that they are conspiracy theory gibberish, like an enormous whiteboard featuring dissonant elements laboriously connected by red string. All of this was conducted in an effort to convince myself of what I *felt* to be true: that I was dying.

Sleep was off the table, fear and sweat and high heart rate were the name of the day, and of course, there were the breakdowns. Breakdowns for breakfast, lunch, and dinner, all served with a side of hysterical sobbing. Can you imagine? The only thoughts I had were poisonous, and I had no way to escape from them. Sometimes I think about what it had been like for my wife at this particular time. Her response when I ask her now: "Not great, Tobes."

I really wish this is where I could say, "And then I discovered trees." But nah. I had loved trees for many years, and the way I "unstuck" myself from this episode was by adhering to the world's most boring prescription of community and family support, therapy, medication, and exercise. I also wrote a one-man show about it, but we don't have to get into that.

(*TOBINCON*: "Pick of the Fringe," "Producer's Award" at the 2019 Hollywood Fringe Festival, no big deal.)

No, having a personal relationship with trees wasn't some cure-all for the woes of my life. But they are a support mechanism. Mental health specialists like to say that you can have either "ego-syntonic" obsessions—meaning obsessions that you enjoy, that enrich your life, that you understand to be an essential part of who you are—or "ego-dystonic" ones—the baddies that interrupt your life and tear it apart.

I understand the origins of my ego-syntonic obsessions as little as I understand my ego-dystonic ones, but I do know that each respective camp is internally related and always has been. My ego-dystonic obsessions are about being devoured—by disease, by parasites, by zombies, by sharks, you name it.

But my ego-syntonic obsessions stretch outwards into nature and into the past: to fossils and minerals, to meteorology and medieval history, to sharks (it's complicated). And, ultimately, to trees.

The special thing about trees is that they have the ability to fill up my entire brain—with lore, with biology, with taxonomy, with adventurous pursuit—in such an all-encompassing way that I can keep the pie chart full enough of positive obsession at any given moment in order not to allow entry to any of the ruminations that get me in trouble.

That's the very non-clinical way that I think of my brain: as a pie chart. And trees are the filling.

Thank you, trees.

Welcome to My Tree Walk, and I'm Sorry

This is just a sample of what it's like to be inside my head on my morning walk. This tree walk traverses my neighborhood in Los Angeles, known as The Hollywood Dell, and takes me exactly twenty-two minutes if I'm feeling spiffy or twenty-six minutes if I drank more than half a beer the night before.

STOP 1

Boom, barely 50 feet (15 m) out of the gate and we catch one of the finest specimens of blue Atlas cedar (*Cedrus atlantica*) in all of Los Angeles. I've often stood below this tree to admire its glorious bunches of blue-needle rosettes, only to be shouted at by my golf-club-wielding neighbor for trespassing. He occasionally exhibits his naturalistic side with a white ash Louisville Slugger.

STOP 2

After another 200 feet (61 m), I love pausing below a remarkable and out-of-place specimen of Colorado piñon pine (*Pinus edulis*). It's nearly 300 miles (483 km) from its native range and one of only a handful in Los Angeles County. It was planted by a magical Norwegian couple who brought various conifers to the neighborhood in the early '80s, then disappeared without a trace. How do I know this? Because I left a note in my neighbor's mailbox inquiring about it and they returned an answer by email. I've done this a few times with a few different trees, and folks are usually willing to oblige. It's lovely!

STOP 3

But directly across the street is an invisible tragedy. Here, before it was cut down ahead of its time like a leafy James Dean and had its trunk ground into the earth to make way for an infinitely less-interesting variety of fruit tree, grew a fabulous sweetgum (*Liquidambar styraciflua*). This species, in addition to being one of the few that gets full color in LA, often makes me think of the kickball yard in elementary school, when I would spend whole recesses reaching for its spiny seedballs.

STOP 4

After another 200 yards (183 m), I reach a small shrub that owes much of its growth to the natural fertilizer of my dog. It's been rewarding to watch it grow.

STOP 5

After a half-mile (805 m), we arrive at the village mansion, bedecked with multi-colored bougainvillea. You may suggest that bougainvillea is simply a vine. You would be wrong. Sorry, I have a published book now, so what I say goes. Therefore, I proclaim it, bougainvillea species are trees. And they're spectacular.

STOP 6

Right as we close the large loop that occupies the second half of my tree walk, we run into a weeping fig (*Ficus benjamina*) trio. This group of heavily buttressed, voluptuous darlings are known to give local visitors the hallie-dallies with their oh-so-smooth bark and have a penchant for driving contractors crazy with their concrete-busting tropical roots. I wink, I nod, I trod on. Tree-ing is not for the faint of heart, you see.

STOP 7

Finally, as we careen toward my front door with increasing exuberance having borne witness to Mother Nature's signature icons, we arrive at a blue Atlas cedar. You may notice that this is the same blue Atlas cedar from the beginning of our journey. But you know the saying: "a tree from the side is a tree renewed." No? Well, that's because I just made it up. I like doing that.

"Why Are You Against Houseplants?": An Explanation and a Diatribe

You know, I get this question a lot. And it comes in various forms: "Why do you hate Monsteras?" "Why can't I find any advice on your Instagram about watering my plants?" and, from the creeps, "It looks like your house doesn't have any houseplants—could I buy you some ;-)?"

First off, creep, I do not need your gifts. That's what nanas are for.

Second, the answer to all of these questions asking if I'm against houseplants is: you bet!

Non-woody plants inside of the house infuriate me. They're a bunch of tickly miscreants that get all dingly-dangly in suspended baskets and overflow into your favorite rare copy of *Dracula*. If you could not tell, I am speaking from personal experience.

I still have a nightmarish memory from Passover 1994, when I was stuck at the Seder table between my grandfather Izzy and my perfect older brother Ethan (see page 24). I had just finished bungling the Four Questions, when, suddenly, an enormous tarantula began to walk down my back! But, stuck as I was, I could only fall backwards in spasms of panic. I landed smack-dab on a tiny cactus that adorned the windowsill behind me. When I came to, I realized that, hmm, there was *no arachnid in sight*. Instead, it was a dingly-dangly *houseplant* that had tickled me so, simulating the *feeling* of a tarantula.

I spent the rest of that evening in tears, nursing and plucking my injury up in my room and envious of all the fun everyone was having downstairs; Grandpa Izzy had brought his favorite Haggadah for the service— 192 pages of 8-point Arial font. *And I missed it.*

Right then and there, with God and Moses as my witnesses, I made a promise to myself that I would never again abide a non-lignified plant inside my house. To this day, I have kept this promise. Well, *I* have. My wife has other thoughts.

Does that answer your question? Or would you like me to recount this night of vertigo-inducing terror to you again?

Hiking Theory: My Personal Thoughts

Hiking is divisive. Even more divisive than figuring out who has to sit next to Uncle-did-you-read-about-what-they're-putting-in-pudding-now-Raymond at Thanksgiving.

Why is hiking so terribly divisive? Because each person has a different idea of what it is.

When I was young, I was what they call an "inside" kid. Sure, I thought that trees, sharks, and minerals were all very cool to look at, but I would prefer to look at them from the comfort of my own home, thank you very much. Ergo, my fascination with pine cones and fossilized shark teeth—they're all quite suited for indoor examination.

In those days, the phrases "hiking," "going on a hike," and even the archaic "hikery" made me feel like I had done something bad. Whenever the order came down from my older siblings, camp counselors, or a friend's overenthusiastic parent that we were to "hike" that day, I felt that I was to be punished by being made physically exhausted, thirsty, and mosquito-bitten for no particular reason. Why couldn't we just enjoy natural objects in the places they were meant to be enjoyed, like in museums or in my basement?

For years, I carried this anxiety with me, even though I frequently found myself greatly enjoying parts of these forced excursions (you know, trees that were actually alive, a spontaneous discovery of a natural treasure, that kind of thing). But for the life of me, I could not figure out why the act of making yourself temporarily uncomfortable was all worth it.

It wasn't until I moved to California that I accidentally discovered the truth while on a walk with my dog, McFly, in Griffith Park. I noticed that McFly, in between wet poops, was pausing and sniffing every spot of pee, every novel plant, and every discarded sock as if it were the Northwest Passage itself.

"Oh," I thought. "Dogs *get it*."

They don't care about the *destination*. They're just *being*, man.

I soon tried this out for myself. I went alone—which I think is a crucial element of finding your comfort in the wilderness (although, of course, it can be dangerous— don't do what I did; go with a friend the first time) into Angeles National Forest at about 5,000 feet (1,524 m) for a three-hour . . . (*shivers*) . . . hike.

During this time, I couldn't have widened my radius of travel to more than 50 feet (15 m) from where I embarked. I found the skeletons of incense-cedars (*Calocedrus decurrens*), pine cones buried on the forest floor, and a variety of other curios that made me feel like a child cracking open a fabricated geode. And I was able to maintain this easy perambulation because there was no source of pressure to keep me *moving* anywhere against my will.

This discovery of a wonderful spot is what I first referred to as "locationizing." But that seemed so clinical. So I changed it to "diddle-doddle-doodling." But that didn't roll off the tongue as trippingly as I might have liked. So, I landed on "meandering," as in:

"Yesterday I went for a lovely meander down by the Old Gulch," or "Meandering is one of my favorite things to do in Sequoia National Park!"

This may remind you of John Muir's famous description of "sauntering." After all, Muir was also a "hiking" skeptic.

But I guarantee you that "meandering" makes "sauntering" look like the Daytona 500.

Meandering is borderline sedentary. From a bird's-eye view, I probably look like a vertical housefly on a horizontal windowpane. But it happens to be the exact pace at which I forget that time exists.

So, my friends, I encourage you to discover whatever pace or energy is required so that time can stop for *you*.

How angry I am that no one told me "hiking" can also be the opposite of hiking!

Trees I Love to Hate and Hate to Love

Being in love with trees is a complex business. Like a great love, one often finds oneself at the intersection of lust and resentment, yo-yoing back and forth between extremes, like a mere serf in service to his Lordship, the Great Outdoors. Such is the nature of Nature!

But I find that cognitive dissonance is one of the most compelling things about having a personal relationship with trees: one day you'll be in love with a certain tree, the next you won't give it a second thought. On Tuesday, you'll find the Callery pear (*Pyrus calleryana*) to be a disgusting and invasive bastardization of all that is good and holy. On Wednesday, you'll feel yourself hypnotically drawn to its lovely flowers like Ferdinand the Bull.

After many years of toggling back and forth on many, many trees (sometimes many, many times each), I've come to find that my feelings are rather stable yet contradictory concerning a special few. These are the trees that I revel in despising and also the ones whose intoxicating allure overwhelms my passionate hatred.

The following are my entries for each category.

Trees I Love to Hate

Sycamore (genus *Platanus*)

I figured I'd start off with a bang here and talk some serious smack on a tree that a lot of you probably love. Sycamores of various types—American, Arizonan, Californian—have been in my life for one reason or another since I was a very young sapling. I believe that I crashed into one when I lost control of the toboggan with my friend Isaac Kastenbaum (whose last name, incidentally, means "chestnut tree"). This was a commonplace event, as I have a well-known lack of athletic grace in winter sports. But here's the thing that drives me completely batty: outside, in my driveway, there is a beautiful 2021 Subaru Forester in forest green, which is the exact car I have wanted my entire life. And it is covered, *covered I say*, with a thick, almost impenetrable layer of pollen and bark dust from the lecherous California sycamore towering above it. And yes, I know I should probably move the car inside the garage, but here's the thing: the Forester craves the outdoors and that would be inhumane. Or something. Regardless, this seasonal disrespect towards my *hog* has turned me against the sycamore for good.

Italian cypress (*Cupressus sempervirens*)

These trees are, of course, native to Europe, and they're eminently familiar to anyone in Los Angeles by their thin, spire-like profile. My intense disgust regarding these trees is a simple reaction to their ubiquity in this godforsaken town, where their presence is meant to signify an "exoticness" only surpassed by those good-for-nothing palms (more on this later). Hate 'em!

Trees I Hate to Love

Italian stone pine (*Pinus pinea*)

In my budding days of tree obsession, I always found the stone pines nearest to me to be blasphemous among pines: they always looked to be on the brink of collapse—their trunks buckling under some invisible pressure—and their wide, rounded crowns simply unattractive to me as a mountain pine enthusiast longing for the spirit of Olympus! But then I came across pictures of stone pines in their native habitat, dotting the Mediterranean coastline like handsome centurions. More recently, I went for a run in Rome (shirtless, which is apparently illegal; Rome, I apologize), and saw how the trees' flattened tops complement the geography of the city. Suddenly, my aversion to them melted away. In my neighborhood, though? Bunch of Roman punks, if you ask me! (Rome and I are complicated.)

Black walnut (*Juglans nigra*)

Growing up in the woods of Pennsylvania, my dad struck a deal with my siblings and me: one-half cent for every green, stinky walnut husk that we picked up, tossed in a wheelbarrow, then threw deep into the forest where they could decompose far away from the house. It was quite possibly the worst five bucks you could make: nails green with walnut stink, nose running from molds untold, inevitable collision of foot and Labrador Retriever doo-doo. Yet even the words "black walnut" bring me back to a time in my life when the most important thing imaginable was to chuck as many walnuts into the woods as I could. Simpler times.

On Tree Huggability

The beautiful thing about placing your arms about a tree—aside from the exciting array of epithets hurled your way by the village philistines—is that it's a completely unmediated experience. Utter weirdos, including me, have been doing this for millennia. Just a couple of life forms getting real, utterly unashamed by anyone seeing them do so. The best tree hugs remind you of a lovely time in your life or a particularly cozy person, or the fact that you're holding a gargantuan life form that doesn't mind.

Unless it's a floss-silk tree (*Ceiba speciosa*). Then they mind. Oh, do they mind!

Hugging is a subject that I've long associated with inner conflict. As a white guy raised in Clintonian America, I was brought up with the idea that it's cool to hug, man, but not too much, you know? Best to throw a pat in there to let the other person know that you don't like them too much, and that it was super weird that you both just hugged like that, whoa!

Only later on did I discover that this approach was flawed, to say the least. And thus, I began my "March Across the Forest," hugging every lignin-lined ambassador I could find. These were long, deep tree hugs. The kind of hugs that I hoped I could one day have with my fellow human beings. You see, unlike people, trees don't judge.

Unless it's a honey locust (*Gleditsia triacanthos*). Then they judge. And you bleed.

The point is, I'm not your average tree hugger. I've done it *a lot.* And wouldn't you know it, I've got a few opinions that I'd like to share on the matter.

Now, a lot of trustafarians would be willing to fly coach for the information that I'm about to give you. But before I do, let me tell you a little bit about the criteria I've used to grade these trees on huggability.

What do I look for in a tree hug? Resin that isn't too sticky. Bark that isn't too sharp or sheddy. A pleasant aroma. A general lack of thorns. Excessive girth isn't a big negative because you can always find a tree of the same species that's a bit narrower, and therefore, open to a big ol' coze fest. And, finally, it goes without saying, a certain *je ne sais quoi*. But, please, before you engage any tree, do your due diligence and make sure you aren't going to grab a wasp's nest or a broken bunch of splinters that used to be a branch.

Okay, let's get down to business and snuggle-wuggle it up.

TREE	HUG-SPERIENCE	PERSON IT MIGHT REMIND YOU OF	GRADE
Northern red oak (*Quercus rubra*)	A preposterously middling hug-sperience. Oaks are marvelous for many reasons, but the rough, gray and indifferent bark of a mature oak overrides its typically perfect diameter.	Your painfully anxious father-in-law	C
Jeffrey pine (*Pinus jeffreyi*)	"Fortune smiles upon the man who hugs a Jeffrey!" This is especially true in the late summer, when the normal heptane in its pitch creates a deep aroma of vanilla and pineapple. Sublime, rare, meaningful.	Your ninth-grade crush	A
Floss-silk tree (*Ceiba speciosa*)	Ouchie! One may be ensnared by the lure of the Floss-Silk's bright green bark (the trunk can photosynthesize! That would be like if your torso could . . . photosynthesize!), but upon further inspection, you would see the thorny barbs of a secretive enemy.	Jon Snow when he kills Daenerys Targaryen (*GOT* spoiler!)	D-
Grandidier's baobab (*Adansonia grandidieri*)	I'll admit I've never had the pleasure of traveling to Madagascar, where Grandidier's baobab grows endemically, but there's something hilarious about trying to embrace the trunk of a tree that keeps expanding and contracting based on its water content.	Your pal at the Halloween party dressed like a Whoopie Cushion	B (presumably)
American sycamore (*Platanus occidentalis*)	As I write these words, I am staring unenthused at the sycamore overhanging my house, and I'm reminded of the bark and dust that fills my nostrils every time I have to clean my gutters. And of my dust-covered Subaru. Thanks, but no thanks on the cuddle fest there, ace.	Your frenemy that just came back from a "rockin' week-long climbing trip," where there was "no running water, but I didn't even care because it was so dope."	D+
Incense-cedar (*Calocedrus decurrens*)	You'll get a whiff of Number 2 (no not that one, you toilet-brain! Pencils!) as this fella is often felled to make them. But damned if that bark doesn't look like it was carved from an extra-jumbo Cadbury bar.	Your typical hot nerd	A-
Coast redwood (*Sequoia sempervirens*)	A fire-resistant shmoople fest. A cozy-wozy, fibrous squeezy-weezy. A soft and squishy clasp of croompy-woompy wigglewuggles.	Nana	A+
Honey locust (*Gleditsia triacanthos*)	A series of sharp barbs that pierce your flesh, stopping your heart, killing your life.	Michael Myers, famed slasher of cinema	F

The Ethan Tree, or Seeing Tree Metaphors in Your Own Life

I love my older brother.

That's something you typically say about someone before you trash them mercilessly. But I'm not going to tear Ethan apart here, because, like I said, I love him very much and we love to hang out. But I do feel deep-seated bitterness towards him. And I suppose you could call that "ill-will."

Why? Well, there's a perfect metaphor in the tree world for our relationship: the two species of Douglas-fir.

The first species of Douglas-fir is that of the famous common Douglas-fir (*Pseudotsuga menziesii*), which represents Ethan. The second species is the lesser-known bigcone Douglas-fir (*Pseudotsuga macrocarpa*). This tree represents me. Let's take a closer look.

The common Douglas-fir is an enormously popular tree. It occupies living rooms at the holidays, provides the most timber of any tree in North America, and even holds a few disputed height records from the pre-deforested Northwest, rumored to be above 400 feet (122 m).

Now here's something: Did you know that when Ethan was crowned Homecoming King in his senior year of high school, the school spontaneously threw him a party immediately afterwards? Reminds me of the effortless charisma of the common Douglas-fir.

I threw a party once. I got dumped at it.

No, my personal brand is closer to that of the bigcone Douglas-fir, which is famous only for its weirdly big cones. In my case, these could be my enormous eyebrows, which were once labeled as "interesting" by a compassionate classmate in seventh grade.

In short, the bigcone Douglas-fir lives a stunted, laughable life in the mountains of California, while its perfect older brother maintains multiple graduate degrees and a successful small business—I mean, is a wonderful hiking mainstay in the Pacific Northwest.

(Now, Ethan, if you are reading this, please understand that I would never resort to fisticuffs or even interpersonal insults in order to express my white-hot contempt of you and your life. So, instead, I've found a readymade relationship between my friends the trees, and I'm exploiting that instead. You're welcome.)

So, dear reader, if you're ever thinking of doing something drastic or saying something you might regret in the future when dealing with a loved one you resent, please consider employing a helpful tree metaphor instead. This can be enormously therapeutic and serve to launder your rage effectively. Here are a few tree metaphors that I'm not currently using but that you may find applicable to your own life:

The Bennifer

For many years, the dawn redwood (*Metasequoia glyptostroboides*) was thought to be extinct. But it was then discovered growing in a pure stand in rural China in the 1940s. It's since become one of the most popular ornamental trees around. Use this metaphor to describe a long-lost lover who has recently made a comeback in your life, just like our pals Jen and Ben.

The Coworker Who Always Takes Credit for Your Work

One of the most popular lies in America is that the ponderosa pine (*Pinus ponderosa*) has bark that smells of pineapple and vanilla, which makes for a transcendent olfactory experience for the lucky sniffmeister. This is actually the work of Jeffrey pine (*Pinus jeffreyi*), ponderosa's anatomically similar cousin that manufactures normal heptane in its pitch.

More on this in the next section. Cast yourself as a hard-working Jeffrey against a scheming ponderosa in a grievance-filled metaphor tailor-made for the office.

A Soulmate Just Out of Reach

It is said that Rocky Mountain juniper (*Juniperus scopulorum*) and eastern red cedar (*Juniperus virginiana*) are nearly identical species, yet their vast ranges never overlap. Pick either the juniper or the red cedar, and feel what longing truly is.

UNPOPULAR TREE OPINION: The Jeffrey Pine is Superior to the Ponderosa Pine

I'd like to kick off "Unpopular Tree Opinions" with something light, à la Pauline Kael on *It's a Wonderful Life*, simply to provoke you all. Something to let you all know that I don't mind courting tree controversy. So here goes.

The ponderosa pine (*Pinus ponderosa*) needs little introduction: it's the most widespread pine in the continental United States, with several subspecies that reinforce its institutional grandeur. Without googling it, and without consulting any of the six reference books splayed out before me, I can tick off four or five pop cultural references of this tree, including Matthew McConaughey's construction of his boyhood treehouse. Pop culture: a thing that trees are not normally a part of. What I'm trying to say is that the ponderosa pine does not need a PR agent.

You know what tree does? The infinitely superior Jeffrey pine (*Pinus jeffreyi*).

Let's delete the entire mythos of the ponderosa for a second. Let's wipe away its legendary status as a Civil War-era tree that powered the Union, its fame as the state tree of Montana, and even its place in the hearts of millions of Americans who just really love pine trees, of which the ponderosa happens to be the platonic form.

Do I sound like the living embodiment of that "well, actually" guy from your first semester freshman seminar? Well, friend, joke's on you, because I can back it up!

You with me? Great. Because now we're going to put two trees into the ring that are quite similar. Both the ponderosa and the Jeffrey are yellow pines, meaning they have tougher wood and bundles of needles in threes, and they occasionally overlap each other's range in the mountains of California (Jeffrey's range is much smaller, hence its poor PR).

But only one of these trees gives off a life-changing, soul-stirring, olfactory treasure chest of vanilla, pineapple, and butterscotch when you stick your nose between its purple-brown ridges: the Jeffrey.

Insanely awesome researchers Tom Chester and Jane Strong have found that 70 percent of all Jeffrey pines have that distinctive odor that expands your mind (caused by heptanes in the sap), while a mere 10 percent of ponderosas do (ponderosas contain terpenes, which often smell like turpentine).

So, while you're busy ticking off the accomplishments of the *oh-so-great* ponderosa pine tree, you can go ahead and add "noted plagiarist" to the mix, because it seems that it's quite intent on claiming the crown jewel of the Jeffrey as its own.

I'd like to throw in an additional few facts about the Jeffrey pine: there's a good case that Jeffrey pines can attain greater age than ponderosas (which have been known to reach one thousand years old) owing to the Jeffrey pine's higher elevations and slower growth patterns. And let me not neglect their visual poetry: I have seen 5-foot-wide (1.5 m) Jeffreys teeming with life despite having melted in upon themselves like craggy trolls.

There are few experiences like placing your nostrils between the protruding ripples of Jeffrey pine bark that has just been warmed by the autumn sun, only to find that the world is a better place than it was a second ago.

Show me a ponderosa that can do *that*.

The Entire History of My Love Life on a Redwood Stump

I was recently touring the warehouse of Angel City Lumber in Los Angeles—who do amazing work with wood that has been salvaged from the local area—and a certain stump caught my eye. It was a coast redwood (*Sequoia sempervirens*), characteristically beautiful in the color and width of its tree rings (these trees simply *love* to grow) and featuring dramatic separation between the pale heartwood and the deep-red sapwood. But what really intrigued me was that, when I counted the rings, the tree seemed to be exactly as old as I was at the time: thirty-four. I consulted the manager on duty, and she confirmed that the tree had indeed been cut that year by an LA resident who could no longer afford the water bill and foundational headaches that the redwood was giving him. A pity.

So, it appeared, this tree was born the same year that I was: 1987. Yes, the Year of the Rabbit. And, after reasoning that my newfound emotional attachment justified a financial investment, I took the stump home, where I plotted out the events of my love life on its growth rings:

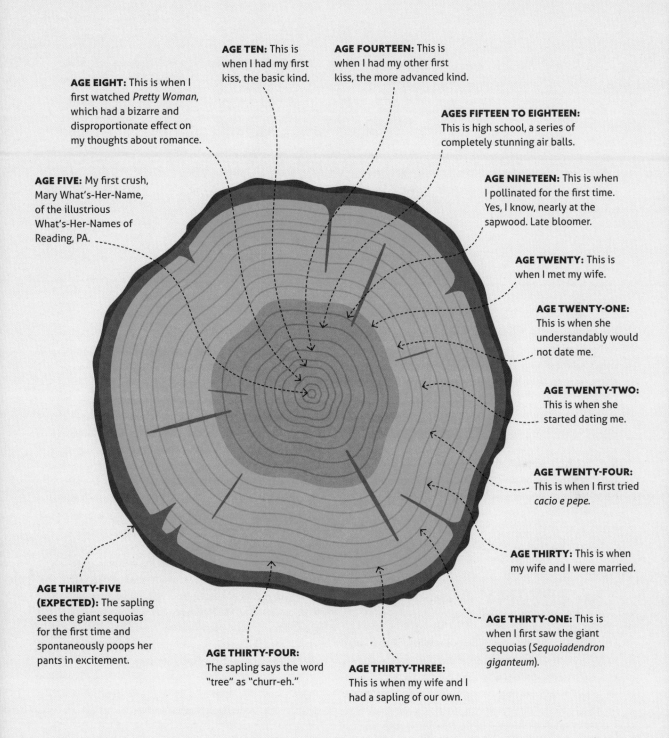

AGE EIGHT: This is when I first watched *Pretty Woman*, which had a bizarre and disproportionate effect on my thoughts about romance.

AGE TEN: This is when I had my first kiss, the basic kind.

AGE FOURTEEN: This is when I had my other first kiss, the more advanced kind.

AGES FIFTEEN TO EIGHTEEN: This is high school, a series of completely stunning air balls.

AGE FIVE: My first crush, Mary What's-Her-Name, of the illustrious What's-Her-Names of Reading, PA.

AGE NINETEEN: This is when I pollinated for the first time. Yes, I know, nearly at the sapwood. Late bloomer.

AGE TWENTY: This is when I met my wife.

AGE TWENTY-ONE: This is when she understandably would not date me.

AGE TWENTY-TWO: This is when she started dating me.

AGE TWENTY-FOUR: This is when I first tried *cacio e pepe*.

AGE THIRTY: This is when my wife and I were married.

AGE THIRTY-FIVE (EXPECTED): The sapling sees the giant sequoias for the first time and spontaneously poops her pants in excitement.

AGE THIRTY-FOUR: The sapling says the word "tree" as "churr-eh."

AGE THIRTY-THREE: This is when my wife and I had a sapling of our own.

AGE THIRTY-ONE: This is when I first saw the giant sequoias (*Sequoiadendron giganteum*).

Chapter 2

"Arbor-Culture"

I'm often wistful for a world in which trees are not only cherished and respected, but are the center of popular culture. Part of this is because I have little time to devote to the latest "shows and flicks" because I'm busy reading tree books and making videos about trees and raising a young sapling. Is it too much to ask for culture to come to *me*?

But think of it: instead of centering ourselves around the Kardashians and all those Marvel super people from the Comic-Cons, trees would be our movie stars, our reality stars, our visionaries.

Intrigued? Read on, friend, read on.

The TREEMY Awards

The movies wouldn't be the movies without a couple of hot young dummies hanging out together in some awesome tree sharing a delicious jar of peanut butter against a setting sun, ignorant of the complete hellscape into which they will be thrust the next day. But trees playing the role of "symbol of youthful nostalgia" is only one of many suitable parts for them.

Last year, after accruing a fulsome account of every tree I've ever seen on film and how dramatically compelling it was, I hosted an awards ceremony for trees that I dubbed the TREEMYS. In terms of hosts, I think I most resembled Billy Crystal due to my lengthy song-and-dance routines and vaudevillian facial expressions. And, of course, the Judaism. The TREEMYS took place in my backyard, and I gave out statuettes carved from my withered bonsai to worthy recipients. The voting body consisted of social media users who could vote more than once, but I think that's still more legitimate than the Golden Globes. Unsurprisingly, no winners came forward to accept their awards, even when I specifically cooked up an honorary award for Treebeard from *The Lord of the Rings*. Imagine not coming forward to accept an award made specifically to attract you to the ceremony! Hmm, come to think of it, maybe the TREEMYS have more in common with the Globes than I'd like to think.

Whatever, it ruled. My wife's guac was killer.

In the following pages, you'll see the categories. The winners are marked with an asterisk.

Best Hero Tree

The Shawshank Tree from *The Shawshank Redemption*

Perhaps the most famous of movie trees amongst Boomer Dads, this two hundred-year-old white oak (*Quercus alba*) from *The Shawshank Redemption* was a remarkably simple symbol of hope for Red (Morgan Freeman), who has finally been paroled from prison after doing forty long years. Yes, the Shawshank tree is an old white guy. The Tree Academy acknowledges its tree bias.

*The *Forrest Gump* Tree

This idyllic live oak (*Quercus virginiana*) has come to represent to so many of us the spirit of human youth and connection between Forrest and Jenny: a refuge from the cruelty of the world. Like some human actors

before it, this tree has received criticism for *doing a mere impression* of a perfect tree instead of giving us a nuanced, realistic *interpretation* of one. But the fact is that voters tend to remember how the trees made them feel as opposed to anything else, so this criticism usually falls flat.

The *Avatar* Tree (Na'vi Hometree)

An extremely gimungoid tree; 500 feet (152 m) tall; 150 feet (46 m) wide. And yes, host to an entire clan of extra-terrestrial neuro-spiritual humanoids. But it is felled by invaders, and TREEMY voters don't like a bummer ending.

Best Villain Tree

Trigger warning! These trees, like their films, are graphic. Skip on to the next category if it's too much.

*The *Conjuring* Tree

Now it would be difficult to label the tree itself as evil here, but Bathsheba (a nineteenth-century Devil-worshipper who sacrificed her child, and then hung herself from the tree—classic!) probably lent the tree—which we can reasonably assume is an old oak from its twisted appearance in New England—a lil' Satan Spice.

The Creepy Sex Tree from *Antichrist*

I don't personally find it surprising that a tree this edgy (Willem Dafoe and Charlotte Gainsbourg do the bone dance on its roots while writhing human limbs appear from its bark) in a film this edgy (please don't make me recount the plot of it) was too much for an academy that likes its narratives conventional and its trees free from human limbs.

Tree of the Dead from *Sleepy Hollow*

This tree, which marks the gateway to hell for the Headless Horseman, is full of human heads. Human heads are, if possible, even less appealing than human limbs to the Academy.

Most Misunderstood Tree

The Whomping Willow from the Harry Potter series

The Whomping Willow changed the entire paradigm for trees on film. Suddenly, trees were expected to be these big-budget CGI monsters, merely meant to *entertain* rather than enlighten. But it still holds true that the Whomping Willow was just sitting there, minding its business, until a couple of underage wizard dipshits drove a car into its seedballs. You might have thrown a few punches too.

*Grandmother Willow from *Pocahontas*

God bless *Pocahontas'* Grandmother Willow, who does everything in her otherworldly power to help that blockhead John Smith get his act together and convince world-historical butthead Governor Ratcliffe that there isn't any gold in friggin' Virginia. *Just listen to Grandmother Willow!*

The Ford Explorer Tree from *Jurassic Park*

A lot of people think that the tree itself was malevolent in this iconic scene, where Dr. Grant and Little Boy attempt to escape downwards from cracking branches. Um, did anyone even notice the *Ford Explorer doing the falling?!* This tree might have won this category, save for its pitiful sixty seconds of screen time.

Lifetime A-tree-vement Award

Treebeard from *The Lord of the Rings: The Two Towers*

He didn't come.

My Full List of Plots for Prospective Tree Films

One day, I hope to make a film that features a tree or trees in large, commanding roles. The following are my plotlines for films that I have abandoned in this regard, presented without comment.

Feel free to use them for your own film scripts, as I no longer feel passionate toward any of them after countless slammed doors and Hollywood heartbreak.

Romance

The Promise Oak

Thirty years ago, Eve Fallow and Luke Crestmayer carved their names into their beloved northern red oak as a promise to each other before tragedy pulled them apart. When they both hear that the oak is to be felled that November, will it reignite their long-lost passion?

The Green Lagoon

In this soaring romantic epic about a love with no bottom, the children of two tragically killed forestry research partners marooned in a redwood canopy at 250 feet (76 m) build a world of their own in the treetops.

Historical

Only God Can Make a Tree

Based on the origin story of the legendary "Tree That Owns Itself" in Georgia, this sweeping 1880s courtroom drama follows a wealthy man's dying wish to give his tree complete sovereignty. Also, there is gold inside the tree.

My Pine Cone Brother

In a French town ravaged by the bubonic plague, a mysterious drifter suddenly appears, accompanied by what he states is his "pine cone brother." One by one, the town folk begin to believe him until the town finally learns to believe in itself.

Horror

The Promise Oak's Revenge

Thirty years ago, Eve Fallow and Luke Crestmayer carved their names into their beloved northern red oak as a promise for happily ever after. Now the oak wants revenge.

A Nightmare on Honey Locust Street

Every night, Eddi Havermeyer has the same nightmare of a thousand thorny barbs on her throat from the honey locust tree outside her bedroom window. But when Eddi's classmates start turning up dead and the tree starts changing position on her lawn, she has to ask herself: Is it all really a dream?

Drama

Falling

After a forestry accident left his partner dead, Miles Hodgkins forsook the modern world to live in a fallen sequoia. Yet when a lonely researcher discovers Miles' hiding place, he must choose between a life unbothered in a tree and a second chance outside it.

Chained

Martin Proudfoot and Terry Longingdale are forest protectors chained to a threatened western red cedar (*Thuja plicata*). As the days pass, they fall in lust, love, rage, and everything in between. Also, there is gold inside the tree.

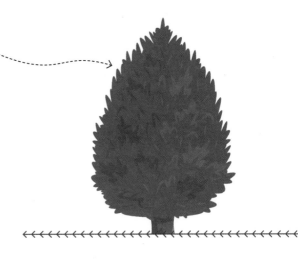

Adventure

Fly through the Branches

Maggie Noguchi is a third-generation American and full-blown member of Generation Z. But when her legendary bonsai master grandfather's favorite tree is stolen, she must dive into an old world she finds alien to her in order to get it back.

Chicago Stump

Things haven't gone so well for Dylan McKenzie's family since his great-great-great-grandfather cut down the famed "General Noble Tree" in 1893. But when his grandfather (x3) speaks to him in a dream, Dylan discovers there is another giant of the forest on the chopping block, and with it, a chance for his family's redemption.

Comedy

Tree Guy

When arboretum specialist Nick Wilkins is fired for public intoxication, he decides to sow revenge chaos in the only way he knows how: switching the labels on the trees during the International Arborists' Conference.

High Hopes

Middle school is hard. It's even harder when you're a 16-foot (5 m) sugar pine (*Pinus lambertiana*).

Pollinate by Prom

(Plot in title.)

Tree People

A Christopher Guest-style mockumentary in which we follow six eccentric tree obsessives competing for the title of "Most Woody" at the twenty-fifth annual Tree and Wood Show.

Science-Fiction/Fantasy

The Tree

When a drilling operation goes awry, a band of oil riggers wake up seemingly glued to a gnarled 1,000-foot-tall (305 m) tree below the earth's crust, which a bus-sized insect calls home. Can any of them escape with their lives?

Superhiker

The sap of a newly discovered pine tree bequeaths powers to the hikers who drink it. But when the United States military wants to turn the tree's sap into a weapon, the super-hikers must make a decision that will affect the course of human (and tree) history.

My Thoughts on People Playing Trees

There's something funny about the idea of a person donning a tree costume, gluing plastic leaves to their arms and hands, and applying very sad makeup indeed to convince an audience that, yes, they are a tree. Maybe it's all of that?

Anyway, that's why I have a lot of admiration for anyone who does it: these folks are paddling against the current, and the current is strong, my friends.

But "people playing trees" could mean a lot of things, so let me first give you a couple examples of what I *don't* mean:

1. People playing trees in a production wherein the tree-play occurs in the fictional universe of the play, film, etc. One could call this "diagetic tree-play." Perhaps the most famous example of this is Birnam Wood from Shakespeare's *Macbeth*, in which soldiers allied against Macbeth camouflage themselves with branches in order to confound the isolated king. I always laugh loud and hard during this scene. It's a real hoot when soldiers silently tiptoe like Bugs Bunny up to a snoozing Macbeth, tap him on the shoulder, then cover themselves with branches when he wakes up and his bloodshot eyes search for the culprit. But these actors are playing *men who are playing trees* in the play, not playing trees themselves, so it doesn't count.

2. People playing "tree-like aliens" or "humanoids with a tree-like appearance." I do not wish to

denigrate the voiceover and CGI work of Vin Diesel and several other actors in the creation of "Groot" from the *Guardians of the Galaxy* films; the character was adorable, gave me copious belly laughs and hope, etc., etc. But the difficult truth is that Groot is not a tree, he is simply tree-*like*. So, again, doesn't count.

What counts? When brave actors risk public mockery in order to suspend our disbelief as far as they can throw it; to convince us that they, themselves, are a living, breathing, sometimes walking tree.

I submit the following actors who have done it and done it well enough to fill mine eyes with tears so thick I might have drowned the wind.

1. Candy Candido and Abe Dinovitch as the Angry Apple Trees in *The Wizard of Oz* (1939). I'll never forget seeing the slinging limbs and apple fastballs of these two remarkable gentlemen as a boy sitting on my daddy's knee. I asked him, "Papa, why did Dorothy wish to grab that apple without asking?" Papa got up and walked to the fireplace, stoking the withering embers. Then he turned slowly and answered me: "What Man cannot understand to be his, he cannot understand." It was a weird night at the Mitnick household.

2. A classmate from my second-grade production of *Hansel and Gretel*. The following is a completely true story: this may shock you, but I was passed over for the role of Hansel and assigned the role of Townsperson #2. But fine, it happens, I'm completely over it. Whatever. Doesn't matter. Barely think about it two or three times a day. But it is tradition to fill the forest background roles of such productions with the less attention-craving children, of whom my extremely tall classmate Zac happened to be one. Every rehearsal, whilst Gretel forgot her lines and Hansel showed off his homemade vinyl lederhosen, Zac would be stick-straight, a stalwart sequoia putting us all to shame in his personification of the evil witch's forest.

That is until one day, when the bright lights of the Cumru Elementary School auditorium overpowered him, sending him toppling over, somewhat unconscious, to the floor, at which point he became *extremely* unconscious. Zac sustained a concussion as a result of his dedicated tree portrayal, it was said, and contracted the flu while in the hospital to add insult to injury. He gave his all for us, and in return, was given a hero's welcome when he returned to school three weeks later, by way of Dunkin' Donuts Donut Holes. He was the bravest tree-player of them all.

A Detailed Examination of the "Chris Pine" (*Pinus crisus*)

For those who don't know, Chris Pine is both a very good and very good-looking actor known for a plum role in the 2006 hitman classic *Smokin' Aces*, among other things. Chris is a big hit with me personally because he has one of the most enviable surnames imaginable. I often wonder what my life would be like if my own last name were Pine, and everybody thought of an autumn night's walk in the mountains when they heard it. Instead, God saw fit for me to be dubbed Mitnick, which translates to "toll collector" in old Ukrainian. If that doesn't make your skin crawl, I don't know what will.

Anywho, when I asked my wife how a Chris Pine (*Pinus crisus*) would appear if she came upon one in the forest, her answer was: "gorgeous." Looks like I will be accompanying her on her forest strolls from now on to make sure everything's on the up-and-up.

But I want to go more in-depth here, and it just so happens I got my hands on a burnt-edged naturalist's description of the apocryphal Chris Pine from the 1870s. Oh, whoops . . . 2023.

Upon Seeing the Chris Pine (*Pinus crisus*) on a Ridge at Late Dusk

The American West is ripe with conifer mammoths—the ponderosa pine, the sugar pine, the Sitka spruce. These capture the public's attention. But there are those outcroppings of tree communities that exist in isolated groves—the foxtail pine, the Santa Lucia fir—which bequeath their rarified wisdom only to the few that seek them out.

But rarer and more sacred still is the singular Chris Pine (*Pinus crisus*), which grows alone in a secret location in Santa Monica, California. To the traveler who breaches its presence, it is said to be a nigh-mystical experience.

At a distance, the Chris would appear fairly unremarkable, at least to the casual enthusiast: a rounded, bright-green crown cascades over the trunk and roots, in similar fashion to the lax ease of a blue spruce, obscuring the appearance of the bark. One could easily mistake it for a common piñon due to its average stature of 55 feet (17 m) and its tendency to hide its canopy with a baseball cap or Panama hat.

But as one moves closer, if one does not involuntarily burst into terrible poetry or various promises to "treat [the Chris Pine] good, baby", the Chris reveals its splendor. Crossing the curtainous threshold of pine needles that guard its inner sanctum, one grabs a handful: a marvelous, unheard-of, and tear-inducing ten-to-the-bundle, smooth cut with azure on the reverse. Branches smooth, pliable.

But lo: One has dropped the bundle of needles—for they have spotted the trunk itself! At 6 feet (1.8 m) in diameter, with plates of silvery bark, rectangular and fair, adorning it like a suit of armor. This is no ordinary Pine.

Approaching the bark, the scent is unmistakable. It can only be described as an intense freshness, wherein hints of traditional pine bark are mingled with lemon and Old Spice. One notices the cones (splendid, admirable) that litter the ground about it. But, one notices, there are no litters of needles themselves. Does this tree not age? Is it of the same ilk as the Elven trees of Tolkien? One cannot say, though he has his charmed suspicions.

One places their arms about the broad trunk, staring upwards into a drapery of glorious limbs. And closing one's eyes, a quick cinematic montage of comfort flashes into being: warmth, summer, home.

It is the Chris Pine (*Pinus crisus*).

My Full List of Plots for Children's Books about Trees That Have Yet to Be Written

One day, I hope to write a children's book that features a tree-centered plot. The following are my own rejected tree-centered children's book plots, available for your use if you so choose.

Leave No Trace

When a child points out that her father's giant sequoia (*Sequoiadendron giganteum*) cone was taken from a National Park illegally, the father takes her on a trip to return it to the giant sequoia From Whence It Came.

Which Way to the Treetop?

A suitcase-toting aphid heading to a mistletoe convention on the top of a white fir (*Abies concolor*) keeps needing to ask directions from different creatures that he sees along the way.

You Never Really Own It

A bonsai-practicing parent shows their child each step to creating a masterful tree, always emphasizing that "you never really own it." Forty years later, the child, now grown, does the same with their own child. Just try holding back the waterworks on this one.

When the Bough Breaks

Young Douglas-fir (*Pseudotsuga menziesii*) sapling Jerry lives next to his mother tree. When he cracks a limb during a storm, mother tree shows him how his cambium works by showing him some of her own old wounds.

No, I'M the Tallest!

When several coast redwoods (*Sequoia sempervirens*) get into a competition of "which tree is tallest," they find out that measuring a tree isn't nearly as easy as it seems!

Always in My Heartwood

At each stage of its life, a mother tree sings the song "Always in my Heartwood" to her sapling.

Grandmother's Live Oak

When young Mabry hears that grandma has a "live oak" in her yard, she imagines different ways in which the tree is alive.

Vincent J. Tree, Private Eye (chapter book series)

Vincent J. Tree, a tree who is also a private investigator, goes around solving various tree-related incidents in his neighborhood.

March of the Larch

A simple counting-book perfect for the youngest readers. It follows ten unruly larches (genus *Larix*) trying to march up a mountain.

UNPOPULAR TREE OPINION: I Really Don't Like the Lorax in *The Lorax*

The Lorax is not great.

Hear me out. I'm not saying that I dislike *The Lorax*, an environmentalist masterpiece by Dr. Seuss that has inspired generations of young people. I'm saying I dislike the Lorax, *the character*. Not because he's a nudge (I'm not huge on the Once-ler either, but he's correct about this) or because he looks like the love child of Yosemite Sam and Chester A. Arthur.

I dislike him because he isn't very strategic *at all* when it comes to dealing with the Once-ler, and the fact is that trees *are* quite strategic. So when he says "I speak for the trees," he's doing a pretty piss-poor job of it.

It's true that the Once-ler suffers from bottomless greed and a stunning narcissism complex. But that's why we need smart representatives who know how to manipulate these cartoon villains into giving the trees what they want. I'd blame the trees and the other assorted creatures who presumably elected the Lorax to speak for them, but, as in life, the buck stops with him.

Consider the following three scenarios, which could have transpired if the Lorax had been the wartime consigliere the Truffula Trees deserved:

Scenario 1:

1. The Once-ler proclaims dominion over the Truffula Trees.

2. The Lorax informs the Brown Bar-ba-loots (which are clearly bears) that their food source—Truffula Fruits—are under threat. He encourages them to organize and march on the Once-ler's house.

3. They do, and are able to drive the Once-ler out of the forest without violence after he sees ten thousand starving, desperate bears on his lawn.

Scenario 2:

1. The Once-ler proclaims dominion.

2. The Lorax informs the Truffula Trees.

3. The trees decide to manufacture a resinous irritant that causes severe skin rashes, leading to endless complaints from the Once-ler's Thneed clientele. He's subsequently buried under emails and lawsuits and closes up shop.

Scenario 3:

1. The Once-ler proclaims dominion over the trees.

2. The Lorax uses opposite psychology, telling the Onceler overenthusiastically that it's "a brilliant design! A marvel! A diamond! The new paradigm!"

3. The Once-ler, who already dislikes the Lorax at first sight, will grow skeptical of his own idea because

of this weirdo's enthusiasm for it. He abandons the Truffula-logging enterprise.

It's interesting that the Lorax has accrued such remarkable goodwill over the past few decades, because if these scenarios show us anything, it's that a good leader is not only passionate but savvy as well.

Four Short Reports on Niche Tree Books

When I first made the outline for this book, it occurred to me that I would be spending an awful lot of time writing about living trees, and I should probably throw a bone to the folks who are more interested in the uses for deceased ones.

So, I picked up four books that addressed this exact issue, intending to write four long (ten thousand-word) analyses of our dependence upon dead trees for our collective sustenance.

Yet, I soon discovered that I had gone too far in the other direction, and that no one would be interested in this. So, I split the difference, and wrote miniature reports on each book filled with fun facts for everyone. If you're a hardcore woodhead who simply cannot go a day without your cellulose fiber research-paper fix, this section was written just for you. And because these are simple "reports" that one might write in fifth grade, I've tried to emulate the style of my own writing from that era of my life.

The Age of Wood by Roland Ennos

I very much enjoyed reading this book. I liked how Mr. Ennos described how wood is the most important material in the history of humanity. The main character in this book is named Wood. Mr. Ennos shows us how Wood goes from being a practical unknown to being the most famous substance in the world, from the ancient Egyptians' use of *Acacia* and sycamore fig (*Ficus sycomorus*) to the modern-day pursuit of tropical wood exploitation. The part I liked best is when Mr. Ennos talked about wood. People are sure to like when Mr. Ennos talks about the specific gravity of wood, and why woods from the rainforest are denser. This is because those trees are slow-growing understory trees that pump themselves full of compounds to prevent rotting in the wet heat. I would recommend this book to anybody who likes wood.

Paper by Mark Kurlansky

I very much enjoyed reading this book. This story takes place throughout history. The good guy in this book is named Cellulose Fibers and the bad guy is named Other Substances. One thing I thought was really funny was when Mr. Kurlansky described how the futile attempts of the nineteenth-century Luddites is an apt metaphor for paper as a technology and the attempt to restrict its use. The part I liked the best was when Mr. Kurlansky lists the percentages of cellulose present in different kinds of trees, with aspen (*Populus tremuloides*) up at 57 percent and hemlock (*Tsuga heterophylla*) at only 48 percent. One thing I learned is that people used to collect linen rags for paper before they thought of wood pulp. I would recommend this book to anyone who is interested in the repeated technological failures by an emerging American paper industry to isolate fibers from wood pulp.

The Pencil by Henry Petroski

I very much enjoyed reading this book. I thought it was cool when Mr. Petroski told us that eastern red cedar (*Juniperus virginiana*) was originally prized as the prime material for pencils before their old-growth forests were nearly logged into oblivion in the early twentieth century, forcing pencil industrialists to find alternative sources of wood that wouldn't split and were strong and scented enough to make for an adequate substitute, thereby ushering in the era of the incense-cedar (*Calocedrus decurrens*) as the go-to pencil resource. Two new terms I learned from this book were "Siberian graphite" and "BOPPS" (broken-off pencil points).

The Toothpick by Henry Petroski

I very much enjoyed this book, and I enjoyed it even more once I realized that it was written by Henry Petroski, who wrote *The Pencil*, which I had just finished reading. One thing that made me sad was that paper birch (*Betula papyrifera*), one of my favorite trees, is considered the A+, gold-star tree for toothpicks due to its softness and tendency to taste like the forest. Because of this, some people call it "the toothpick tree." I think those people are cowards. I laughed when I read how some toothpick industrialists would intentionally design their products to break prematurely in the user's mouth so that the user would have to use four or five toothpicks at a time, thereby upping their sales revenue. I would recommend this book for anyone who has ever had anything stuck in their teeth.

In conclusion, I would recommend these books for anyone who likes books about dead trees.

Anton Chekhov: The Ultimate Tree Obsessive

There once was a man named Anton Chekhov, who died in 1904. He was a devoted lover of trees, especially those that grew in his homeland of Western Russia. He was obsessed with birches (genus *Betula*), and how their meaning might change for someone with shifting tides of emotion, from representing imprisoning bars to emblems of freedom. But it didn't end there: he also loved willow, alder, fir, maple, beech, oak, poplars, plum, cherry, pear, crabapple, pine, acacia, linden, spruce, horse chestnut, apples, and olives, and wrote about them all.

He wrote about these in his short stories with the goal of lending mood, atmosphere, and symbology. He also included them in his plays—*The Seagull, Uncle Vanya, The Cherry Orchard*—the best since those of William Shakespeare. When he wasn't writing, he was tending to his country farm at Melikhovo, planting trees for the benefit of his family.

The reason I want to talk earnestly about this gentleman for a hot second before we pass on to the rest of this silly book about trees is because the way he writes about trees makes me feel things, then cry, then think about trees some more.

A lot of Chekhov scholars and biographers (and there are many) like to emphasize that he was an extremely forward-thinking person in the realm of ecological thought. This is incorrect, because he was actually nigh-on prophetic. He lent his characters beautiful monologues extolling the wonder and purpose of forests, protecting old growth, and even theorizing about climate change a century before it became proven science. He also lent them visions of a frightening future in which the forests were completely cleared in order to give the characters a sense of passion and purpose. I wish I could quote all of these passages at length right now, but just check out the first act monologues of Astrov in *Uncle Vanya*, or perhaps the Act III scene between Astrov and Yelena. Never has a monologue about deforestation been so sexually charged, I promise you. It's good stuff.

Elsewhere, like in *The Cherry Orchard*, he uses the haunting symbolism of the cherry trees on an estate as symbols for enslaved serfs who once worked the land. Thus, the trees' ongoing existence denotes the continued exploitation of enslaved peoples' labor.

Understandably, it's these grand visions of conservationism and humanitarianism that get the most attention in his writing, which basically invented subtext (the idea that people don't actually say what they mean very often).

But what everyone tends to underestimate is the power of the trees themselves for Chekhov, apart from any usefulness that they might have as symbol or stand-in.

All one has to do is read the final words of Tuzenbach from *Three Sisters*, a character about to meet his doom in a duel and knows it. He's a committed pessimist and cynic. But as he begs for a single parting word from the woman he loves unrequitedly, he suddenly looks up with comfort in his place of imminent death:

"I am happy. It is as if for the first time in my life I see these firs, maples, beeches, and they all look at me inquisitively and wait. What beautiful trees and how beautiful, when one comes to think of it, life must be near them . . . There's a tree which has dried up but it still sways in the breeze with the others. And so it seems to me that if I die, I shall still take part in life in one way or another."

Write Your Own Tree Poem

Obviously, the most famous poem about a tree is "Trees" (1913) by Joyce Kilmer, which is mostly known for the line "I think that I shall never see / A Poem lovely as a tree", and the assertion that "Only God Can Make a Tree." While some poetry scholars might sneer at Kilmer's sixteen-line naivete, I find it quite lovely. No Herculean efforts here, no blank-verse metaphors for 1960s tax laws, just a guy having a good time feeling small next to a tree.

Or you could take the Emily Dickinson tack. In her poem, "'Hope' is the Thing with Feathers" or "314" (1861–1862), she gives a real Old Testament spin on Mother Nature, writing "Nature—sometimes sears a Sapling—Sometimes—scalps a Tree—Her Green People recollect it—when they do not die—." "Her Green People": very extraterrestrial, very terrifying.

Or you could go all Johnny Keats on your trees, lulling your audience into a place of sensuous paradise with your imagery, like in "To Autumn" (1819): "To bend with apples the moss'd cottage-trees, / and fill all fruit with ripeness to the core"; *Delicioso*.

But if the prospect of starting from scratch scares you, or you find yourself wracked with the anxiety of influence from others and their tree words, I've created this handy template for you so you can sort of write your own. It's in Shakespearean sonnet rhyming structure, meaning ABABCDCDEFEFGG and ten syllables per line (iambic pentameter).

Is it a little like Mad Libs? Sure, but was anything ever more fun than Mad Libs?

"*A Tree Poem*" by [Your Name Here]

Forsooth is't not the [two-syllable tree] of mine youth?
Whose [two-syllable adjective] leafies maketh mirth of poe?
And is this not the [one syllable part of a tree] that charmed mine tooth—
A'laying [two-syllable adverb] where they did once grow?

Alas! Thy [two-syllable adjective] barkskin lies in twain,
Askewing all thy [two-syllable word for seeds] mishy-mash'd,
And splinter'd is the [one-syllable word for branch] where I did reign,
A [two-syllable word for ruler] once; now all my realm is dash'd!

Yet what find I, in [two-syllable word for dirt], rock, and rot—
The greenest [two-syllable word for baby tree] yet beheld by me!
From deepened earth thy [two-syllable word for leaves] fully wrought,
To make a life so new so [three-syllable adjective meaning "bitchin"].

From life's departure maketh thee thine gate,
To open every [the tree, possessive] heart to fate!

Tree Pun Acceptability

As we speak, our society barrels towards ruin. The culprit? Puns. Specifically, those that are terrible and easy. And tree puns, my word! The worst of them all! I worry that this trend will soon make its way into the ordinary dad shed and perhaps even into our halls of government. I take no pleasure in reporting this.

Now, look, I'm a dad, which means I have a predisposition towards these linguistic monstrosities. So why do dads love puns? Puns are often the first jokes that a child can understand because they think, "Hey, wait, why is that idiot screwing with the language he spent years teaching me? That's hilarious." Puns in general are low-hanging fruit in this regard, and once you get a laugh from the very young, it's tempting to go back to the same tree for everyone else in your life.

Soon, average dads like me—not me, and you'll soon see why, but dads *like* me—could be causing an eye-roll epidemic of such massive proportions that it will make optometrists our busiest, most-valued citizens.

So, I'm making this chart that I hope will soon become unwritten folk law. It's an assessment of each tree pun and where they fall in the following categories: *Audible Sigh* (use at will), "Ugghhh!" (use sparingly), or, the worst, "#CANCELDAD" (use absolutely never upon pain of potential minor emancipation).

PUN TYPE	MY ASSESSMENT	JUDGMENT
The Everyman: "Leaf it Alone," "I have a Tree-t for you!," "WOOD you mind helping your old dad with this?"	Look, I'm not a heartless monster. I know that certain puns are unavoidable. The everyman is a classic, and completely inevitable in the parent-child relationship. Just be careful, okay?	"UGGHH!"
The Bank Shots: "Cambium!" = "Can't Be Him!," "Olive It!" = "I Love it!," "Walnut me!" = "Well, not me!"	Three words: degree of difficulty. Respect.	*Audible Sigh*
The Stumper: [sits on stump] "Well . . . I'm stumped!"	Nothing much to assess here. You're just a benevolent goof who loves sitting on stumps.	*Audible Sigh* (with involuntarily smile)
The Ivy Leaguers: "Really Poplar guy," "Do you remember/the 21st day of Septimber?", "Love this Deodarant!"/ "Gross—got some phloem rising in my throat."	Seems like you have specified knowledge and perhaps a horticulture degree. More respect.	*Audible Sigh*
The Back Pockets: "Fronds like these," "Bough before me," "I was pining for some outdoors time," "The Park Ranger assured me it was root-ine."	Universally recognized puns are actually quite useful if you find yourself with a bunch of six-year-olds but don't want to resort to the slightly more reprehensible use of the Everyman (see above).	"UGGHH!"
The Nihilists: "Why don't you ash-k her?", "Genus Christ," "I'm really pithed off," "Oh, I was just ponderosa-ing the question."	Does language mean nothing to you? Does it thrill you to butcher humanity's signature mode of communication? For you there is only power, I suppose.	#CANCELDAD
The Depraved Ones: "Yew and me," "Stick with me," "What's it all fir?" "Gonna go ahead and plant myself here." Anything with "bark."	A story, friend: once you had a body and a mind and experienced the miracle of creation. You felt the wind in your face. You witnessed the tender smile of a newborn babe. But now you have become death, destroyer of worlds, and there's not a snowball's chance in hell that you can be redeemed.	#CANCELDAD

Chapter 3

Bonsai—A Wonderful Way to Torture Oneself

Words cannot express how happy I am that you've made it to the bonsai chapter, because now you can join me in experiencing the most exquisite torture imaginable. No, not of the trees—but of yourself.

But hold up—let's do this quick, because I want to give this question the space it deserves: Is bonsai actually tree torture?

No. Moving on.

So, you want to feel the sweet, sweet pain of an all-encompassing hobby in which you need to fail innumerable times before you have a bit of pay-off around year three? Then you're *my kind* of stubborn masochist.

Bonsai History

I owe you a little straight talk here about such a storied and significant cultural practice. Bonsai is a Japanese word that means "tree in a tray," which comes from the older practice of Chinese penjing, which means "tray scenery." The difference?

Sometime in the cultural transfer between these two countries about a thousand years ago, the Japanese practice began to focus on only one of three aspects of Chinese penjing (the others being landscape [shanshui penjing] and water and rock penjing [shuihan penjing]). And, boy, they really went for it.

Harvesting old, gnarled junipers and pines from the mountains of Japan (collecting trees known as *yamadori*), Japanese bonsai practitioners began to prune, pluck, and wire these genetically normal trees into marvelous, tiny-scaled versions of what they look like in the wild. Cut to one thousand years later and Japanese bonsai trees with remarkable histories (some date back five hundred years) can fetch a million dollars at auction.

The art form has boomed worldwide as well. Bonsai has developed cultural and geographic idiosyncrasies that vary by country and continent, but most are based on trees native to the country in question. For example, bonsai artists in Indonesia and Southeast Asia make great use of *Podocarpus*, a tropical conifer, and shape it into the classical Japanese "Darth Vader helmets" of foliage. Their North American counterparts have a burning passion for the coast redwood (*Sequoia sempervirens*) and ponderosa pine (*Pinus ponderosa*), typically developing the foliage with an eye for a naturalistic, spare character that only the most aged trees possess. European bonsai artists are always diving deeper into the world of deciduous trees, experimenting with excellent results on everything from a collected birch (genus *Betula*) to the myriad cultivars (cultivated variations) of Japanese maple (*Acer palmatum*).

What can I say, folks, it's a bona fide bonsai *movement*!

"Wow, that's all great, Tobin. Where do I start?"

Not so fast, Mr. Rash-and-Curious. Have you seen my backyard? Do you want your trees to look like *that*? (Well, except for an exceptional coast live oak [*Quercus agrifolia*] yamadori and a piñon pine [*Pinus edulis*]— those are papa's little gold stars). Let's be honest, out of perhaps fifty trees that I've worked on in the past few years, the results are thus: fifteen dead, ten on the brink, ten in less-than-fantastic shape, ten healthy but boring, and only three or four winners.

That's a sad tally, folks. So, I'm not going to sit here and pretend that I can teach you a thing about it. That's what the internet is for. But what I can tell you is *how* I obtained these trees, or *material*, as the calculated brutalists refer to it:

I purchased three as bonsai in a pot ($$$), twenty as simple nursery stock, ten as pre-bonsai (younger trees that were trained early to have desirable bonsai characteristics), collected five as urban yamadori (trees which were going to be cut down anyway), four as mountain yamadori (permitted forest collection), and obtained five from other methods (air-layerings, plantings, clippings).

Obtaining your trees through one of these methods is the fun part. Well, one of the fun parts. It really is all quite fun—buying material, thinking about the material, wiring the material, potting the material, watering the material, reading up on the material, neglecting household duties in favor of looking at the material some more—until, poof! One day your beloved redwood that

you spent hours upon hours getting to know millimeter by millimeter—you know, that one tree you had huge plans for, and to which you also felt a kinship; that rare interspecies dialogue shared only by beloved childhood pets and certain probiotics when you're all backed up—withers and dies. No answers as to why. No one to share your grief but the mycorrhizal fungi that would have been delighted to grow on its root system.

Needless to say, this tree would have still been flourishing had a landscaper planted it in the ground, or even back at the nursery, where a clumsy clown like you wouldn't have been able to get his grubby hands on it.

But then you, *wonderful* you, came along, full of pomp and delusion, like some sort of Time Warner Music Collection infomercial host, and you pointed to the redwood and said, "Mine." And the redwood paid the price. And so did you.

Ay: bonsai.

Bonsai Styles

Though the lines have been blurred quite a bit in recent years, there are twenty-one classic styles of tree in bonsai. But for the newbies, I've tried to pare down the styles in this section to some of their most recognizable incarnations.

It's important to note that species work well with particular styles according to their growth habit. Take, for instance, the *cascade* (in Japanese: *kengai*) style. This dramatic label refers to when a bonsai tree falls over the side of the pot, *cascading* below its bottom boundary. What works well with this intense, modern, perhaps even sensual style? Trees that have an intense, modern, perhaps even sensual growth habit in the wild, of course, i.e.:

- Junipers (genus *Juniperus*), which have a melty, mystical vibe about them.

- White pines (several species in genus *Pinus*), whose mountainous regions often find them pouring themselves downwards onto the craggy crags below.

- Satsuki azalea—a cultivar of *Rhododendron indicum* that makes for luscious locks of lovely leafies.

What doesn't work well in cascade style? Well, take the coast redwood, for example, whose vertical growth habit can hardly be matched. Trying to bend that baby against all it knows to be good and true is just going to make for a trash can full of scented splinters.

I know there's someone out there right now going, "But Tobin, there are EXCELLENT versions of redwood yamadori that exist in the cascade style!" Sure, there are always exceptions when you have a hunk of mostly dead wood and a single live vein that you can manipulate. But I guarantee, I can *personally* guarantee—me, Tobin Mitnick, a Jew Who Loves Trees—that if you find a redwood growing in a nursery container and you get the bright idea to go all cascade on it, it will end in tears. It will probably end in tears regardless, but doing it *that* way it will *definitely* end in tears.

Here are another few greatest hit tree styles and what species works best for them.

duty, these fellas prefer it straight-up. Species that work well in Formal Upright include a great deal of deciduous trees like elm, but also several conifers like the true cedars (genus *Cedrus*) or even deciduous conifers like dawn redwood (*Metasequoia glyptostroboides*).

Informal Upright (*moyogi*)

Here's where things get twisted. These trees ditch the bowties and slap on a bolo in order to get all informal on you. They still point generally upwards, but there's a fabulous curve here or a bend there that gives the tree lots of movement, like in the wild. Picture that Hebrew school carpool mom putting on some early Sheryl Crow and just feeling it. Many suitable species here: junipers, pines, Japanese maples, just to name a few.

Formal Upright (*chokkan*)

Now this is where we *should* find his majesty the coast redwood. Unyielding as a mom on Hebrew school carpool

Semi-cascade (*han-kengai*)

These trees look like they've had one too many. They're bent sideways, with perhaps some foliage below the rim of the pot. Again, many suitable styles from white pine to genus *Cotoneaster* to pomegranate (*Punica granatum*).

Windswept (*fukinagashi*)

Mountain and seaside blasts of wind are meant to be seen in the shape of these bonsai, whose limbs and foliage are wired and pruned to look as though they're twisting in the breeze. Conifers are typically best here, as they tend to be more flexible for the bending, although I have seen several Chinese elms (*Ulmus parvifolia*) in this style that would blow your socks off.

Literati (*bunjin*)

Ah, yes. The "sensitive child" of bonsai. The term *literati* comes from a class of Chinese artists and poets who lived during the first millennium CE who would shape trees inspired by the paintings they did of the mountain trees in the distance. It makes sense that *wabi-sabi*, the later Japanese concept of beauty contained in transience, follows in these footsteps. The tree shape? Some scant bit of foliage at the end of a long, curvy trunk. A very, very sensitive child, indeed. Species: mostly juniper and pine.

Quiz: What Style of Bonsai Tree Are You?

1 You are a tree. But right now you're in the middle of Saturday night self-care: a nice Birch beer paired with repeat viewings of the "Seasonal Forests" episode of *Planet Earth* along with a piñon pine-extract bath. Suddenly, "knock, knock!" Your tree friends are outside and want you to get canopy crazy at TREEBAR with them! Do you:

A Cower in fear and recite tree poetry to comfort yourself.

B Roll your eyes and lip-sync David Attenborough: "It is the very essence of wilderness."

C Tell them "sure," but only until your sap crystallizes.

D Throw off your blanket to reveal a tunic made of loblolly pine cone scales. Let's do this!

2 You get to TREEBAR and notice that there are some *very* well-formed angiosperms looking in your direction. What's your approach?

A Ignore them. No pollination necessary on tree friends' night.

B Play hardwood to get and stay with your tree pals.

C Walk over and ask one to buy you a groundwater.

D "Your forest or mine?"

3 You and your tree crush have made your way outside TREEBAR. It's clear that you're both gazing at the other's bark like a couple of cork harvesters. Who makes the first move?

A Neither of you do. This conversation about exotic acorns is stimulating enough.

B They do, by gently stroking the leaves in your crown.

C You do, by executing the classic "accidental brush up the trunk."

D It's hard to remember when their twigs are on your pollen sacs like that! Yee-haw!

4 Things are getting pretty Zone 10 up in here! They look you right in the eye and ask the question you've thought about since first seeing them, "Wanna come back to my mountain? It's in Yosemite . . . " How do you respond?

A "Yosemite? Isn't there white pine blister rust there? No, thank you!"

B You slap them right across the apex—you're not that kind of burl.

C "I'd love to. Just let me pay for my carbon dioxide sliders."

D "Shhhhh . . . my place in Grand Teton is just around the corner."

Results

0—2 POINTS

You are the **Literati** style: not only is your trunk wispy and your foliage fragile, but so is your personality. You're sensitive to a fault and would rather curl up with a good trail map than risk snapping a branch out there in the scary, scary world.

3—4 POINTS

You are the **Formal Upright** style. Though you might enjoy a good conversation every now and then, your idea of a good time is a straight-laced and conservative game of pine cone chess. And your tree opponent better follow the rules if they know what's good for them!

5—6 POINTS

You are the **Informal Upright** style. Your tree friends trust your sense of judgment and can rely on you to tell them when the sap is all dried up on a night out. But you're also likely to be a wound-up evergreen who holds on too tight to their leaves to really let go.

7—8 POINTS

You're the **Semi-cascade** style. Somehow, you've managed to strike the perfect balance of party tree and cultured aesthete. You've certainly had your walks of shame back to the forest, but that doesn't mean that you don't know when a relationship is phytotoxic.

9—10 POINTS

You're the **Cascade** style. You're the pith of the party and a surefire growth-ringleader during wild nights out. But beware, your wandering branches might find you with a great deal of pollen partners but no long-term mycelium networks.

11—12 POINTS

You're the **Windswept** style. Okay, if there was such a thing as a bonsai tree combined with an extreme weather event, you are it. Fast winds, fast limbs, fast trees. But all this fun and games often leaves your tree pals in the lurch—how can they depend on a tree with such an unquenchable thirst to get blown all the time?

Key

<<<<<<<<<<<<<<<<<<<<<<<<<<<<<<<<<<<<<<<<<<<<<<<<<<<<<<<<<<<<<<<<<<<<<<<<<<<<<<<

A: 0 points,   B: 1 point,   C: 2 points,   D: 3 points

Bonsai Myths

I don't need to tell you this, but we live in an unprecedented era of tree misinformation. Depressingly, this extends to our discourse concerning horticulture, gardening, dendrology, and yes, bonsai.

As much as I'd like to blame the internet for this, the truth is that bonsai myths have been floating around for centuries, sometimes as a result of xenophobia or racism concerning Asian cultures and sometimes as a result of simple Hollywood nonsense.

Pretty much everyone who takes up bonsai needs to spend a good amount of time countering these common misunderstandings:

1. **It's pronounced "bahn-zai."** Nuh-uh. It's pronounced "bon–" (like "bone" but shorter, similar to "bon" in "bon-bon," coming from the Japanese word for "tray") and "–sigh," which means "tree." The pronunciation "Bahnzai" comes from the word "Banzai," which was American shorthand for a Japanese military charge during World War II. The later innovation of a fighter-guy holding a bonsai tree as a fighting symbol is, uh, weird to say the least.

2. **Bonsai is a type of tree.** No. They are regular trees made small. Bonsai can also be a noun ("this oak is a bonsai"), a verb ("I'm going to bonsai this oak"), and an adjective ("this is a bonsai oak").

3. **Bonsai is an inside thing.** Almost never. Maybe if you can replicate sunlight with lamps using tropical trees. But, for the most part, trees really enjoy being outside.

4. **Bonsai is only done by zen masters and clip-clipping old ladies who serve you hot cocoa on Sundays.** False: strapping lads like me do it. And some zen masters and old ladies who like to serve you hot cocoa on Sundays (Hershey's . . . score!).

5. **A person owns a bonsai.** Allow me to get a little hoinky-shnoinky for a minute. There's a saying in bonsai that you never actually "own" a tree, you just take care of it for the next generation. It's slightly corny, but this maxim can be practical as well: it centers the tree as opposed to you, and encourages you to think long term for the tree, instead of just for today. This serves as an overriding metaphor for all bonsai.

So You Want to Gift a Bonsai Tree?

The time comes in every tree enthusiast's journey when they become interested in bonsai. And the time comes in every bonsai enthusiast's life when that enthusiasm yearns to break free and invade the hearts of everyone you know like an unwelcome but harmless parasite. All this is to say that bonsai evangelism is a completely natural outgrowth of tree love. Regardless, it is all-consuming when it strikes. Goodness, me, the nature of passion!

Anyway, you're going to want to give people bonsai trees as gifts. You just are. What better way to trap them into the same kind of hobby that you do willingly? Suffice to say that I have given many a bonsai tree as gifts for birthdays, weddings, bar mitzvahs, you name it, and each one has had a piece of my soul—or my wallet—attached to it.

And what do the recipients of my gifts nearly always do? They let them die. Just like the legendary love fern from *How to Lose a Guy in 10 Days*. The recipients often dissemble, claiming the tree is "doing great, yeah!" while completely overdoing the exclamation point.

But folks, I *know*. I *always* know.

It's important to me that you use my painful experiences to spare yourself some needless agony. Therefore, I made a chart for you that breaks down the life expectancy of a bonsai tree given to different people in your life.

Bonsai Gift Life Expectancy

RECIPIENT	TREE LIFE EXPECTANCY (IN YEARS)	NOTES
Moms	5+	Helicopter moms are obviously desirable here. But if yours is more laidback, get the woman a *Ficus* or an olive and it'll still work out great. Why? Because she's your mom. If you can trust her not to tell anyone that you cried when you found out that you were cast as Lefou instead of Gaston in the seventh-grade Spring Swing, you can trust her with anything.
Significant Others	3 to 4	If it's meant to be, the tree could last a lifetime. If it's not, you can kiss that baby goodbye as soon as you hear the front door slam shut behind you.
Your Stoner Younger Brother	1	This guy has asked you repeatedly to get him a bonsai tree ("treeeeessss!"). But one day when he shatters his best bong ("ooh . . . whaaaat?!"), that Juniper trunk will start looking mighty carvable.
Your Influencer Friend	0.1	"Today I'm going to show you how I made an elm tree gazpacho using just ingredients that I found in *my own backyard*!"
People with Aggressive Squirrels	0.00	The squirrels will immediately savage the bonsai tree.

Coping with Inevitable Failure

Nothing can match the highs of getting into bonsai.

First is stage one. Suddenly the world is green and new and tiny and magical. A host of fresh information and factoids fill your brain, then your bookshelf, then finally your hands as your skill with wire and fertilizer convinces you that you've really done it: you've found a long-sought-after passion to fill your cold, dead adult heart.

Then comes stage two. And stage two sucks, because, despite your best efforts, stage two is the moment of inevitable failure. Your Japanese black pine (*Pinus thunbergii*) that you lovingly and painstakingly shaped to within an inch of its life decides to punish you for doing so and withers after six months. You overwater your Chinese juniper (*Juniperus chinensis*), causing a fungal infection that slowly saps the color of the foliage until it looks like it was fashioned from burnt English muffins. You forget to close the door to your porch and your cocker spaniel zips out, smashing your delicate white pine (*Pinus parviflora*) and the Japanese Tokonome pot that held it. Then, to add insult to injury, he urinates on it, long and proud. Bad dog.

Something like this will happen, and when it does, it may strike the tree you love most. Maybe even your first tree. And if that's the case, it will most certainly strike the heart of your resolve as well. Why go on with this hobby/passion/practice/lifestyle if it is bound to break your heart over and over again?

The best analogy I can give here is falling in love with a human being. Similar to stage one of bonsai immersion, puppy love is the best feeling around. Boundless excitement and curiosity coexist with obsession and attentiveness. A heavenly lightness beyond words.

But after about a year, you might have your first real blowup, and you might have to dig deeper to find that sense of mystery that used to shake you by the lapels.

So it is with a full season of bonsai.

At this point, you have a choice before you: Will you let disillusionment envelop you to the point that the only way to free yourself of it is to . . . free yourself of it? Or is there something deeper than that initial passion? Something that might convince you to head back to the nursery to find a shrub passed over by others for its "ugly" trunk, and to bring it home, where you can care for it while helping it reach its full potential?

The long practice of bonsai requires more than just infatuation in order to pick up the pieces where you've failed.

Like being in the embrace of a great love, bonsai requires giving something of yourself.

Bonsai requires devotion.

Chapter 4

Around the House and Neighborhood

Along with bonsai, there are a great many ways that you can integrate the arboreal arts into your everyday life. Maybe even into the cozy cave in which you're reading this book.

I tread on dangerous territory here, because I've previously mentioned that I like my living room free of dingly-dangly houseplants and bonsai—well, at least those that aren't meant to be there. But this chapter is about bringing that tree *spirit* inside with you, while hopefully leaving undesirable flora and fauna outside.

This is what I like to refer to as "tree domestication," wherein one brings the greatest features of the outdoors *indoors* and comes one step closer to dissolving the walls that block the trees from one's sight and senses.

Get Yourself a Comfort Cone!

I have a memory of sitting in my room at seven years old and watching my father chat with his best friend Mohamad.

Mohamad was laddering his fingers through a series of beads on what looked like a bracelet while he talked. I asked him what he was doing.

"These are my prayer beads," he said.

"Are you praying?" I asked.

"Not right now," he said, "but my prayer beads have many uses."

Um, whoa, I thought. "Many." Whoa.

Later, on "Culture Day" in second grade—yes, Culture Day—I learned that Mohamad had been using his tasbih—his Muslim prayer beads typically used for keeping count of prayers—in a manner akin to the *kompoloi*, the "worry beads" of the Greeks. That is to say, as something to pass the time, or perhaps as the precursor to the fidget spinner.

Prayer, worry, fidgeting, idea generating, they're all part and parcel of the "many uses" suited to an innovation of my own: the Comfort Cone.

No, I'm not talking about the thing we strap around dogs' heads in order to humiliate them after surgery. I'm talking about a cone—pine, cypress, or otherwise—that you can hold in your hand to help you get you through the day. I can't recommend this enough, partly because I like attaching meaning to particular naturalistic objects, and this is a great example of one that might actually be deemed socially acceptable.

Here's a little bit about mine, and why I like it so very much.

It's durable as all living hell.

My comfort cone is from a giant sequoia (*Sequoiadendron giganteum*), which makes it a cypress cone. Cypress cones are excellent choices for long-term durability and resistance to sweaty palm rot, partially because they're quite hard and often dense. This is in contrast to other similar-sized cones like the lodgepole pine (*Pinus contorta*) cone, which will both slice up your fingers and wither away after a week or two of frequent use, or the Douglas-fir cone, which will get you cute looks for its fun protruding bracts but isn't really practical in a long-term sense.

It's loaded with personal significance.

If I'm flipping my comfort cone between my fingers in jittery unrest because, say, my piece of salvaged black ironwood (*Krugiodendron ferreum*) is late in the mail and I'm fretting it's lost, like at the very second I'm writing this, I can also remember that I picked up

the cone from the foot of the Boole Tree, my single favorite tree on planet Earth. This was when my wife and I were pregnant with my daughter, and that's one of the warmest memories of my life. So, the lost ironwood isn't too big a problem in the grand scheme of things. (For those of you who are curious, the Boole Tree sits in a national forest—not a national park—where it is okay to collect a cone with a ranger's permission. No takey-takey from national parks, everyone.)

Finally, it is an excellent conversation starter. You know what will really take your mind off of whatever you're worrying about? When someone gives you permission to talk about a thing that you really like by asking you about it. I love this feature of the comfort cone.

The Ultimate Christmas Tree Rankings

Before I am anything else—a self-described naturalist, a middling TikTok celebrity, a father— I am, of course, a normie. That means that I like normal, boring, popular stuff—you know: The Beatles, dogs, *Christmas trees.* And being a normie first and foremost, I never let my Judaism stop me from obsessing over Christmas trees every year and butting my nose into everyone's tree choice. If, one December, you find yourself strapping your newly purchased red cedar (*Juniperus virginiana*) from Chris's Discount Christmas Trees to the top of your car and someone snickers as he walks past you, it's possible that you were just publicly mocked by yours truly.

To the rankings.

The Five Best Christmas Trees

5

4

3

Fraser fir (*Abies fraseri*)

North Carolina once named its state tree as the hilariously vague "pine tree." But it seemed as though they got wise to this goof and soon adopted the Fraser as a companion tree in 2005 to seem more legit. And with good reason: super-short, toddler-friendly needles adorn every sturdy branch of the Fraser, making it a popular holiday tree for the folks who are looking for an intersection of convenience and aesthetic pleasure.

Norway spruce (*Picea abies*)

The Norway spruce may not be the best literal fit for your living room, as they tend to grow rather large, but every Rockefeller Plaza Christmas tree for the past forty years has been a Norway spruce, and, therefore, it earns a spot on this list. I also want to take this opportunity to say that, before you read the annual hit pieces on how utterly screwed up this year's tree at 30 Rock is, you must understand that it takes a few days for the branches to fall into their familiar cascading arrangement. This information never silences the haters, but also those people are haters, so, by definition, they *are* going to hate.

Eastern white pine (*Pinus strobus*)

This is a "degree of difficulty" entry. Anyone willing to forgo the amiable, workable branches of a fir in favor of a true pine's weaker, bushier needle arrangement simply for the love of the tree is a true baller in my book. Go you.

Nordmann fir
(*Abies nordmanniana*)

This may not be the obvious fir choice, but the benefits of having a Nordmann in your home are undeniable, my god. A native of the Caucasus Mountains, it conveys a certain wildness about its needles and branching that other tamer firs, such as the noble or balsam, don't typically have. Dark green, glossy, and slightly curved, the foliage of this uncommon suitor will have your captive handyman audience saying, "cool tree, but did you want me to snake the kitchen sink as well?"

Douglas-fir
(*Pseudotsuga menziesii*)

The Douglas-fir is perhaps the most studied conifer in the world, with reports of trees reaching nearly 400 feet (122 m) before modern logging cut them down to (sub-redwood) size. If simply imagining the contrast between forest giant and living-room adornment isn't an emotional enough experience for you, take this to the bank: slightly up-angled branches make excellent ornament hangers, and the scent of a Dougie will fill your house. Also, it's just rugged enough to let people know you're not a complete noob at this.

So those are the best. But, look, I care about you. You bought this book. And I do not want you to accidentally commit to a tree that will make me or anyone else burst into hysterical laughter. These are three unfortunate picks that you'd be wise to avoid:

The Three Worst Christmas Trees

Red cedar (*Juniperus virginiana*)

I used this as an example in the opening paragraph as something I would laugh at. Why? Well, this is a common type of cypress tree on the East Coast that is well-known for its use as a hedge. What I imagine when I see one of these being used as a Christmas tree is that you chose to dig up your neighbor's hedges to enact some kind of vengeance, in a kind of a Hallmark movie, Hatfield/McCoy-type scenario, and that makes me laugh because I love those kinds of movies. Sorry: *films*.

Torrey pine (*Pinus torreyana*)

When I see a Torrey in your house, it initially makes me think of the dreamy island of Santa Rosa off the coast of Santa Barbara, CA. But then I realize that this is one of only two places in the world where these pines grow naturally, that they are a critically endangered species, and that you are a tree thief and amoral monster for stealing a protected tree. Hope you enjoy community service.

My tree (*Arboris tobinus*)

Everyone knows that I have the hottest, most fashionable tree in my house every December. Last year was a concolor fir, this year was a blue spruce, next year is . . . wow, nice try. You almost got me. For the love of God, don't just try to copy mine from last year *this* year—that has been a complete disaster for everyone who has tried in the past and they'll all testify that it will just be a really, really embarrassing experience for you and your whole family. Matter of fact, it's best if you didn't copy *any* of my tree picks, just to be safe. I'm just trying to look out for you.

Pine Cones and Whisky: Pairings to Stimulate the Senses

I don't know about you, but as my age increases, my definition of "partying" tends to become more and more bespoke. Whilst in a past life I frequently hit the "clurbs," looking for a fine hunnie with whom I could trade sensual bonsai secrets, I have since found my hunnie and created a small hunnie to boot. Needless to say, these days I do less "clurbing" and more "watching *Titanic* at 1.5x speed."

But I also enjoy an excellent philosophical conversation with friends wherein we lament the pains of the world and seek out elemental truths and watch hilarious YouTube clips. In times like these, I like to be positioned with a brown liquor in one hand and a pine cone in the other. Perhaps it is the woodiness of a marvelous bourbon or the peaty smoke of a lovely single-malt Islay that makes such liquid delights a symbiotic partner to a balanced pine cone. But, like Hamlet, I often find my most penetrating insights come forth when I balance Poor Yorick in one hand and Old Pulteney in the other.

The following are my favorite pairings with their corresponding philosophical inquiries.

"What Is Action?"
Giant Sequoia Cone and Bowmore 15

For when the order of the evening is tackling the enormous problems of the world, such as climate change, pair the cone of the giant sequoia (*Sequoiadendron giganteum*) with one of my favorite peaty single-malt Islays: Bowmore 15. I guarantee you that the combination of a cone that withstands an intense grip during heated discussion and a Scotch that pulls no punches in complexity will make for a lively exchange.

"What is Gentleness?"
Jeffrey Pine Cone and Hibiki Suntory Harmony

I have oft described the Jeffrey pine (*Pinus jeffreyi*) cone as the Tom Hanks of pine cones: gentle, lovely, rounded, a real crowd-pleaser. And, when cradled alongside a glass of the gentlest blended Japanese whisky around, the Hibiki Suntory Harmony, you'll find your personal genius longs to seek out the meaning of mercy and kindness. The blended nature of Hibiki Harmony is also a fantastic complement to Jeffrey's middle-range elevation of 7,000 feet (2,134 m).

spurs you on also commands their attentions, and its poetic balance is made manifest in your two palms. In your right: that rarest of Speyside single-malt Scotch whiskies, Glenburgie Aged 21 Years, whose fruit nearly equals its malt. In your left: a 15-inch (38 cm) sugar pine (*Pinus lambertiana*) cone—the longest of nature's pine cones and one of her crowning achievements.

"What Is Love? (Baby Don't Hurt Me)" Red Pine Cone and Well Whisky

It is true that after so much time spent pondering the heavier elements of existence and perhaps after two or three previous pine cones and their accompanying whiskies, you may feel the urge to rise from your seat and give in to the beat of Trinidadian–German Eurodance artist Haddaway's 1993 classic "What is Love." In this case, juxtapose your gyrations with something you won't mind spilling or stepping on, like a Maker's and soda and the barefoot-friendly red pine (*Pinus resinosa*) cone.

Building Your Own Tree Library

"What Is Beauty?" Sugar Pine Cone and Glenburgie 21

For this, the ultimate question for tree-loving aesthetes, I have the perfect combination. Picture it: you recline languorously like a modern-day Aristophanes, ready to volunteer your theory for why the conical tree canopy is the ultimate expression of floral beauty. Your companions are rapt, for the same inspired trance that

Knowledge: Some people think it's out of fashion, but I happen to like it.

That's why my tree library—which is my primary center of knowledge accumulation and enhancement on the subject as opposed to the internet, which is full of tree misinformation (I literally just saw a meme that stated the Angel Oak's age as fifteen hundred: a brazen falsehood)—is a treasured spot in my house. My wife was sympathetic when I told her that I wanted the Indiana Jones-like experience of quickly running my fingers along a series of related book spines until I found just the title to quench my query, so she allowed me to have my own bookcase where I could exploit this fantasy. Thank you, madam—my heart is yours.

I've since organized it into several tree subsections. From each, I encourage you to have at least one bibliographic example as you build your own tree library in order to diversify your tree knowledge. I haven't created my own system for indexing yet, but I'd imagine that it would be rather dewy.

Bottom Shelf

Coffee Table Inspo (*right*): These tomes saturate the blank mind with imagery and wonder. My own entries include *The Oldest Living Things in the World* by Rachel Sussman, *Wise Trees* by Diane Cook and Len Jenshel, and *Gnarly Branches, Ancient Trees: The Life and Works of Dan Robinson–Bonsai Pioneer* by Will Hiltz.

Straight-Up Tree Guides (*left*): These heartbreaking works of staggering genius are the real heavy-hitters of the tree world, and the intrepid researchers and taxonomists who write them are nothing less than heroic. It's good to have at least one continent-wide guide, like David Allen Sibley's *The Sibley Guide to Trees*—peerless in every respect—and another, more local guide. For me, this is Matt Ritter's *A Californian's Guide to the Trees Among Us.*

Second Shelf from Bottom

Deep Dives (*left*): This is my favorite section, where special trees get special attention in masterful works of research. Highlights include Ronald Lanner's *The Bristlecone Book*, and Robert van Pelt's inimitable *Forest Giants of the Pacific Northwest.*

Climate Change (*Leave some space between deep dives and bonsai on your shelf for the coming boom of books about climate change and trees.*): It's early days yet,

but *A Trillion Trees* by Frank Pearce gives some great insight on how reforesting the world is much more complex than dropping a thousand saplings all over your yard.

Bonsai (*right*): While it's completely your call whether bonsai is your bag, I highly recommend having at least one book in this section—if just to intrigue your guests. I have sixteen. Try one of Peter Chan's nine books on bonsai, such as *The Bonsai Beginner's Bible.*

Second Shelf from Top

Naturalist Corner (*left*): This is a great place to store the works of the personalities long associated with tree-dom, such as Suzanne Simard's *Finding the Mother Tree* or *The Collector: David Douglas and the Natural History of the Northwest* by Jack Nisbet. But it's also a good place to examine the shortcomings of nigh-mythical figures such as John Muir, and to put their sometimes-harmful ideas about who has the right to enjoy the outside world into modern context with a book like *The Adventure Gap: Changing the Face of the Outdoors* by James Edward Mills.

Tree-Adjacent Fiction And Poetry (*right*): The most popular section for visitors. For me, this includes all of J.R.R Tolkien, Richard Powers' *The Overstory*, and plenty of John Keats, Mary Oliver, and Anton Chekhov.

Top Shelf

Tree-Related Children's Books (*right*): If you haven't looked into this, look into this: the world of arboreal children's literature is boundless. Revisit these when you've lost your way. Titles include *The Peace Tree from Hiroshima* by Sandra Moore, *Little Tree* by Loren Long, and yes, *The Lorax* by Dr. Seuss.

Curios (*left*): These works are often the products of intimidatingly probing minds whose thirst for ultra-niche expertise leads them to exciting new frontiers in tree lore. I currently have *The Pencil* and *The Toothpick* staring back at me, both exhaustive biographies penned by Henry Petroski, and both of which I touched on earlier (page 37).

When a Tree (Your Tree) Falls: How to Write a Tree Eulogy

Sometimes there's a disturbance in the tree force. At those moments, it's best to be prepared.

It's a harrowing thought that you might look out one frosty morning upon the horizontal frame of what used to be your favorite woody neighbor. There should be time for mourning, but the greatest honor you can give your fallen friend is to let others know how wonderful they were!

The rules of writing a eulogy for a tree are the same as writing one for people: the cooler they are, the more colorful and compelling and moving and funny the eulogy is. The—how do I put this?—more *garden variety* they are, the more useful generalizations become. The only thing to note is that you should stay away from character defects, such as a compartmentalized fungal infection or accusation of excessive sap production.

Here's the general structure of my eulogy for Tree 103, which was a 346-year-old eastern white pine (*Pinus strobus*) and the tallest tree in New York State until it buckled underneath the weight of a neighbor. Folks, this eulogy—there's no other way to put it—killed.

Start off by being your wonderful and gracious self, and remind people why you are their rock in this heavy moment:

"Good morning. First off, I'd like to thank the Saplings, Seedlings, and entire dendrological network of Tree 103 for inviting me to speak today. It's an honor, plain and simple. I hope my words can give you comfort in this difficult time . . . "

Even if you don't mean any of this, it gets 'em every time. Next, you're going to get personal, or arboreal as the case may be, while you warm up the crowd:

" . . . It's wonderful to see so many familiar faces filling this room with love and lignin, all of whom loved Tree 103, and all of whom Tree 103 loved over the centuries. Manny, your skills as an arborist assured that Tree 103's golden years were filled with the finest foliage. (Applause starts.) Ellis, you are a good squirrel and a good boy. (Applause gets louder.) And, of course, who could forget those whom Tree 103 called his 'little Truffle-makers': his plot of mycorrhizal fungi (enthusiastic screams from the 'Truffle-makers') . . . "

I anticipated this uncouthness from that wild bunch, and threw in a joke to take back control:

" . . . Alright, alright, the wake isn't 'til eight, you loons!"

Huge laugh, control mine again. The crowd is now warm, it's time for the "old guy" joke:

" . . . Tree 103 rode this earth of ours for 346 crazy trips around the sun. Three hundred forty-six. Or just a couple less than Johnny over there . . . (moderate laugh) . . . well, Johnny's a bristlecone pine so I guess that's to be expected. (Larger laugh.) And of course, Tree 103 went the way most of us would want to go: with our neighbor collapsing on top of us (enormous guffaw)."

Now that you've given them a whole lotta hoots, you can do the boring but necessary stuff—lists of positive attributes, tender memories, the whole shebang. But make sure you loop it around back with a realistic, off-the-cuff, and totally rehearsed piece of hilarity that demonstrates how much larger than life your subject was . . .

" . . . oh, man! I remember, for the coronation ceremony for New York's tallest tree, Tree 103 leans over to me in the middle of Leo DiCaprio's speech introducing him and whispers, 'Enough already! When's the sunlight buffet?!' And right when Leo's about to call him up to the stage, Tree 103 lifts his roots and lets out this enormous CRREEAAKKK!!!"

Here, you'll have 'em in stitches, basking in the memory and warmth of their wild friend. And all you have to do now is let them down gently:

"Oh, my friend, my friend (push away tears of laughter and pathos) . . . no one made the days sing like you did. (Put your hand over your heart to steady yourself for the final gut punch.) You used to say it to me, but now I'm saying it back to you: (Silence—Tree 103 can't talk).

Standing ovation.

UNPOPULAR TREE OPINION: I Admire the Bradford Pear, and I Don't Care Who Knows It

As I write this, there is a popular strain of tree content that unnerves me. That frightens me. That enrages me.

We all know the Bradford pear is an unholy menace. We know about its creation as a sterile offshoot of the Callery pear (*Pyrus calleryana*), itself an import from Asia whose promise to revive an American pear die-off in the early twentieth century led to its establishment as the go-to tree of suburban sidewalks. We know about its tendency towards messy structural collapse after year fifteen. We know about its invasive ability to gobble up the sunlight from native flora. We know about its smell, the one that the vulgarians among us have compared to a certain reproductive fluid found in the human male. All of this we know.

But it seems we know all of this *too* well. Because now there's a pile-on effect happening. Everyone wants their fifteen minutes of Bradford pear Internet Hatred fame. From green-screen TikToks to your whack uncle's GeoCities, everyone is an angry, righteous citizen who just *cares so much*! "Look how much I despise this tree—the tree that is bad!"

But here's the thing, folks: *I don't buy it.*

Because I'm familiar with the great texts of civilization (*Frankenstein, Jurassic Park*), I understand that it isn't the Bradford pear you're angry with. What you're *actually* angry with, you pitchfork-wielding, tree scapegoat-obsessed mob of outdoor enthusiasts, is a civilization that made it possible for the Bradford pear to exist in the first place. A civilization whose hubris begot the distorted illusion that the Bradford pear would remain sterile, as opposed to finding fertility through pollen transference with other similar cultivars.

Do I sound like Jeff Goldblum here? Chastising you for believing that life will not, indeed, "find a way"? I suppose that's fine, because we've unleashed this unholy monstrosity upon ourselves and we'll continue to witness the carnage we've wrought.

For me, it is hard not to admire an invader of our own creation who so nimbly preys upon our weaknesses. One might say that obeisance is the only course of action, for when the reckoning comes:

"Thou didst seek my extinction, that I might cause greater wretchedness; and if yet, in some mode unknown to me, thou hadst not ceased to think and feel, thou wouldst not desire against me a vengeance greater than that which I feel."

Mary Shelley, *Frankenstein* (1818)

A Note on Garden Fashion

In my early days of tree-play and garden exploration, especially when I was first diving into the wonderful world of bonsai, I was spending a lot of time outside. I don't have to tell you what you should wear for an arduous trek or a cold jaunt through the limber pines (*Pinus flexilis*)—that's meandering territory for meandering gear. But what should one wear in their own backyard when they're just poopin' around, smelling flowers and bending juniper branches?

You might think it makes a lot of sense to dress like those frumpy people in those English films where elderly people fall in love: you know, big sunhats and flowered frocks over soft mittens meant to repel the morning dew. They all look like friendly grandparents, don't they? Isn't that lovely? Don't you just want to run up to them and ask them if they have an extra gooseberry to munch on?

But most of the time, what you're seeing is just the film's costume czar showing off how good at their job they are. Any real gardenhead knows the truth: Unless you're planning on sharing it that day with a grandchild or a grandparent, garden time is *your* time. The likelihood is that you're in the garden to be left alone doing your thing, be it digging or planting or smelling or sitting. It's a time for the warmth of the sun and the cool of the grass. And there's nothing that can ruin that like a child shouting "Mommy, ew, tomatoes, I hate them, ughhh . . . " or a spouse throwing some sexual innuendo at you. Not right now, dear!

So, what I recommend for garden fashion is to dress yourself in the most comfortable, albeit hideous, rags you can find. This way, you'll simultaneously feel right as rain and frighten any loud children or fresh spouses back into the house where they belong.

Each to his own, but here are the fundamentals of my most successful garden fashion. As you can see, I've smartly subtracted all sartorial intelligence.

Hat: A visor is preferable. That way it's both functional and completely horrible to behold.

Sunglasses: None, preferably. Sunglasses have the potential to arouse a lusty partner. If you must wear something, wear those enormous square sunglasses that cover the entire top half of your head like my grandparents wore when they vacationed in Boca. Consult your local drugstore.

Top: I love this part of the outfit. There are so many options. I have several dependable T-shirts that scream "get away from me." One is a fifteen-year-old Turkey Trot shirt with crumbling decal lettering, another is one of my own Bar Mitzvah T-shirts ("Who Wants Toby a Millionaire?"—again, the lettering is nearly dust) and the third is a freaky stoner bonsai number that I bought from a random website.

Bottom: I only have one piece for a bottom. They are my brother's (yes, Ethan, who I both love and envy) old black-and-white striped gym shorts. The crotch is a bit too high, so they look really uncomfortable, even though they aren't that bad at all. But the potential awkwardness involved makes even the chattiest neighbor keep their distance. They're perfect.

I usually throw in a pair of dog-torn sandals or shit-stained running shoes to complete my ensemble.

And, remember: Don't be afraid to mix-and-match.

Your Neighborhood Tree Super Team

Sometimes it's nice to look out the window and into our arboreal paradises to see those that actually serve the trees hard at work. I'm talking about the various professionals in the tree trade who help make our world beautiful. I often fantasize about building a murderer's row of these ecological superheroes for a children's show, like "Captain Planet" but so much more niche.

Bryce, Super Arborist: While your everyday, normal arborist has a wide swathe of duties from diagnosing pathogens to making the hard calls for unavoidable tree felling to having an intimidating understanding of ropes and rigging, Bryce is different. He has the *superability* to cut through multiple layers of municipal red tape with his SuperShears and get the job done faster than anyone else (and with super rates too!)

Lena, Super Forester: The forester has historically looked after the use of wooded communities for both ecological health and the use of human beings. But there's a reason Lena is a *Super* Forester: she knows what the forests need, because she's the only one the trees actually *talk back* to!

Amanda, Super Nursery Manager: Uh-oh, you hear the term "manager" and your tree-brain immediately shut off? Well, how's this for a new superpower: Amanda, your super nursery manager, has the power to control the weather within her ten acres of pristinely kept saplings, guarding them from triple digit temperatures in the summer and late frosts in the spring!

Rodrigo, Super Dendrochronologist: Researchers who study the effects of weather and historical climate events through the anomalies present in tree growth rings are some of our most valuable seers of the past. But Rodrigo has SuperSight (rumored to be 20:0.000001) that allows him to see micro-events in a tree's xylem that other researchers simply cannot see! Like when, in 1589, a grizzly bear ate some bad salmon, paused by a Sitka spruce (*Picea sitchensis*), and let out an enormous fart.

Arden, Super Silviculturist: It's a given that silviculture is the practice of creating sustainable forests for tree-farming and ecological function, so you'll oftentimes find Arden working closely with Lena to find the best solution. But Arden has a different trick up her sleeve: she can create networks of mycorrhizal fungi just by running her hands along the ground!

Chapter 5

Look on My Pine Cone Home, Ye Mighty, and Despair!

Hey, you.

Yeah, you. Stop looking around. I'm down here.

No, not over the side of the cliff. Down here. Beside your foot.

Do you see me? No? I'll give you a hint . . .

. . . I'm inside this pine cone.

Oh, don't look so astonished! Haven't you ever seen a Jeffrey pine cone before? Rounded, toasty brown, with kindness and comfort radiating from beneath each and every scale?

Yes, that's it. Bend an ear down here, there's something I want to tell you. Closer, please.

Look closely now, beneath the third scale from the top . . .

. . . rotate 30 degrees clockwise . . .

Hi.

Okay, please stop screaming now and hear me out: I know I'm a tiny person who lives inside of a pine cone and that might be alarming for several reasons. But I just want to say . . .

. . . that I know why you're out here. Alone. Among the trees. In your coziest flannel, with your coziest hat, and your tastiest treats.

I was once like you. I couldn't take it anymore, being down there in the city with everyone else. It felt raw and sad and fake, almost as if we were all a bunch of hamsters on hamster wheels. And when you're a hamster, you have to eat hamster food too. And you have to look at all the other hamsters eating hamster food too. And suddenly you realize there is no dignity in hamsters, or in being a hamster. Did I take this metaphor too far? Okay, let me just say . . .

. . . that I know what it's like for all meaning to go out of the world.

Allow me to tell my tale.

I came up here because I wanted an answer to my question. The same question that you have: Will the trees make me forget that I'm a hamster? Will they do away with my humiliation? Will they cloak me in their arms and take away the emptiness, just for a little while?

And you know what? They did. I was a glowing guest of the trees who let me crouch below them, silent and smiling, like a resting newborn. They said nothing. I said nothing. I simply ate and drank what provisions I had, making my bed upon the humus of time.

But I see the question in your curious eyes: How did I get so tiny?

Well, one day, my time was up. I had eaten my last Nature Valley bar, infinite crumbs and all, and I was parched with thirst that sultry July evening. "You must go now," the trees seemed to be saying. "But I don't want to," I cried out. "I want to stay here, forever, where I am no instrument of an invisible hand, cranking the dreaded hamster wheel, again and again . . .

. . . I wish to renounce the world of men! I wish to be a part of the forest!"

And at that moment, something marvelous happened: a golden mist enveloped me, and I felt all my sorrow and loneliness leave me, and I felt my body becoming smaller and smaller, and the forest became grander and grander, until it was as big as creation itself. And as I stood on the tip of a tiny mushroom, I found myself no longer fearful of the world, or wanting of peace, for it was mine. Mine! I was resplendent and blessed, and my worth radiated from within me like a star in my heart, and the magnificent world all around me shone back on my face like the self-same star. I was home.

I regretted nothing about leaving my previous life. I had life anew! I spent my days seeking out the mysteries of nature contained within the smallest granules of tree bark. Those who might be tempted to consume me instead offered me a hairy leg to climb. I hitched a ride on their magnificently spiky thoraxes like a jockey upon a stallion.

It was as if the meaning that had eluded me in my previous life was suddenly everywhere—every miniscule grain of dust was a treasure chest of knowledge and beauty worth careful study and love.

One day, while finally cresting a small rock I dubbed Mount Superlatus, my ant antennae cane gave way near the summit. I tumbled down with joy—for this was a common occurrence in my travels—until I came to rest, laughing, at the foot of a great pine cone. It was the one you currently hold in your hand, wrought from God's finest materials and fashioned in the form of his servant Jeffrey. I took up residence inside of it, building for myself a castle beyond the imaginings of our greatest wonderers.

I made for myself a pine cone kitchen, with a tiny stove for a late breakfast, because I usually don't get up until nine-thirty or ten. See it? And here's my pine cone great room, which is the kind of cavernous living room that only truly exquisite residences possess. Down there is my pine cone garage, where I drive a really nice seed over to that sugar pine across the way for some fresh sap every afternoon.

And of course, up there, way at the top, is my pine cone bedroom. See it? I added a fireplace and a chimney made of minute pebbles. When my cone is tossed and tumbled in a gale, I rest easily in my pine cone bed and fall asleep to the sounds of crunching needles and heavy raindrops on the lower pine cone scales.

But after many seasons of wandering and wondering, after uncountable days and nights living in peace and relative fulfillment, after immeasurable years full of meaning and laughter and tears of joy, I have come to a simple truth: each season the wonders are fewer, each day my fulfillment seems less so, and every year my existence seems less like that of solace and more like that of solitude.

Suddenly I, who thought only of humanity with contempt, felt a yearning for a shared experience with another human being.

I called to the Tree Gods, "Tree Gods! Give me leave for one afternoon that I might return to the city, to tell the people of my exploits, and to feel the warmth of a common smile!"

But the Tree Gods were silent. I had made my exchange, you see. There was no going back. I could not have the life of man and the life of the forest.

When I saw that I would receive no answer, I wept bitterly. I rent my garments like an infinitesimal King Lear, taunting the canopy above as the mad king did his winds.

Finally, my anger gave way to despair. I had all the glory of creation at my fingertips, but was instead cursed to solitary confinement within its wonders by way of my abandonment of my brethren.

And I see the same pain in your eyes: the longing for a life of warmth and comfort and splendor, away from the death and the sickness and the cruelty.

And I see you imagining our untold days as grains of sand, tumbling back and forth over the soil like angels amidst the jewels of creation, gazing up at the trees, now higher than your eyes can touch, their trunks occupying an entire afternoon in your patient circumnavigation.

And I see you imagining a life of meaningful friendship with another tiny person inside this pine cone castle.

Eating breakfast together in our kitchen. Sharing a bottle of pine cone wine at night. Only a laugh or two may fit in here, but they'd be ours! And when we're done, we'd climb into the pine cone dumbwaiter and arrive at the top of the pine cone castle in our pine cone bedrooms to retire. There, we'll brave the winter winds against the windows, away from the world, under the trees, alight in their grace, our scars healed over, with no memory of the time before or time at all. I must admit, I have long desired this kinship. Hoped for it. Prayed for it.

But alas! The years have stolen from me my selfishness. So this I say to you now:

You must not give in to temptation.

You must return to the horrors of the world of humans. For who will guide them if not you? Who will tell them about the trees and the life inside of them? The endless sweetnesses that await them, one arm around a tree, the other around their fellow?

Don't become like me: rich in treasure alone. You are the one who can tell them of my folly, and you are the one who can bring them here, from whence they came, and show them that the hamster wheel only runs when they run on it.

Now, now, don't cry. Remember that it does you no good to mourn a life you have never known.

Chin up. It's time to make your decision.

Chapter 6

Climate Change and Trees

It seems as though every day brings a new tree-related calamity as a result of a warming planet. My most rabid critics might think, "Well, it's easier to consider things like trees and animals as opposed to the fates of human beings." But that's a red herring, because I need not tell you that the fates of all living things are bound to each other—in the air we breathe, in the homes we inhabit, in the way we make our existence thoughtful and meaningful and not just a story of mere survival.

There are harsh truths to face about our most iconic trees, which we risk losing—some within the next ten years—as a result of spreading bark beetles, uncontrolled wildfires, and other new phenomena that are a direct result of carbon emissions. But there are so many unknowns when it comes to the future of trees, that sometimes it can be easier to list what we *don't know* in order to find some sort of Stoic calm amidst the chaos.

And then, once we open ourselves up to all of the confusion, terror, and genuine ugliness that ignorance affords us, we can begin to reassemble those tiny parts of what we *do know*, and see what we have.

What I Don't Know

Should I give my enthusiast's opinion on the vast and frightening topic of climate change with respect to the trees I love so much despite my lack of scientific qualifications? I don't know.

Will the rapid warming of Earth due to infrared absorption of carbon dioxide be the end of life as we know it? I don't know.

And will the water stress from drought that makes trees more susceptible to disease make them part of a global extinction? I don't know.

Will the bark beetle lay waste to every white bark (*Pinus albicaulis*), sugar pine (*Pinus lambertiana*), and limber pine (*Pinus flexilis*) as it migrates up the mountains as temperatures increase? I don't know.

And will it finally lay claim to the bristlecones (*Pinus longaeva*), ending the longest continuous plant record on the planet as it turns their home into a wooden graveyard? I don't know.

And will our methods of forest fire management in an era of hotter temperatures still lag behind indigenous practices which emphasized controlled burns to limit the intensity of fires? I don't know.

And will the increasing volumes of dead trees provide ever more burnable fuel for these fires? I don't know.

Will late frosts kill the young spring tissue in many angiosperms, threatening them as well? I don't know.

But can we use the benefits of fast-reproducing generations of healthy mycorrhizae to help transition their slow-growing tree partners to higher latitudes? I don't know.

And can we perhaps utilize the fast-growing, carbon-storing potential of birch and aspen as our primary arboreal weapons against climate change? I don't know.

Am I wrong to have doubts about the current vogue of private and corporate tree-planting movements? I don't know.

And is their marketing an insufficient Band-Aid for climate change, given that keeping warming below a certain threshold will come from government regulation and cutting of emissions? I don't know.

Isn't even the act of carbon offsetting through tree-planting a good excuse for wealthier people to continue their unfortunate behaviors, like flying on private jets, through "paying" for it via an unproven system of balance? I don't know.

And why does the public conversation stop at the actual planting of a tree, as opposed to the maintenance of that tree, or the consequences of planting that tree, such as the possibility of reduced albedo (the reflection of solar radiation) in new forests from the dark greening of the earth that will actually absorb *more* infrared light from the sun before the forests can reach maturity after one hundred years to absorb sufficient carbon, leading to temperature *increases*? I don't know.

And why isn't more energy directed towards maintaining our current carbon sinks of old-growth forests, where the oldest and largest 2 or 3 percent of trees store more carbon than 50 percent of young growth? I don't know.

Shouldn't prevention of deforestation in this regard be the tree community's primary objective, as opposed to creating more trees? I don't know!

Oof, is it shameful to have more emotional access to sadness on behalf of an old tree being cut down than to human beings who will be immiserated? That's a bummer of a thought, and I don't know.

What does that say about the meaning of my own life in a world where I feel alienated from other people but very close to trees? Ugh, I don't know.

Man, I just don't know.

What I Know

I know that it feels nice to be sitting on a cushioned chair after spending four hours outside.

I know that the dirt that I couldn't get out from beneath my fingernails feels like a reward of some kind.

I know that I'll have to pay special attention to the American elm (*Ulmus americana*) sapling in a plastic pot while it regains its strength after being transplanted from a neighbor's yard.

I know that the biggest challenge in removing the sapling was understanding where the roots of the tree ended and where the messy, dead roots of all the other crap began, and where to cut. Also, that it was in deep clay, which isn't the best to deal with.

I know that I'm thankful its parent elm above me gave me shade on a 96-degree day.

I know that it feels good to tell my neighbor that her seemingly ordinary tree was actually remarkable.

I know that it was a good idea to leave a note on her fence inquiring about the enormous American elm in her front yard, which is a rare sight in America after its devastation from Dutch elm disease, and an even rarer sight in Los Angeles where it does not grow natively.

I know that the original owner of the house planted it sometime around 1940, and that her name was Elizabeth, and that she was English, and that when she died at ninety-four her family requested that trees be planted in her memory.

I know that I'm anxious to hear back from her granddaughter about whether Elizabeth planted the tree because it reminded her of the English elms (*Ulmus procera*) that must have surrounded her in her youth in England. Those are mostly dead now as well.

I know that sometimes trees offer simpler truths than overwhelming history lessons or critical energy fables, like that kindness across time feels like shade.

I know that the oft-quoted proverb, "Society grows great when the Old plant trees in whose shade they know they shall never sit," isn't good enough for me. It should continue," . . . and when the Young plant trees to sit under when they are old."

After all, planting a tree can be a sign of hope for oneself as well.

Part II

A TREE, BASICALLY

Having said my piece, I will say no more—about myself and trees, that is.

My aim in part two of this book is simple: I want to position you squarely in that hard-to-find sweet spot of education and fun. Some call this "edu-tainment," but I prefer "fun-utation" or "edu-funion." Regardless, with too much education you risk falling into boredom. And with too much fun, you risk falling out of a ponderosa.

If I succeed, I bet that the next time your pals ask you to meet them in the woods you'll practically jump at the chance to identify trees, wonder at trees, jive with trees, and, ultimately, make dirty jokes about trees, which many people will tell you is the purpose of every nature walk.

So: Botany, biology, ecology. Tomato, tom-ah-to, to-mo-tah, right?

Wrong. And the difference between these terms has life-and-death implications for all mankind, so you'd better listen up. I'm joking . . .

I'm also slightly not joking. Read on.

Botany is the study of plants specifically. We'll dive into this first so that we can cover leaves, needles, seeds . . . that type of stuff. It's the field with which we associate terms like apophysis, petiole, and rachis—none of which I will be using again in order to maintain your attention. It's also where the word "botanicals" comes from, so prepare to get crunk with a twenty-five dollar aloe-infused margarita and a hemp-extract face mask. Just kidding again—this guide is anything but chill.

Biology is the study of life, obviously. This will be the second part of this section where we look at a tree as a larger living organism. Most of the time there's a marvelous gestalt effect, with the tree becoming greater than the sum of its parts. But I've also seen the opposite happen with some scrubby lodgepole pine krummholz and, Lord above, that is a sorry sight.

Ecology is the study of life's ecosystems. What systems and species does a tree support? How does it function in a forest? In the world? Is it planning on voting in its local elections? What happens when there's a tree plague? Answers to these questions and more in the Tree Ecology portion of this section (page 82), which seeks to understand trees as bigger than themselves.

And look, if you choose to skip part two and go straight to part three, I won't blame you. It's probably what I would do if I were in your shoes. But I've tried to make this section as simple and palatable as possible for the hecklers in the cheap seats because it's my sincere belief that the road to wisdom is paved with knowledge, and the road to knowledge is paved with uncomplicated explanation. With a few jokes thrown in.

Behold: A tree, basically.

Chapter 7

Tree Botany

The history of botany and how it applies to trees can read like a murderer's row of competing naturalists, all strong-arming each other in a race to the top. But it's mostly a slow and exacting science wrought by careful observers in illustration, then explored more deeply by people with very cool microscopes. The main thing is: this is all the tiny pieces, and this is what they do.

Tree Botany I: Leaves— Broadleaf Trees

I love leaves. They're amazing. They house the organic chemical chlorophyll in chloroplasts, which take in energy from the sun, carbon dioxide (CO_2) from the air, and water and nutrients from the tree's roots in order to make glucose. Glucose builds the tree. Then the leaf poops out oxygen through the stomata, which are kind of like a butt and a mouth at the same time. Couldn't be simpler, right?

But "**broadleaf**," yikes. As a wise man once said, "Willis, brother, of what do you speak?"

Well, it's pretty intuitive. "Broad" + "leaf" = a leaf that is broad and not needle-like. These are also known as the leaves that look like leaves. They're featured on the **angiosperms**, which include most **deciduous** trees (which have leaves that fall at least yearly), but a few **evergreen** trees (you know this one) as well, such as the Olive and many tropical trees. The angiosperms also all have flowers as their reproductive organs as opposed to **gymnosperms**, aka **conifers**, which bear cones instead.

(Fun fact: Some methods of taxonomy group broadleaf trees under the division Magnoliophyta as opposed to Pinophyta for conifers and Ginkgophyta for ginkgo trees, but this technical terminology would also include those damned, dirty palms and I will not be giving them the satisfaction of their inclusion in this section or any section. Until I talk some smack on pages 204 to 205).

In short, the larger the leaf, the more sunlight it is designed to absorb. This greediness can be explained by a few different causes: the tree grows in a region with a ton of sun, such as the tropics, where it has evolved to accommodate more light absorption; the tree grows in a highly competitive understory (a lower level of the forest) and it's desperate for more sun; the tree is simply a show-off and needs to be publicly shamed.

What really matters here is the organization of the veins, which structure the leaf. In broadleaf trees, veins run out like nets to the edges of the leaf, and contain pathways for xylem and phloem, which are specialized cells for water, sugar, and nutrient transport. I won't be getting any deeper than that. Also, that would be where my expertise gets spotty, so this works out for both of us.

Leaf Shape and Arrangement

Check it out, noobs: Leaves have a few features that help you identify what tree you might be looking at.

1. **Is it lobed?** Oak leaves, yes. Elm leaves, no. Lobes are the shaped, pointy, or rounded borders of a leaf.

2. **Check the edges**. Are they smooth like a weeping fig? Or **toothed** like a thankless child? I mean, a Birch?

3. **Is there just a single leaf attached to the leafstalk**? Or are multiple leaves (**leaflets**) attached to one leafstalk? The former is a **simple leaf**, the latter is a **compound leaf**. Or as I like to call it, a "leaf made of leaves." There are also leaves that are **bipinnately compound**, or leaves made of leaves made of leaves. There are even **tripinnately compound** leaves. That's right, folks: leaves made of leaves made of leaves made of leaves.

(PS: If you've got leaflets on two sides running parallel on your leaf, it's called pinnately compound. If they're radiating from a center point, you've got a **palmately compound** leaf. Palm = your hand. See what botanists did there?)

4. Are pairs of leaves springing up **opposite** each other on a twig? Or do the buds take turns, resulting in an **alternate** arrangement?

Why do trees drop their leaves? And why do leaves change color?

Simple answer: They get tired of them. Literally! They suck the nutrients out of their leaves and into their trunk and branches to toughen up for cold weather, then give a big ol' middle finger to their leaves.

But the joke's on the tree, because just before they do their final, explosive, Travolta-in-the-hellmouth-at-the-end-of-"Stayin' Alive"-dance to the ground, the leaves freak out. They generate a variety of beautiful pigments as if to say to the tree, "Good luck finding this again, jerkwad!" (Spoiler alert: It will.) As the chlorophyll breaks down, eliminating the leaf's greens, we see yellows, which were always present, along with red and brown toward the leaf's final days. Some trees, like the sweetgum (*Liquidambar styraciflua*), will feature multiple leaf colors on each branch as their leaves are all in different moments of despair simultaneously.

Tree Botany II: Leaves— Needles and Scales

Oh, thank God the broadleaf section is over and done with. I think I did a pretty good job pretending that I like those trees. I mean, I do. Just not as much as I *adore* conifers.

Conifers—the cone-bearing trees that make up the botanical grouping gymnosperms—are my inter-biological kingdom soulmates. I won't gush on too long about them here, because we've got to get to **needles and scales**, but suffice to say that they light a fire in me that I can only describe as **pyriscent**. That's an incredibly dirty joke if you want to look it up, but there's no time for me to explain it here.

You may presume that all conifers are evergreen. Simply not true. Larches (genus *Larix*), dawn redwoods (*Metasequoia glyptostroboides*), and baldcypresses (*Taxodium distichum*) all lose their needles annually.

Now, I'm a merciful man, but I won't forgive you if you fail to text this fact to at least twenty-five of your closest friends and relatives immediately.

The needles and scales of conifers function identically to broadleaves in photosynthesis, except that their veins are parallel and tightly packed, producing a needle or scale that's tough, darned tough! And the rougher the atmosphere—these suckers can grow above 10,000 feet (3,048 m) with regular gusts of 100 miles per hour (161 kmh) pushing them around—the thicker the cuticle, or waxy protection on the needle that seals up its stomata in order to protect precious water. Anyone who has held a handful of Great Basin bristlecone pine (*Pinus longaeva*) needles knows what I'm talking about. Those bad boys are *dense*.

So, why needles instead of broadleaves? Now, if I were a bonafide rapscallion, I would answer "divergent evolution." So, divergent evolution. That basically means that needles and their aforementioned toughness do better in cold temperatures, while broadleaf trees in milder climates have adapted more expansive ways to express themselves.

But the most compelling thing about conifers, to me—aside from their romantic representations of age, their head-swimming aromas, and their typically isolated geographic locations which make journeys of the head and the heart and the soul and the road not only a feature but a necessity—is the mystifying variety in the shape of their needles and scales.

Pines (genus *Pinus*), famously, have needles in bundles enclosed in a **fascicle**, a word which *sounds* dirty (a little like pyriscent), but is not. We traditionally divide up pines into yellow pines, which have three needles a bundle, and white pines, which have five. But it can be a bit more complicated than that. The Western United States, for example, is blessed with lodgepole pines (*Pinus contorta*), two needles; parry piñon pines (*Pinus quadrifolia*), four; and single-leaf piñon pines (*Pinus monophylla*), one. The classification of these pines as yellow or white is, well, up for debate.

Redwoods (*Sequoia sempervirens*), the tallest trees, have flattened needles that run pinnately on their stems. Bonus fact: the stomata of these needles are evolved to actually *absorb* water from fog, so that water goes *into* the leaf. Leaves don't usually do this. It's extremely rare and breathtakingly cool.

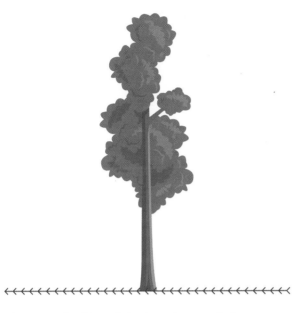

Giant sequoias (*Sequoiadendron giganteum*), the most massive trees, have tiny, compressed, and pointed scales around their stems which might leave you saying, "Hey, where are the leaves because I cannot see them, for this tree is superlatively large and I expected proportional chloroplast containers?"

Spruce (genus *Picea*), which can certainly be nasty if you please, have sharp needles that grow 360 degrees around the stem.

A lot of people tend to have difficulty telling apart firs and spruces, so here's a poem I often recite to remember them:

"When gripping thus the fir tree grand,
One knows the softness of the land,

When gripping thus the spruce tree grand,
Oh, God, oh, shit, my hand, my hand!"

Firs (genus *Abies*), which typically grow at higher elevations, have blunt, flat, thick-cuticled needles that grow on the sides and top of the stem. Break a bunch of California white fir (*Abies concolor*) needles in your hand and you're in seventh heaven, my dude.

True cedars, which fall under the genus *Cedrus*—such as the breathtaking blue Atlas cedar (*Cedrus atlantica*)—have what are called rosettes: circular bursts of needles that are at once poetic and fascinating.

False-cedars, which get *called* cedars a lot of the time but are really just a bunch of nouveau-riche scallywags across several genuses, such as the admittedly lovely incense-cedar (*Calocedrus decurrens*), have flattened scales which fan out horizontally.

Tree Botany III: Flowers and Fruit

Do trees have sex? That's mostly a question for J.R.R. Tolkien, and I'd imagine that if they did it would be loud and distracting. But on this particular earth no, they don't, and we should be thankful because that would be painfully awkward to explain to young people.

But one could say that they do have a sexy *time*—the spring—when they aim to pollinate. Some trees do this with flowers, and some do this with cones and pollen.

We're going to rely on our botanical Jets and Sharks, the **angiosperms** (the mostly deciduous broadleaves) and **gymnosperms** (the mostly evergreen conifers) in order to make an important distinction that someone will probably take an exception to in the coming years: our guys the angiosperms? They have flowers. The gymnosperms do not.

See, flowers are an organ (oh my God, get your head out of the gutter. No, wait: keep it there. This is where stuff gets NC-17). They're made up of multiple "parts," like the male-classified **stamen**, which have pollen on the anthers, and the female-classified **ovary,** which contains

Junipers (genus *Juniperus*) mostly feature scales of a similar bunching arrangement, but a few, like the common juniper (*Juniperus communis*), are sharp and cruel. But I understand: if someone kept calling me "common," I'd be peeved too.

an egg. Outside these "parts" are the petals and the sepals, which get nice and smelly and colorful in order to attract bugs and other pollinators, like birds and bats and you. Then a bug or a bat or your nose carries the male sperm cell in the form of pollen to another flower and WHAM!—you got yourself a fertilized egg. From there, a fruit grows around it, which usually takes a few months to ripen.

Sometimes, like in oak flowers and maple flowers and other extremely boring flowers, the flowers rely on the wind to carry their pollen to other trees. Sure, a tree can occasionally self-pollinate, but, like a grateful teenager will tell you, it tends to be less successful. It's also not great for genetic variation.

This all might be a bit simplistic, since some trees feature flowers with different sexes on the same tree, and some angiosperms produce entire trees with different sexes, like American Holly (*Ilex opaca*). But that's the gist, and I'm sure that about 99.4 percent of you don't care to go any further anyway.

Oh, did you have a few comments?

I'm sorry, I don't remember the "fruit" on angiosperms such as oaks, maples, and elms. Well, Sonny, perhaps you neglected to notice the **acorn** on the oak and the winged "keys" on the maples and elms. The acorn is a fertilized fruit known as a "nut," and the keys are marvelously evolved to flutter their asses all over creation in order to make more of themselves.

So, you're telling me that apple I just ate had fertilized seeds in it? Yes, I am. And that apple tree (genus *Malus*) you got it from is just praying that you'll do a number two in some soil with a moderate pH. Just bring a trowel.

Whoa, whoa, my man. I hang with a flowering dogwood (*Cornus florida*) and he says that he flowers year-round, not just in the spring! I am sorry to break it to your arboreal friend, but he's wrong. Those are actually specialized leaves called "**bracts**," not a part of the flower proper. Bougainvillea has these too.

Tree Botany IV: Cones

Cones are often one of the first introductions of young human beings to the world of nature. It's why so many of us have such nostalgia associated with them: cozy feelings of hot soups, cold winters, and the crickle-crackle of a Duraflame log keeping your butt snuggly whilst reruns of *The Beverly Hillbillies* play on Nick at Nite.

But enough about me. Let's be objective for a second: cones are the best things in the world.

Notice I did not say "pine cones," because *cones* refers to any and all locations of female reproductive organs on the gymnosperms (the conifers), including those of the true cedars (which fall apart every year), the firs (same thing there), the spruces (which are slightly heartier but still get dashed to pieces on the forest floor), the cypresses (which are round and solid), the giant sequoia (which are the size and toughness of golf balls), and all others in the gymnosperm category.

And, last but not least, the pine cones, which refer to the cones of trees in the genus *Pinus*.

Gymnosperm, of course, means "naked seed," because, folks, I don't see no fruit around that thing! And, while they don't have "flowers" as defined by true nerds, the cone is the equivalent thereof.

Cones work in simple, beautiful ways. In general, the process is as follows:

The **pollen cones**, which are the male reproductive organs that form on the lower part on the conifer and go to pieces like clockwork (much like our own species), burst in the spring. This releases pollen that floats up into the canopy of another tree, where the female woody cones are awaitin'.

The pollen then pollinates and fertilizes those developing cones by landing on a cone scale—a single woody outgrowth on the cone—and releasing sperm into the ovule.

Then, get this, the cone seals up, grows for anywhere from six to eighteen months, then opens in order to release its seeds when they're all cooked.

There are some caveats here—the cones might be **serotinous**, opening later by design, including due to fires melting the cone's resinous "glue." Or perhaps they rely on squirrels or rats or birds to gobble up the fertilized seeds for secret stashing, only to have them sprout years later.

There really are so many wonderful things to say about cones, and pine cones in particular for their woody staying power and their humanity-wide ubiquity. You might even find yourself *enjoying* the botanical terminology, for a change. For example, the end of a cone scale is called an "umbo," and the prickly ones, like the ponderosa, have what's called a—get this—"prickle" on the end. I mean, it's as if two warring botanists got together in 1823 for the purpose of naming the parts of a pine cone and simultaneously said, "Hey pal, let's set aside our differences and just get cute right now." Which makes sense, because, when examining the wide variety of cones from the adorable Douglas-fir (*Pseudotsuga menziesii*) with

its papery bracts to the teensy-weensy cones of the mighty coast redwood (*Sequoia sempervirens*), you have a feeling that God was doing the same thing nearly six thousand years ago.

Wait, what?

I really enjoy putting content out into the world about cones—mostly pine cones—and so I'll get a lot of questions about them, but these are the two most common ones that I'm asked:

Where do "pine nuts" come from? This may blow your mind, but yes, they come from pine cones. There are a few species that are more popular than others on an industrial *scale*, such as the Italian stone pine (*Pinus pinea*), but for my money, the most delicious pine nuts (which are just the fertilized seeds atop each scale) come from the single-leaf piñon (*Pinus monophylla*). Sumptuously oily and nearly sweet, they're perhaps the most important food sustenance in the history of the indigenous peoples of the Americas.

The claws, sir, the claws on some of these beasts! Why? I can only assume you're referring to our spiky, frightening, and mace-like friend the coulter pine (*Pinus coulteri*), whose pine cones can grow up to 8 pounds (3.6 kg) in weight and to 15 inches (38 cm) long and have prickles that resemble the velociraptor claw from *Jurassic Park*. The answer here is to ward off predators, or *megafauna*, as they were known in the evolutionary days of yore.

But didn't they rely on these "megafauna" to disperse their seeds? Oh, uh, yes. I mean the claws are there to, uh, ward off, uh, young men who would use the cones as, uh, weapons in local, uh, things.

What? Sorry, that's the end of this section.

Tree Botany V: Twigs (yes, really)

Twig. Funny word, eh? Almost onomatopoetic as it rolls off the tongue.

How do you understand the progressive scale of your twigs? I'm willing to bet, for you, it goes something like this: twig, branch, trunk.

But the botanist's flow goes a little something like this: twig (meaning this year's growth), branchlet (last year's growth), branch, trunk, tree, forest, Earth, Universe, *The Matrix*. Sorry, folks, what the botanists say, goes.

What I want to say about twigs is this: there's a lot of excessive terminology involved here that might make you want to pull your hair out—axillary bud, leaf scar, bud scale—but there are a few simple things that are good to know in order to identify the tree you're looking at.

The first is alternate versus oppositely arranged buds. This is straightforward: If a pair of buds or leaves sprout together on a twig, one on either side, they're **oppositely arranged**. If there's only one bud or leaf, then a ways down the twig there is another on the other side, they're **alternately arranged**. All maples grow with opposite buds. The sweetgum has alternate buds. Good to know!

The second is concerning the **buds** themselves, which I've mentioned already, and you're probably like "yes, yes, small green thing which turns into a leaf," which is sort of true. But buds—which form in the summer, hang out for the fall and winter, and push (cool word) in the spring during bud burst (cool term)—are specialized for either leaves *or flowers* in the angiosperms.

This means that, in a tree like the saucer magnolia (a genus *Magnolia* cross), the flower buds are mad swole, while the leaf buds are somewhat less swole but can still show their faces at the local Crunch. Different trees have differently colored and sized buds for flowers and leaves. Keep that in mind when trying to figure out a naked angiosperm in the middle of winter.

A couple other things that happen in twigland that make our world marvelous:

The exploding, meandering shape of oaks (genus *Quercus*) is due to the tendency of their buds to cluster up at the end of each year's growth near the **terminus**. Hmm, a bajillion buds within a couple inches from each other—which way will they go? The answer is "everywhere," which gives us the random, yet graceful, swoop and movement of oaks.

Also, think about this the next time you see one of those enormous, ball-shaped, spiky weirdnesses amidst the branches of that oak or incense-cedar. Those "**witches' brooms**," as they're called, are caused by pathogenic invasions into the tree. You know, mildew, fungus, that sort of thing. What those pathogens do is short-circuit the growth of twigs, causing them to wig out uncontrolled in all directions like a freaky-deeky brain monster. Twigs!

Chapter 8

Tree Biology

We're zooming out, folks. Now we can get a glimpse of the tree as a whole and maybe even get a hint of its ultimate aims. You're going to like this section, because, just for a second, we can leave behind the mind-numbing distinctions between our old pals the gymnosperms and the angiosperms because everyone's the same here, man!

That's not technically true, like, at all. But I'll try to keep the nerdity to a minimum.

Tree Biology I: Oh, Good, a Trunk Cross Section, Thanks, Tobin

The aim of the tree's trunk is two-fold: to support the branches (which in turn support the leaves), and to transport water, nutrients, and carbohydrates throughout the tree so it can live long and prosper.

On the following page, you'll find the all-too-common cross-sectional diagram of a tree trunk, which grates terribly on the young folks, I know. Don't worry, I've

spruced it up a bit with some contemporary vocabulary to make it more palatable for Gen-Z. Sorry, boomers, my editor said I had to.

Pith: One could say the pith's drip is iconic. Centrally located, it's alive, spongy, and really into transporting water and nutrients via its **xylem cells**, which TBH are the absolute GOATs of the tree vascular system. (This is in contrast to the **phloem cells**, which absolutely spill the tea throughout the tree. The tea here, of course, being glucose and other tree-building organic molecules).

Heartwood: "I'm dead."—The heartwood. No, seriously. It's dead. The heartwood is the centermost portion of the trunk wood. It no longer transports water. Therefore, it is made of structurally important, but empty and soulless, wood cells. You know: dead. You might notice that the rings here vary in size. This reflects either biological inclination (yews [genus *Taxus*] grow slow AF and have thin rings, sequoias [*Sequoiadendron giganteum*] grow fast and have thicc rings), environmental conditions (big snowstorm that year? Might be thinner), or maybe tree health (fungal infections will leave the rings shook).

Rays: These guys actually transport materials *horizontally* toward the pith. Savage!

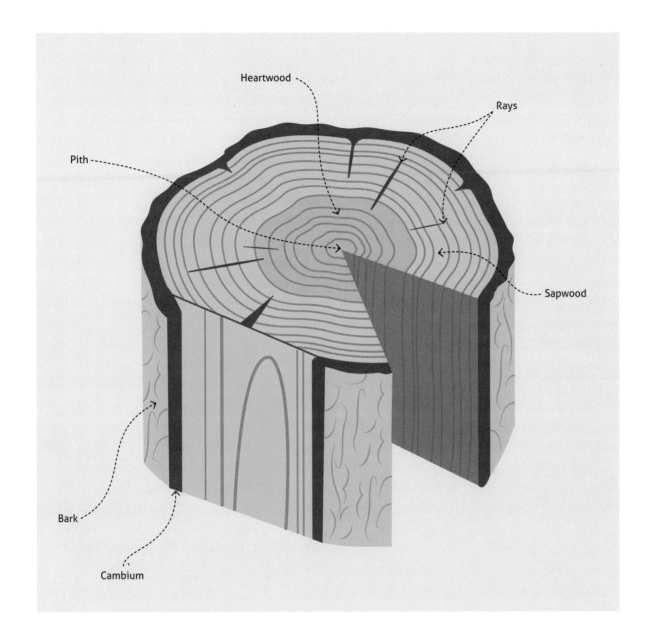

Spring wood versus autumn wood: Within each growth ring there's an inner, thicker, lighter section and an outer, thinner, darker section. Seems sus, right? No worries, it's just the spring wood (also known as early wood), which forms in the spring and has fewer xylem cells to color it, and the autumn wood (aka late wood), which grows later in the year and has more xylem cells to color it. Yas!

Sapwood: The sapwood is the outer portion of growth rings, and I stan the sapwood. Here's why: the sapwood is full of xylem cells, which conduct water and nutrients from the roots up the tree through specialized xylem pipelines, all the way to the leaves so that they can photosynthesize and respire. Quite a mood, really.

For a long time, everyone thought that xylem cells transported water and minerals up from the roots to the end of the leaves, unidirectionally. End of story. But the last few decades of research have shown this to be speculative at best! The coast redwood (*Sequoia sempervirens*), for example, is a tall fellow—like a 400-foot-tall (122 m) kind of tall fellow. It's tough work to transport water all the way up to the tree's crown with that stupid gravity thing happening all the time. So the needles have developed an adaptation: they suck in water from the fog through their stomata, and reverse the xylem flow down towards the roots. Damn, Gina!*

Gen-Z: You do know this was a catchphrase from a successful 1990s television show entitled, Martin, correct? That show was the absolute bee's knees!

Sap, Pitch, Resin, Amber: What's the difference? Well, you got the order right. Sap is phase one: sugary, watery, nutritious stuff that flows throughout the tree in its phloem cells in order to lend growth materials to the parts of the tree in need. It's what maple or birch or sugar pines give off when tapped. Pitch is phase two: the sticky, frustrating stuff that's impossible to remove from your fingers and clothes. Resin is the third stage: when the pitch has hardened into a crust. And amber is the fossilized version: the place where dinosaurs come from.

The Cambium Layer: This is where the tree gets its glow-up. The cambium layer is the gooey growth layer between the wood and the bark where the cells are constantly dividing. This year's growth layer becomes last year's growth ring. But it also becomes . . .

The Bark: There are two layers of bark (major flex). There's the innie bark (technical term), which is known as the phloem layer and is, you guessed it, full of phloem cells which transport glucose and other carbs. The cambium creates a new one of these every year, which totally slaps. There's also the outtie bark, which comprises multiple layers of dead cells that protect the tree in various ways, from fire to insect invasion. You know the type: covered in lichens, maybe peeling, maybe fibrous, maybe plated.

Slay, Bark! Okay, gonna see myself out.

Tree Biology II: The Tree as a System

Hopefully by now you're seeing that we are building towards the tree as an entire organism with a distinct purpose: to be a good tree.

But there are a couple major tree features we haven't touched on yet. The first is the root system.

The **roots** serve a two-fold function: to absorb water and nutrients, and to keep the tree upright. If they fail at either one of these, the tree's kaput.

The roots are the first part of the tree to grow when it emerges out of its embryonic stage as a seedling, and consequently, they're the first to ball out in the spring, when they expand via their root caps (their tiny tips) and sprout literally a bajillion separate tiny root hairs. These Tiny Tims are the ones that actually do all the absorbing, and they appear most frequently in the top 18 inches (46 cm) of soil, though they can spread out far from the trunk laterally.

But what about those huge roots—what's *their* deal? Simple: to anchor that baby down. They're structural. *Finis.* But that doesn't mean they aren't fascinating in and of themselves. Structural roots can stand higher than a human being in certain *Ficus* trees and other tropical species that have evolved to stay anchored in wet soils. And, of course, there are the aerial roots of the strangler figs (certain trees of the genus *Ficus*). The seeds of these trees implant themselves upon another mature tree, send their roots down through the air, and eventually subsume the original tree.

Some root systems are even shared between trees that reproduce asexually as clones, like the great Pando cluster of quaking aspen (*Populus tremuloides*) in Utah's Fishlake National Forest.

A tree with both anchor roots and plenty of functional root hairs has everything it needs below the surface of the soil (excluding symbiotic mycorrhizal fungi. You can read plenty of books on that but definitely not mine, because that subject is *involved,* man).

So now we have all the ingredients for the tree to work as intended and be a good tree: the root hairs absorb water and minerals, those then travel up through the xylem cells in the sapwood of the trunk, and then out into the leaves, where they are used as an ingredient in photosynthesis as the leaf takes in carbon dioxide and light. Then the leaf **transpires** water as a byproduct along with oxygen and sends its new carbs throughout the sapwood and phloem layer via specialized phloem cells. These take the carbs to the parts of the tree that need building and growth. Voilà!

But in order to be the *best tree it can be,* the tree must adapt its shape to the available sun and fortify itself against the elements. This is where the final major tree feature comes into play: growth habit.

A tree's natural growth habit is defined in its DNA, such as the broad, spreading shape of a southern live oak (*Quercus virginiana*), swirling all over in order to let its broad leaves have the maximum exposure to light in a phenomenon known as phototropism. This also goes for a conifer such as the Sierra white fir (*Abies concolor*), whose conical shape allows the most exposure for its needles while conserving effort to push water up against gravity in such a tall tree.

But while the natural growth habit of a White Fir might be the most aesthetically pleasing, they might narrow their shape a bit in a dense forest where there's a great deal of competition for sunlight. Ditto on a rock face where they stare down 75 mile-per-hour (121 kph) winds all winter with frequent snow—a broad set of limbs might find itself creaking and cracking all too frequently in these elements.

Similarly, the oak might find itself top heavy in a competitive area as it reaches upward to snag that good sun.

All this is to say that, well, trees are smart. They know, through both their genetics and their environmental adaptations, how best to grow and function. It's this flexibility in the tree as a system that gives them the physical variety that we love when we both traverse a desert landscape and climb a mountain path.

Chapter 9

Tree Ecology

We are now fully zoomed out. We're looking at a tree as a part of something larger than itself, and several things have become clear: trees are veritable cities for their plant and animal inhabitants, they work in enormous groups called forests that affect the climate of the world in interconnecting patterns, and it's pretty damn scary when something threatens a great deal of them at once. These are the ecological dynamics that come into play when a tree branches out.

Tree Ecology I: A Tree in the Forest

Holy moly, look at this: an old-growth Douglas-fir (*Pseudotsuga menziesii*)! She's getting up there in age at nearly seven hundred years old and approaching 8 feet (2 m) in diameter. But after reading the previous chapters (you *did* read them, right? I mean, I wouldn't, but you should), we *know* this tree now: we know how her needles do their thing, how her cones do their thing, how her anchor roots and tiny root hairs and bark and phloem all do their thing. We're basically besties.

But this tree is also a member of the forest community. Not only that, she's basically the mayor around here ("here" being a radius of roughly 100 yards, or 91 m, in the wet, temperate forest of the Pacific Northwest). And that means she's got *responsibilities*.

First off, she's got a successful cooling and oxygen-production business. Being so epic in her soft-needled **crown**, trees like her are responsible for about 50 percent of Earth's oxygen as well as excellent sun shading and functioning as **carbon sinks**.

Now, in every reelection campaign, which she always wins, she's got her supporters. For example, there are a good many animal citizens who appreciate her. The red tree vole (that obtains water from her needles) and the spotted owl (that digs for truffles at her base) are completely dependable boosters even if their fundraisers are a bit garish.

Then there are those in the middle: the swing-voter types. These include the benign fungal growths such as mosses and lichens that are present for every town meeting but rarely contribute anything of value. There's also myriad bird life that always want to build, build, build into the trunk for safety's sake. This will compromise the Douglas-fir's own health way down the

strike, creating a sea of biological detritus that will stock the forest floor with many tons of yummy supper for a variety of fungi, insects, bacteria, and other trees as a **nurse log**.

For she has raised and readied an army of saplings to take her place!

Tree Ecology II: A Forest in the World

Finally, let's look at the impact trees have on the world-at-large as forests.

There's a bunch of types of forests: boreal, tropical, woodlands, temperate, with the modifiers "sub" and "seasonal" thrown in there a bunch to differentiate them all. But the main difference between these ecosystems, which we call **biomes**, is temperature and precipitation.

In general, the closer you get to the equator, or tropical rainforest, the higher the diversity of both plant and animal species. The closer you get to the poles, where you find boreal forests dominated by conifers, the less species diversity you will find.

But this seventh-grade geography lesson only works if I'm assuming that these forests are **old-growth**, meaning forests that have not previously been cut for human use. Much of the protected forest on the West Coast of the United States is old-growth, and the functional remaining Amazon rainforest is old-growth as well. But a forest that is secondary or managed growth, like nearly all of the Eastern United States, hasn't yet achieved the diversity of species that it once had five hundred years ago, since it's only had perhaps fifty years to recover since its last clearing.

Why am I saying all of this extremely unfunny information? Because I want to be unfunny for a little while longer while also showing you how the fates of Earth's forests are intertwined.

line when the wood there begins to rot, but, hey, got to give the tweeple what they want sometimes.

And, of course, every mayor has her detractors. Few citizens of the forest are as good at bringing down our mayor as **bark beetles**, who feast on the cambium of living trees. Too many of them can even mean death to our mayor. Ditto for dwarf mistletoe, a parasitic plant that sinks its roots into the Douglas-fir's wood and sucks up her water and nutrients whilst it grows larger and stronger.

But this lady isn't sweating her opponents, because she's got a veritable political machine below the forest floor. Her roots are connected to the various saplings around her via **mycorrhizae**: microscopic strands of various fungi that produce a complex, molecule-trading network that researcher Suzanne Simard has compared to the neurobiology of our human brains. In fact, our mayor tree is what Simard calls a "Mother Tree," due to her irreplaceable ability to foster young trees through her so-called "wood-wide-web". Thou shalt not mess with Dr. Simard.

So while the bark beetles and mistletoe continue to thrash her at community meetings, Madame Mayor has no fear of the day she falls to the ground from a lightning

Functional old-growth forests are critical for weather, temperature, and carbon regulation across the planet in a way that secondary growth forests cannot be, at least for a long time.

In an old-growth forest, like Olympia National Park, you're going to find a great deal more enormous trees. This is because while trees top out in height, they never stop growing in width. And that creates huge, old trees that are great sequesterers of carbon, or **carbon sinks**, which is contained in both the tree itself and the tree's ability to take in carbon dioxide and return it to the ground. In fact, the largest roughly 2 percent of trees are responsible for storing 50 percent of all tree-based carbon. And the only place where these trees appear is in old-growth forests, where they've been allowed to grow undisturbed.

If they are cut down, then we will lose, at the bare minimum, 50 percent of the carbon-storing capacity of trees worldwide. Considering that the sum total of all the biomes removes about half of our carbon emissions yearly, this would, in a word, suck for the prospect of containing climate change. It would also suck when we eventually decide to change our minds and reforest the planet, because the temperatures would then be too high to do this in most places.

But there are also more local effects here. Take, for instance, the idea that trees are responsible for launching a great deal of water back into the atmosphere through respiration and evaporation from their leaves (especially in tropical rainforests). Fewer forests mean less water in the atmosphere, which would raise temperatures and obstruct normal weather patterns. Countless species from different biomes depend on temperature and weather regulation, and both excessive heat and drought might spell ecological catastrophe for geographic interiors, such as those areas east of the Rocky Mountains.

There's even a growing body of evidence of intercontinental atmospheric water patterns, dubbed "floating rivers," which means that my current climate in Los Angeles will be supremely affected by the deforestation of the Amazon.

All this is to say: might be best to keep the old-growth forests.

Tree Ecology III: A Tale of Two Tree Plagues

Unfortunately, tree diseases are a great way to demonstrate the centrality of trees in our own lives. It's also kind of scary how analogous they can be to similar diseases in human beings.

Take these two, for instance: the American chestnut blight (caused by a fungus) and *Xylella fastidiosa*, a bacteria which causes olive quick decline syndrome (OQDS).

In the first half of the nineteenth century, chestnut blight arrived in the United States from Asia through imported trees. It completely wiped out the American chestnut tree (*Castanea dentata*), which previously represented one quarter of the hardwood trees in the Eastern United States. The story of chestnut blight reads like a horror miniseries. It was discovered in 1904 in the Bronx, then proceeded to creep slowly outward at a pace of about 35 miles (56 km) a year, killing every chestnut tree in its path. American scientists were

powerless as they bore witness to the destruction of a tree whose ubiquity and significance we can't begin to imagine in the present day.

This unstoppable march bears freaky similarities to our own pests, namely COVID-19 and the 1918 influenza pandemic. This is because the blight spread by fungal spores in the wind and rain, just like the airborne transmission of the COVID-19 and influenza viruses. The blight creates a canker in the tree's cambium layer, then eventually girdles it, meaning that it circumnavigates the trunk like an unholy Magellan, choking off the tree's ability to send and receive water and sugars. No containment measures could have worked, even if we had enacted them. Which we mostly didn't. Shout out to my home state of Pennsylvania, which tried and failed spectacularly. By 1950, the American chestnut was effectively eliminated. A few original trees, and even a few groves of trees, survived, but their numbers continue to dwindle to this day.

Besides the loss of a favorite snack, entire forest communities were impacted, including deer and squirrels (whose numbers crashed for a few generations before they switched over from chestnuts to acorns), and even marine populations who were suddenly getting an influx of acidic water due to massive tree decomposition in the forests. But the greatest impact occurred in rural populations, where the most dependable of all lumbers had suddenly disappeared, and countless workers in Appalachia found themselves without a crop. Chestnut blight crushed these people and those who depended on them.

Presently, there are a few different efforts to revitalize the American chestnut through hybridizing with the Blight-resistant Chinese or Japanese chestnut. And let me tell you, I have seen some cool stuff on TikTok about it. Also, as a card-carrying member of the American Chestnut Foundation, I can tell you that there is an insane amount of energy toward making this happen in what might amount to the largest grassroots science experiment of all time. Watch this space, folks.

In a more contemporary example, an ugly little bacteria named *Xylella fastidiosa* is currently wreaking havoc on southern European olive trees (*Olea europaea*), having wiped out billions of dollars of olive oil production and thirty-three thousand jobs in the Puglia region of Italy in the ten years since it was introduced. It multiplies in the xylem of the tree and blocks the sap flow, causing trees to wither away and die.

But the spread seems to be waning now. Why?

Well, because this little schmuck doesn't spread as easily as the chestnut blight and we're using our smarts to exploit that. This bacteria depends mostly on replication in the gut of the spittlebug, which jumps from tree to tree and spreads infection, not unlike the fleas who carried the bubonic plague.

In contrast to the death march of chestnut blight through the air and the rain, it's within the realm of possibility to limit the spread of a pathogen that depends upon a host to get where it's going. You stop the rats, you stop the plague. You stop the spittlebugs, you limit Xylella's destruction.

Of course, the olive tree industry has a lot to recover from. But thanks to a mixture of luck and scientific forbearance, hopefully we can continue to turn the tables on this little shit of a tree plague.

Part III

A SLIGHTLY OPINIONATED GUIDE TO NORTH AMERICAN TREES

I t's the Night of the Big Game at Tree High North America!

Hold on to your butts:

Did you know there's a high school where things *don't suck?* Furthermore, *they don't suck ever all the time for everybody*? Sure, this high school has all the usual characters that we've come to know and love and exploit for a new Freeform series. But in *this* high school, they all pretty much like each other and *they all get along*. Yes, it's wild. It makes zero sense.

Except that it does, because we're talking about trees. I'm talking about a little place called *Tree High*. Tree High is a high school where the student body is solely comprised of actual trees. There's only one tree high school in North America. Likewise, there's only one on every other continent except Antarctica, where there are exactly zero trees. Have to say, I never did understand what that Ernest Shackleton was on about.

Anyway, Tree High North America has been around for millions of years in its current form, though every few thousand years a tree will transfer in or get expelled (evolution, extinction—you know the deal). During the past two hundred years, however, with the advent of global trade, there's been a flurry of activity in and (sadly) out.

Trees never were as good as people at making up games, so Tree High takes its cues from one of the most popular human sports on the continent. Right now, it's football, but there was a good six hundred years when it was lacrosse, started by the Indigenous Haudenosaunee peoples of Eastern North America. And, as you'll probably glean, since travel is already such a schlepp, separate continental Tree Highs do not play each other in the Big Game every Friday night. Instead, Tree High North America splits itself in two so it can play itself. It's radical.

While the geographic location of Tree High has remained hidden to all human folk these past many millennia, I happened to snag a press pass when I told them I was doing the first extended write-up on the biggest personalities in the student body. And lucky you, because tonight is the opening Big Game of the season, and I got an extra ticket.

Let's get out there, give 110 percent, and see who we can find.

Chapter 10

Spotting Your Tree Pals at the Big Game: How to Use the Tree Guide

If you didn't understand it by now, Tree High is an extremely advanced metaphor. It represents the collection of trees across North America. Well, actually, it's a *selection* of trees across North America. I can't include everybody. This isn't a yearbook, folks. For that type of breathtaking depth, you're going to want to grab yourself a copy of *The Sibley Guide to Trees,* by David Allen Sibley, for trees in North America or one of a handful of other mind-bendingly comprehensive guides.

How did I decide which trees to highlight here? First off, I simply had to include North America's most iconic trees (for example: coast redwood, red oak, sugar maple). No-brainer there. But I also included trees that I found otherwise remarkable (like alligator juniper for its bark or the common paw-paw for its fruit), and others that I thought were rather undersung (blue ash) or had truly sensational personalities (black cherry). What I'm trying to say is that I went with my gut to whittle down a list from seven hundred to one hundred, and I hope you'll indulge me on this decidedly unscientific journey.

Anywho, when you and I walk into the stadium for the Big Game tonight, here's the system that we'll use to identify everyone:

First off, you'll see the most common name for the tree, then the nerdical botanical taxonomical scientifical name, then a few less-common names for each tree. Under those is the most important part: the epithet that shows who this tree is at Tree High. Then you'll see a completely unopinionated blurb about the tree that tells us a little bit more about its "character."

And, finally, we'll have three modes of identification:

"In the Bleachers": This is what the tree looks like from afar—the crown, shape, and height—as well as the appearance of the roots and branches.

"Hold Me": This is what the leaves, needles, flowers, fruit, and cones look like in your hand.

"Stadium Habitat": This is where you can find the tree on the night of the Big Game, corresponding with the elevation (high up in the bleachers means high up in altitude, and vice-versa), cardinal directions (corresponding with its location on the North American continent), and the general conditions of that cozy stadium spot.

On occasion, I was able to get direct quotes from the trees themselves. On rarer occasions, I was even able to get trees to dish on each other.

Folks, you best start believing in tree stories . . . you're in one.

Welcome to Tree High!

A note on groupings: Trees are grouped and described by family then genus, unless only one or two members is present, then I try to include that information in the tree('s) description.

A note on pronouns: Coding trees and their component parts for biological sex is a constant of botanical history. But when it comes to gender at Tree High North America, I imagine a place that's a lot like any other contemporary American high school, where many trees identify as he/him or she/her, some identify as they/them, and some identify as a different combination. At Tree High, some trees eschew the use of anthropomorphic pronouns altogether, preferring only to be addressed as "the tree." My labeling is mostly arbitrary for storytelling's sake, of course, but it goes without saying that the trees at Tree High, like so many young people, are curious, compassionate, and complex. The variety of pronouns here matches this complexity.

Chapter 11

Gymnosperms

Well, here we are at the Big Game, and, gosh almighty, a lot of these tree folk look similar, at least to the unacquainted eye. That's because they're all gymnosperms, or conifers. With similar conical growth and needles that range from long, round, and pointed to short, flat, and blunt, it's easy to see how they may fool you into thinking that they're all alike. But in terms of their personalities, nothing could be further from the truth.

That's certainly the case with the illustrious Pinaceae family. Not only are the pines themselves represented here, but also the spruces, the firs, the hemlocks, the larches, and the *true* cedars. These iconic and commercially valuable trees positively dominate the gymnosperm scene at Tree High North America. It's said that they've been around for 130 million years or so, starting with the greatest genus in all of tree-dom . . .

The Pines (genus *Pinus*)

You know the old saying: "If your genus is '*Pinus*,' might as well be 'your highness.' " Though you can find them at nearly every elevation and geographic region, the pines retain a few common characteristics that lend them their storied status: they have long needles bundled at the base in a fascicle, their winged seeds are dispersed by wind or animal, and they have glorious, wooden pine cones that spread their influence far and wide.

They group themselves into the white pines and yellow pines, with the former usually having five needles per fascicle and softer wood, and the latter having two to three needles a fascicle and harder wood. The pine cones of the yellow pines also tend to be thicker and tougher. But these morphological differences mask a trait shared by all pines: they're the elite and, boy, do they know it.

PONDEROSA PINE (*Pinus ponderosa*)
aka western yellow pine, yellow pine, bull pine
"The Homecoming Quing"

We all know them, and, yes, like it or not, we all love them. Ponderosa pine is the most popular tree in America: they've got the looks, the rare ability to socialize in every, count 'em, *every* USDA hardiness zone, and their wood is legendary for its use in Matthew McConaughey's childhood treehouse. We should also note Ponderosa's groundbreaking campaign to award both a Homecoming "Quing" and Homecoming "Royal" in order to better accommodate gender-neutral trees such as them. And then, of course, they won. Incredible flex.

In the Bleachers: The ponderosa is well-known for their more conservative aesthetic qualities: conical, broad, very tall (up to 250 feet, or 76 m), with huge puzzle pieces of orange bark that sparkle like a perfect set of braces at magic hour. Simply dreamy.

Hold Me: Three long needles (6 to 10 inches, or 15 to 25 cm) inhabit each fascicle, occasionally two, while the prickly, midsize cones (4 to 6 inches, or 10 to 15 cm) carpet the forest floor until cleared away by wind or fire. What's not to like?

Stadium Habitat: True to form, the ponderosa pine is rushing up to say hi to Jeffrey pine at the top of the stands (nearly 8,000 feet, or 2,438 m), then rushing back down again to nearly sea level to give the canyon live oak a good-natured ribbing on the field. A tree of all soils and altitudes. As my mom once said, "Why can't you be more like Ponderosa, Tobin?"

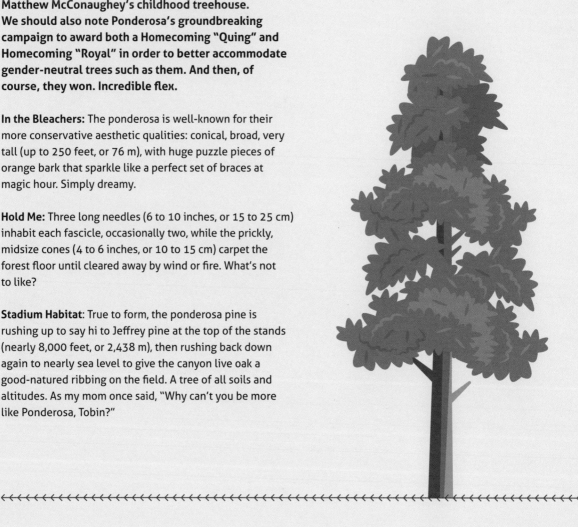

2

EASTERN WHITE PINE (*Pinus strobus*)

aka Weymouth pine

"The Prep School Pine"

The eastern white pine will be the first to let you know that he's from New England: "Maine, in particular. You can even find me on the state flag. My family has a lot of influence there." The eastern white pine's nose may be high up in the air, but that's not without justification: this tree is constantly in demand for lumber, and rumor has it that he's been recruited to play for Bowdoin's basketball team due to his height.

In the Bleachers: Stick straight, with upward-blown branches styled by the wind itself. (But one can be skeptical of this "I-just-rolled-out-of-bed-this-handsome" look—is he trying to hide a receding crown-line?)

Hold Me: As he's sure to let you know, needles come five to a bundle ("as it should be" . . . uh, gee whiz, dude), while his pine cones are 4 to 8 inches (10 to 20 cm), delicate, thin, and white-tipped (manicured?).

Stadium Habitat: Well, you can usually find eastern white pine in the first row of the bleachers, at around 1,000 feet (305 m), hanging with pals red spruce and balsam fir while sipping a Tom Collins in a water bottle, but lately he's been playing with the idea of a career in politics, and for that reason he'll occasionally creep up to 5,000 feet (1,524 m) to glad-hand some Appalachian Mountain trees.

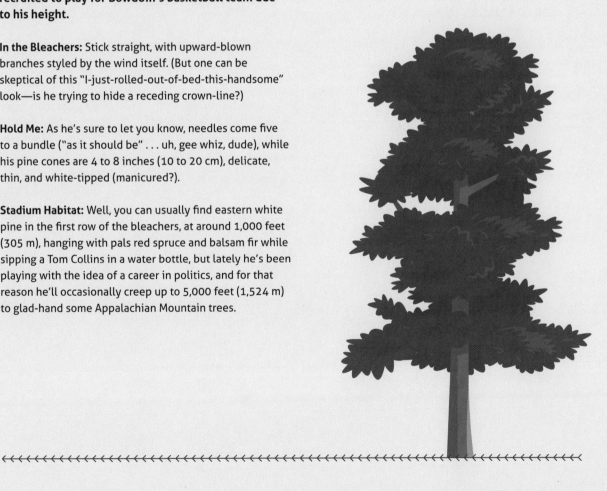

3

SUGAR PINE (*Pinus lambertiana*)

aka big pine

"The Consistent Overachiever"

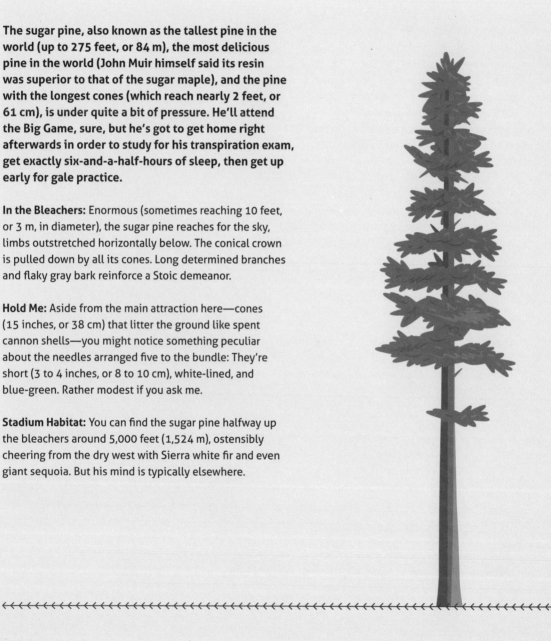

The sugar pine, also known as the tallest pine in the world (up to 275 feet, or 84 m), the most delicious pine in the world (John Muir himself said its resin was superior to that of the sugar maple), and the pine with the longest cones (which reach nearly 2 feet, or 61 cm), is under quite a bit of pressure. He'll attend the Big Game, sure, but he's got to get home right afterwards in order to study for his transpiration exam, get exactly six-and-a-half-hours of sleep, then get up early for gale practice.

In the Bleachers: Enormous (sometimes reaching 10 feet, or 3 m, in diameter), the sugar pine reaches for the sky, limbs outstretched horizontally below. The conical crown is pulled down by all its cones. Long determined branches and flaky gray bark reinforce a Stoic demeanor.

Hold Me: Aside from the main attraction here—cones (15 inches, or 38 cm) that litter the ground like spent cannon shells—you might notice something peculiar about the needles arranged five to the bundle: They're short (3 to 4 inches, or 8 to 10 cm), white-lined, and blue-green. Rather modest if you ask me.

Stadium Habitat: You can find the sugar pine halfway up the bleachers around 5,000 feet (1,524 m), ostensibly cheering from the dry west with Sierra white fir and even giant sequoia. But his mind is typically elsewhere.

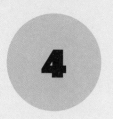

4

GREAT BASIN BRISTLECONE PINE (*Pinus longaeva*)

aka intermountain bristlecone pine, ancient pine

"The Super Senior"

High up in the stands, away from every other tree at Tree High, is the oldest, wisest student of all—the Great Basin bristlecone pine. She's spent nearly five thousand years (many presume longer) going to the Big Game, so there's nothing she hasn't seen. If you approach her to say hello, you might get a warm nod. But all the while, this oldest of trees will have a heavy look in her eyes as if to say, "A lot of memories here. Wish I had someone to share them with."

In the Bleachers: With her short (less than 60 feet, or 18 m), crumpled, irregular crown and bunches of foxtail-like foliage, the Bristlecone is unmistakable. Just to look upon her exposed, twisted, golden deadwood is to know that there is little you could say that she hasn't heard before (at her advanced age, the bristlecone gives very few shits about very few things.)

Hold Me: The density and short length (1 inch, or 2.5 cm) of the bristlecone's needles (bunched in fives), give them a feeling like an old shipman's rope, just in case you've held one of those lately. An old shipman's rope where the needles themselves can be fifty years old. Cones are bristly as advertised (3 inches, or 8 cm).

Stadium Habitat: Few venture up to 10,000 feet (3,048 m), where the bristlecone hangs, perhaps an odd limber pine or two. But while the bristlecone's view of every game is unmatched, her isolation is complete. The rocky, dolomitic soil of the mountainous west is the only place where she feels comfortable. Here, she's free to remember those distant days when she had just entered Tree High, when her crown was conical and her xylem transport abilities unmatched. Those days, dear friends, are long gone.

5

SINGLE-LEAF PIÑON (*Pinus monophylla*)
aka nut pine, pinyon pine
"The Earnest Do-gooder"

Unlike its fellow pines, the single-leaf piñon has the miraculous ability to keep its ego in check. Along with its other nutty pals—the two-leaf piñon, the parry piñon, the Mexican piñon and others—the single-leaf piñon leads whatever the opposite of a gang is. Wherever they go, the piñones spread generosity and compliments, offering up their delicious pine nuts to whoever is in need. The Indigenous peoples of the American West, including the Paiute–Shoshone, have known the wondrous harvest of the piñon for thousands of years, but I count myself fortunate enough to have sampled its bounty alone at 5,000 feet (1,524 m), whilst admiring its single needle in each fascicle—a unique trait amongst pines that lets you know the truth: this tree is very special, and it wants you to feel special too.

In the Bleachers: Diminutive from a distance, with seemingly scrubby branches reaching upwards to no more than 40 or 50 feet (12 or 15 m). At first blush, not a looker.

Hold Me: You prise open a 3-inch (8 cm) cone (quoth the tree: "I'm happy for you to take it!") to find a large white nut on the inside of one of the scales and place it in your mouth. Softer than a macadamia, it practically melts as you feel your strength renewed. Grasping the thick, bluish, single needle per fascicle, you break it apart to smell the inimitable scent of a piñon. "Marvelous," you whisper. "You are the marvelous one," it whispers back. A single tear on your cheek.

Stadium Habitat: It makes sense that the piñon is constantly moving up and down the stands from 3,000 to 10,000 feet (914 to 3,048 m), since it enjoys bringing its tree classmates joy and treats more than actually watching the Big Game. But its sweet spot is traversing the dry piñon-juniper woodlands of California at around 6,000 feet (1,829 m), looking for a sad soul to soothe.

6

LODGEPOLE PINE *(Pinus contorta)*
aka tamarack pine, shore pine
"The Survivor"

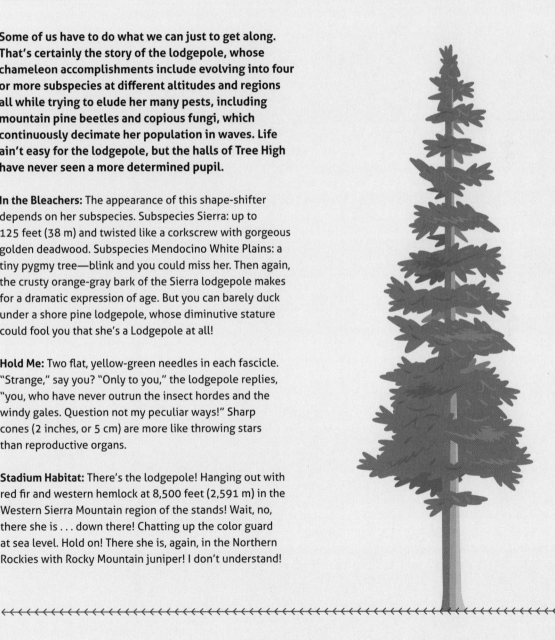

Some of us have to do what we can just to get along. That's certainly the story of the lodgepole, whose chameleon accomplishments include evolving into four or more subspecies at different altitudes and regions all while trying to elude her many pests, including mountain pine beetles and copious fungi, which continuously decimate her population in waves. Life ain't easy for the lodgepole, but the halls of Tree High have never seen a more determined pupil.

In the Bleachers: The appearance of this shape-shifter depends on her subspecies. Subspecies Sierra: up to 125 feet (38 m) and twisted like a corkscrew with gorgeous golden deadwood. Subspecies Mendocino White Plains: a tiny pygmy tree—blink and you could miss her. Then again, the crusty orange-gray bark of the Sierra lodgepole makes for a dramatic expression of age. But you can barely duck under a shore pine lodgepole, whose diminutive stature could fool you that she's a Lodgepole at all!

Hold Me: Two flat, yellow-green needles in each fascicle. "Strange," say you? "Only to you," the lodgepole replies, "you, who have never outrun the insect hordes and the windy gales. Question not my peculiar ways!" Sharp cones (2 inches, or 5 cm) are more like throwing stars than reproductive organs.

Stadium Habitat: There's the lodgepole! Hanging out with red fir and western hemlock at 8,500 feet (2,591 m) in the Western Sierra Mountain region of the stands! Wait, no, there she is . . . down there! Chatting up the color guard at sea level. Hold on! There she is, again, in the Northern Rockies with Rocky Mountain juniper! I don't understand!

7

LOBLOLLY PINE (*Pinus taeda*)
aka bull pine, rosemary pine, North Carolina pine
"The En-tree-preneur"

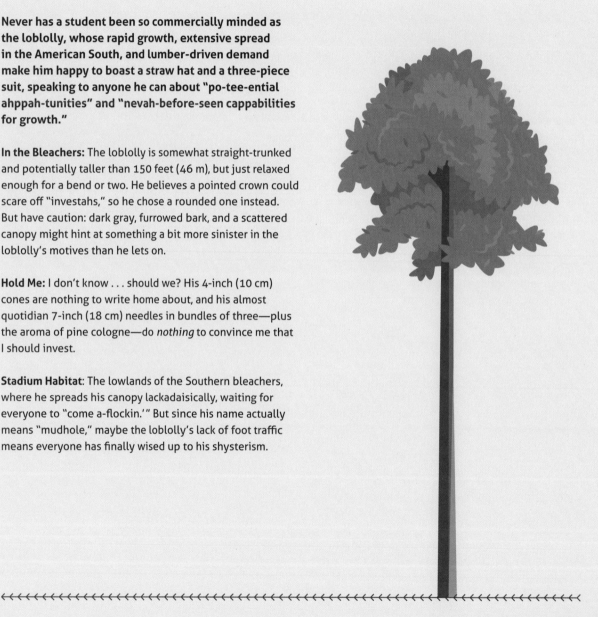

Never has a student been so commercially minded as the loblolly, whose rapid growth, extensive spread in the American South, and lumber-driven demand make him happy to boast a straw hat and a three-piece suit, speaking to anyone he can about "po-tee-ential ahppah-tunities" and "nevah-before-seen cappabilities for growth."

In the Bleachers: The loblolly is somewhat straight-trunked and potentially taller than 150 feet (46 m), but just relaxed enough for a bend or two. He believes a pointed crown could scare off "investahs," so he chose a rounded one instead. But have caution: dark gray, furrowed bark, and a scattered canopy might hint at something a bit more sinister in the loblolly's motives than he lets on.

Hold Me: I don't know . . . should we? His 4-inch (10 cm) cones are nothing to write home about, and his almost quotidian 7-inch (18 cm) needles in bundles of three—plus the aroma of pine cologne—do *nothing* to convince me that I should invest.

Stadium Habitat: The lowlands of the Southern bleachers, where he spreads his canopy lackadaisically, waiting for everyone to "come a-flockin.'" But since his name actually means "mudhole," maybe the loblolly's lack of foot traffic means everyone has finally wised up to his shysterism.

8

JACK PINE (*Pinus banksiana*)
aka scrub pine, gray pine
"The Tree with a Van"

The Jack pine is who Timothée Chalamet wishes he were in *Lady Bird*. His motto? "Sometimes it's good to pack up only what you need and head north, brother." He'll meet up with his cousin the lodgepole pine in Canada to compare notes about life on the road. He won't be seen at every Big Game, since the open road is often calling and Jack pine travels further north than any other North American pine. But the charismatic mystery of the Jack pine and his tiny, essentialist needles make him an admired, if often missed, student at Tree High.

In the Bleachers: The Jack pine has the outline of a tree bound for drifter glory. Crooked, short (30 feet, or 9 m), and spare in his open crown, you can find him colonizing rocky slopes whilst rhapsodizing on how we need so little yet take so much. Here's a secret: the whole pine family is secretly envious of Jack pine's romantic essentialism and lack of vanity.

Hold Me: Two needles per fascicle, like his clandestine cousin the lodgepole. And their infinitesimal length (1 inch, or 2.5 cm) proves a point that we've made thus far about this tree: "A life for show ain't a life, you know." Ditto with his pine cones (1 inch, or 2.5 cm).

Stadium Habitat: The craggy Canadian hills down by the equipment shed at only 500 feet (152 m), where he watches the Big Game from a distance, checking his star chart to make sure he'll have time for a quick make-out with tamarack before the sun rises.

9

RED PINE (*Pinus resinosa*)

aka Norway pine

"The Mean Girl Pine"

If there were a power ranking of the students at Tree High, red pine would be near the top. Not because she's the most populous or the longest-lived or because she loves to style herself after Rachel McAdams in *Mean Girls* ("honestly, Oscar-worthy performance"), but because she grows with a vengeance and not without justification: Jack Pine colonized a great deal of her native territory that had been logged and burned, and now red pine is using her majestic beauty and strategic mind to claw her way back to dominance in the Great Lakes wing of Tree High.

In the Bleachers: A round-crowned tree, haloed with thick-tufted bunches of rich green needles, whose stately height (up to 150 feet, or 46 m) and upright habit belies a knowing smile underneath the foliage. Flaking bark of silver and red adorns this fiery looker.

Hold Me: Even in the palm, the red pine's two-bunched needles (5 inches, or 13 cm) seem kind, lovely, and attentive, like her delicate pine cones (2 inches, or 5 cm).

Stadium Habitat: Red pine stays at a middling elevation (2,000 feet, or 610 m) in the northern Midwest, enough to watch the game at an average distance but mostly to keep an eye on her sworn enemy, Jack pine, as he makes out with tamarack by the equipment shed. One can occasionally overhear red pine's bitter diatribes to her terrified friends, balsam fir and bur oak: "Gosh, Jack Pine is just *so* charming, isn't he? Wouldn't you just *love* to be near that *crooked, gray trunk*! Tamarack must be having such a *wonderful* time!"

10

JEFFREY PINE (*Pinus jeffreyi*)
aka western yellow pine, bull pine
"Pineapple Express"

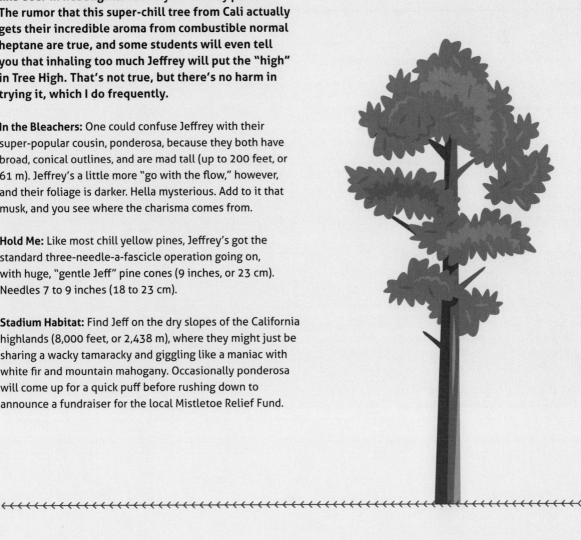

How about this for an excellent tree: a complete knockout, but one with a distinctive scent of pineapple, lemon, and vanilla amidst their bark and twigs that has all the firs following them around like deer in headlights. That's your Jeffrey pine. The rumor that this super-chill tree from Cali actually gets their incredible aroma from combustible normal heptane are true, and some students will even tell you that inhaling too much Jeffrey will put the "high" in Tree High. That's not true, but there's no harm in trying it, which I do frequently.

In the Bleachers: One could confuse Jeffrey with their super-popular cousin, ponderosa, because they both have broad, conical outlines, and are mad tall (up to 200 feet, or 61 m). Jeffrey's a little more "go with the flow," however, and their foliage is darker. Hella mysterious. Add to it that musk, and you see where the charisma comes from.

Hold Me: Like most chill yellow pines, Jeffrey's got the standard three-needle-a-fascicle operation going on, with huge, "gentle Jeff" pine cones (9 inches, or 23 cm). Needles 7 to 9 inches (18 to 23 cm).

Stadium Habitat: Find Jeff on the dry slopes of the California highlands (8,000 feet, or 2,438 m), where they might just be sharing a wacky tamaracky and giggling like a maniac with white fir and mountain mahogany. Occasionally ponderosa will come up for a quick puff before rushing down to announce a fundraiser for the local Mistletoe Relief Fund.

11

COULTER PINE (*Pinus coulteri*)
aka bigcone pine, the widowmaker
"The Reckless Meathead"

It's all fun and games until someone kills a logger with only his pine cones, as the coulter pine did on occasion in the nineteenth century. Somewhere along the timeline of evolutionary radiation, and millions of years before Arnold even pumped his first iron, this pine was mainlining PEDs (Pine Cone Enhancing Drugs). Consequently, this aggressive weirdo now sports the heaviest cones of any pine, some measuring up to 8 pounds (3.6 kg) and 15 inches (38 cm). And, of course, this bellicose pine didn't stop there—he thought it would be cool if each of them were covered in talons like a mutated turkey vulture. If you see him coming towards you in the hall on Monday, best just to walk the other way.

In the Bleachers: Coulter isn't one to show off with great height or a unique growth habit—he's got the common conical shape and doesn't typically rise above 100 feet (31 m). But he's a bulky bro, for sure.

Hold Me: My mom, a nurse, once said she's only been afraid of one child in her care, and that he had "the blackest eyes. Completely unfeeling." Now the coulter pine doesn't have eyes, but he does have the equivalent of twenty cluster bombs, 12 inches (31 cm) each, hanging above your head just waiting for you to make an untoward move. Needles are 10 to 12 inches (25 to 31 cm), three-to-a-bundle, but who cares about that when you could experience sudden death at the hands of a tree undergoing sociopathic 'roid rage?

Stadium Habitat: From 3,000 to 5,000 feet (914 to 1,524 m) in the stands, where he challenges any neighbor on the dry slopes of California, be it bigcone Douglas-fir or incense-cedar, to a branch-wrestling contest.

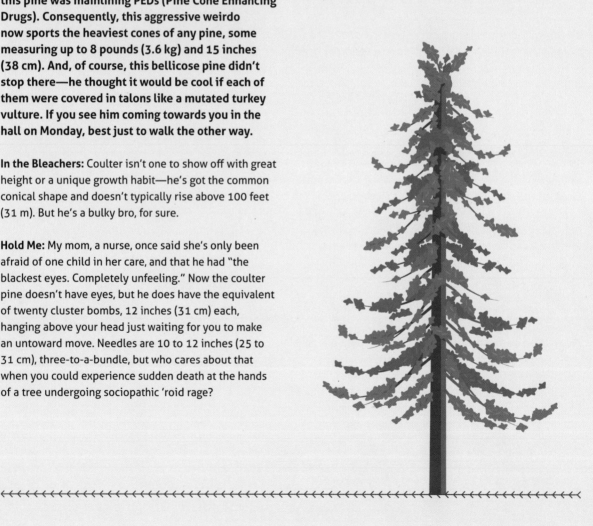

12

FOXTAIL PINE (*Pinus balfouriana*)

aka bristlecone pine

"The Hermit Tree"

Foxtail pine mostly keeps to himself. He calls California his one and only home, and, even there, he's a rare sight up in the Klamath or Sierra Nevada ranges. He's often confused with bristlecone because they appear so similar, but foxtail has none of that Oldest Non-Clonal Organism Energy (ONCE). He simply goes about his business, confident in his ability to live perhaps three thousand years, dazzle any onlookers with his windswept limbs, and photosynthesize all through the winter at temperatures below zero. The foxtail is respected, if not well-understood, amongst his peers.

In the Bleachers: Like a ghost army, bands of foxtails appear together at the ends of the earth rarely reaching more than 50 feet (15 m). In the north, they're straight but squat, but, in the south, all bets are off: sweeping curves of orange bark create the backdrop for a series of seemingly fossilized roots.

Hold Me: The foxtail's foliage is like an upcurved bottle brush made up of hundreds of five-needled bundles (1 inch, or 2.5 cm), and his cones (4 inches, or 10 cm) are soft and simple in shape yet deep purple before they fall.

Stadium Habitat: You can spot the foxtail in the high Western corner of the bleachers (9,000 to 12,000 feet, or 2,743 to 3,658 m), yet isolated from the Bristlecone. Why's he even here? What's he even doing? Only the foxtail could tell us, but he probably wouldn't even give us the time of day.

13

VIRGINIA PINE (*Pinus virginiana*)

aka scrub pine, Jersey pine

"Average and Proud of It!"

Sometimes Virginia pine just has to shake her head at all the other members of her esteemed family: they just try *so hard*. Don't get her wrong, Virginia pine is a hard worker, but she's not concerned with being anything other than her average, wonderful self. You won't hear her bragging about her age or her height or her "big cones or whatever, gimme a break, dweebs" because Virginia pine is happy to be in the moment at the Big Game, where close symbiotic friendships and momentary joy are things to be celebrated.

In the Bleachers: Honestly, you might miss her, "and that's okay, no harm done!" Virginia pine has an irregular crown that only grows to about 35 feet (11 m). "Go ahead, say the 's' word: shrub! I don't mind! Now come take a swig of this turpentine with me and Tulip-Poplar!"

Hold Me: Needles come in small bunches of two (2 inches, or 5 cm), while her tiny cones (2 inches, or 5 cm) each have a small prickle: "Ha, I love my prickles. Lets 'em know I got a little spunk in me!"

Stadium Habitat: Though you might try to approach her, Virginia pine will be too busy cheering on the Big Game with her East Coast pals down near the front of the stands (1,000 feet, or 305 m). "Look at all this! Did you ever think you would be this lucky to have such a great time with great friends at such a great educational institution?!"

PINO DE OCOTE (*Pinus oocarpa*)

aka Pino de Colorado, Mexican yellow pine

"The Tree Who Likes That 'Other' Football"

14

Pino de Ocote, the national tree of Honduras, is always willing to share his thoughts on the Big Game. After all, this Central American tree is more inclined towards *fútbol* than American football, which makes sense given the popularity of fútbol in his native range. But because the stands of Tree High North America are often stuffed with American football fans alone, Pino de Ocote frequently finds himself speaking up to defend the integrity of his beloved soccer. "I don't worry," he's been known to say, "another twenty-five years and fútbol will be more popular than whatever this is." (He points to the field.)

In the Bleachers: Pino de Ocote's southerly style also brings a change in growth habit: up to 120 feet (37 m) with a rounded, mushrooming canopy and brown and gray bark fissuring into plates with age.

Hold Me: It's uncommon for a pine this far south to bear yellow-green needles (8 inches, or 20 cm) in bunches of five, but this pine knows that maximum photosynthetic area will lead to a bright future. There's no time wasted on showy pine cones either (2 inches, or 5 cm)—this is a tree of patience and confidence.

Stadium Habitat: Pino de Ocote takes up residence at 4,000 to 6,000 feet (1,219 to 1,829 m) to escape the heat, biding his time until "the beautiful game" takes its place in the sun.

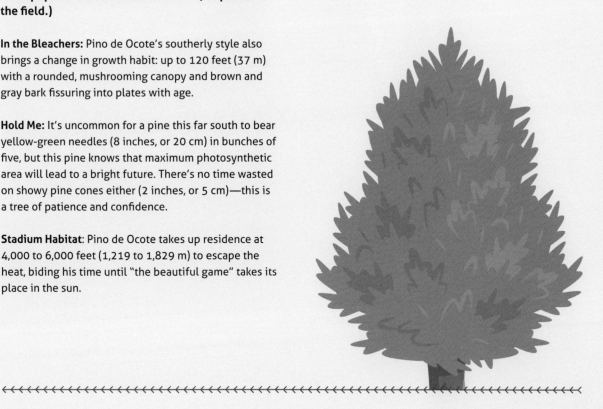

The Spruces (genus *Picea*)

While the spruces may take a backseat to the fame enjoyed by the pines at Tree High, they're no less deserving of it. Or, perhaps, deserving of *infamy*. That's because the Spruces—as opposed to the Firs, their frequently misidentified cousins—have extremely pointy needles that surround their twigs on all sides, making them poor bedfellows and difficult personalities in general. This quality, along with their thinly wrought and hanging cones, makes them well-suited to the northern haunts of Canada and the Rocky Mountains, where it's considered rude to question such peculiarities.

15

BLUE SPRUCE *(Picea pungens)*
aka Colorado spruce, silver spruce
"The Muse"

It's anyone's guess what trees were within a 100-foot (31 m) radius of John Denver as he penned "Rocky Mountain High," but I'm willing to go out on a limb and say that, since he was in Aspen, it was quite possibly the blue spruce: Colorado's state tree and a moody boon to the experience of anyone who comes upon him in the wild. This beautiful fellow may not have the drive or vertical ambitions of other spruces, but what he does have, in spades, is the ability to drive anyone near him to poetry, song, and dance. Oftentimes this culminates in all types of public humiliation (John Denver is an exception).

In the Bleachers: Are you bedazzled, or is it the elevation? Regardless, the blue spruce casts a spell with ordinary growth habit (conical), ordinary height (usually topping out at 100 feet, or 31 m), but with an unreal bluish-silver glow (referred to as glaucous) from his marvelous foliage.

Hold Me: Holding a spruce too close is ill-advised, for the prickliness of the needles (1 inch, or 2.5 cm)—even if they *are* the color of Paul Newman's eyes—could spark a rash or two. Spruces are dotted with cones (3 inches, or 8 cm), whose scales seem wrought of leathery paper compared to woody pine cones. Each scale has irregular toothing on it, as if to say, "What is beauty without a bit of imperfection?"

Stadium Habitat: Brushing shoulders with the similarly ethereal quaking aspen at up to 11,000 feet (3,353 m) in the Rockies, the blue spruce stands as a point of prayer to whomever needs a momentary infusion of creativity.

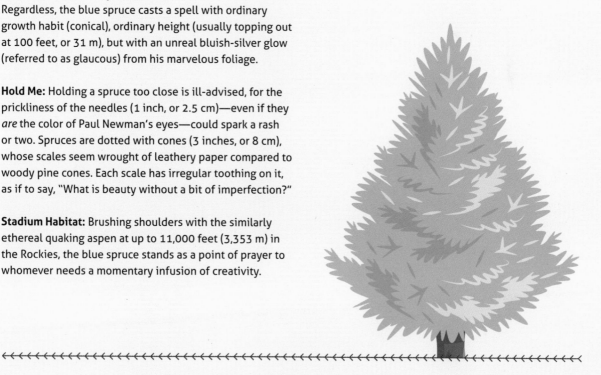

BLACK SPRUCE (*Picea mariana*)
aka bog spruce, swamp spruce, double spruce
"The Unfriendly Twin"

Man, is this guy ever going to give his sister a break? It's completely insane that white spruce and black spruce are twins who cover an identical stadium habitat and range, yet one is so obviously cool and outgoing and the other is such a bummer! It's not like everyone hasn't tried to be nice to black spruce: recently, bur oak invited him to "summer in Illinois," but all black spruce had to say was, "Sorry, Bur. I'm way too busy colonizing bogs while assuming sparse and frightening forms to ever hang out with a sap like you." Jeez!

In the Bleachers: This scrubby denizen of the north doesn't often grow taller than 35 to 40 feet (11 to 12 m), and his uneven, irregular habit and sparse foliage make it look like he always needs a new needle conditioner or something. You might think that nuzzling into one of black spruce's trunk buttresses might make for a decent poem-reading experience, but remember: You. Are. In. A. Bog.

Hold Me: His foliage is black spruce's pride and joy, of course (perhaps to deflect from mere 1-inch, or 2.5 cm cones). What better way to offend anyone than by making your needles shorter (½ inch, or 1.3 cm), spikier, and denser than average?

Stadium Habitat: It's as if this tree simply *lives* to needle its twin, because everywhere the white spruce is (3,000 to 4,000 feet, or 914 to 1,219 m in wet soils), there the black spruce seems to be as well, making life unpleasant for everyone at the Big Game who isn't a lichen.

17

WHITE SPRUCE (*Picea glauca*)
aka Canadian spruce, skunk spruce
"The Friendly Twin"

You've got to admire the white spruce, who does the Lord's work in taking her unfriendly twin black spruce to every community function with her, including the Big Game. White spruce is a joy. It would never even occur to you that she's actually one of three trees who grow above the Arctic Circle along with tamarack and, ugh, yes, black spruce. The white spruce is duty-bound and is always asking what she can do to make everyone's life better: Feed a deer? Make a piano? Appear fortuitously alongside a rainbow? "Really, anything!"

In the Bleachers: Sometimes reaching heights of 150 feet (46 m), the lovely conical shape is topped with a pointed crown. Graceful branches gently slope down over your head as you admire the whitish interior of her scaly brown bark. To your right, a squishy bunny eats fallen spruce foliage. "What a responsible tree," you think. Unlike her twin.

Hold Me: "Be gentle," she's quick to warn you, "I may be a kind lady, but, hey, I'm still a spruce!" You laugh at the charm, and it fortifies you to bear the burden of handling the 2-inch (5 cm) cones and relatively gentle needles, which are bluish-green and have slight white lines running on their undersides. And who cares if they smell a little funky when you crush them? She's so nice! Unlike her twin.

Stadium Habitat: Geographically, this tree covers quite a bit of territory, from 5,000-foot (1,524 m) mountain slopes to, yes, bogs. What an awesome twin. Unlike her twin.

18

SITKA SPRUCE *(Picea sitchensis)*

aka coast spruce, Tideland spruce, western spruce

"The Waterboy Who Gets Called Up"

There's a lot that the Sitka spruce and the mighty coast redwood have in common: size, girth, and, most importantly, enthusiasm for water. But while coast redwood gets thirsty as the central player in the Big Game, Sitka spruce is on the sidelines, using his athletic prowess (read: enormity) to rush to every parched player's side to give them a cool cup of Washington rainfall from his annual intake of nearly 100 inches (254 cm) along his range. But don't think that the Coach hasn't noticed; Sitka spruce is often called in when redwood sustains an unexpected logging.

In the Bleachers: It's easy to spot Sitka spruce: he's the only spruce that towers 150 feet (46 m) on average and up to more than 300 feet (91 m) when he's feeling especially pumped. He combines the classic conical spruce shape with a trunk that is as straight as the game is honest. Whoa, did you see that?! Redwood just took a nasty poach to the burl and may need a replacement!

Hold Me: But before he runs off for his "Rudy" moment, the Sitka drops you a single 4-inch (10 cm) cone, papery and orange, down his buttressed purple trunk. His 1-inch (2.5 cm) needles are a different breed from other spruces. Where everyone else's needles are normally round, these are flat, and where they're normally pointy, these are . . . *extremely* pointy. But, shh, that's his secret weapon!

Stadium Habitat: Nothing thrills the Sitka spruce more than being at sea level or just above, watching the game up close in the foggy, rainy Northwest all the way up to Alaska.

The Hemlocks (genus *Tsuga*)

Underneath the stands lurk the hemlocks. Trading on their notoriety since Socrates was condemned to off himself with hemlock in 399 BCE (actually the poisonous herb hemlock and not the tree, but these lunatics don't care, it's a great backstory), the hemlocks have leaned in harder and harder to the darkness ever since. With their short, flat needles and loads of hanging cones, the Hemlocks most often signal their dangerous ways with twigs that droop treacherously at the ends. Bunch of drooping *psychos*, if you ask me.

19

EASTERN HEMLOCK (*Tsuga canadensis*)
aka Canada hemlock, hemlock spruce
"The Anarchist"

Ever since she was afflicted with the invasive hemlock woolly adelgid (HWA) seventy-five years ago, the eastern hemlock has been on a steady decline into entropy. Witnessing herself waste away from her familiar haunts, she's been known to whisper to herself: "Just like the chestnut blight." While the search for an eastern hemlock might prove more difficult than it was previously, you can rest assured that her slow, moody growth will greet you with a pamphlet containing her favorite quotes from the collected works of Mikhail Bakunin. "Uh, he was an anarchist? Duh?" she says to your blank stare.

In the Bleachers: Peering down through the stands, you might spot a slightly drooping madam, whose twiggery belies her conical form with what some would call "lazy branches." But what some call lazy, others call realistic. Up to 70 feet (21 m).

Hold Me: The tiny, feathery cones (¾ inch, or 2 cm) make eastern hemlock an excellent study in communal regeneration. What would normally be a collection of oppositely arranged, flattened needles with a deep green hue are now brown and brittle, having had the life sucked out of them by woolly adelgids, which siphon sap like some sort of capitalist parasite.

Stadium Habitat: It's difficult to shake the eastern hemlock from her cool valleys under the Eastern Coast stands around 1,500 feet (457 m), where she can read and theorize the living hell out of her own personal decline.

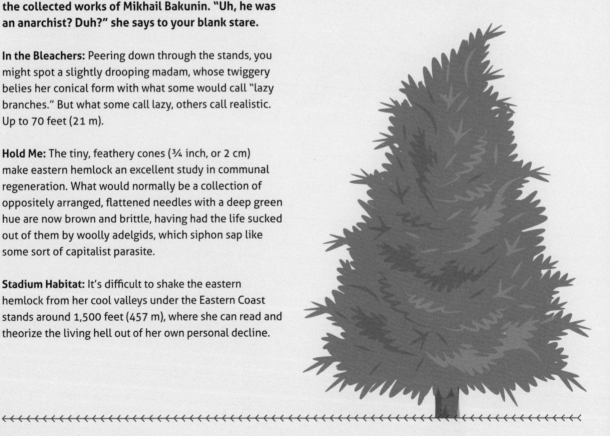

20

CAROLINA HEMLOCK (*Tsuga caroliniana*)
"The Existential Nihilist"

While the eastern hemlock wants to find a way to make sense of it all, the Carolina hemlock has already decided that there is simply no sense to be made. For this reason, the needles travel all around the twig on the Carolina hemlock—a truly shocking choice that has scandalized the student body and made the Carolina hemlock a feared, yet rare, presence in the halls of Tree High. Some trees just want to watch the world burn.

In the Bleachers: If you're brave enough to approach one, the Carolina hemlock won't present any differently from the eastern hemlock: conical and drooping, reaching heights of 50 to 60 feet (15 to 18 m).

Hold Me: Go ahead, take the trunk in your embrace. Then grab a handful of fallen foliage and feel the barbed-wire effect of grabbing the spiralized needles of a branchlet that doesn't care for you or your existence at all. If you look closely at each cone (½ inch, or 1.3 cm), you might see the cone scales flying out horizontally like an addled fighter pilot.

Stadium Habitat: The Carolina hemlock has sequestered itself to, you guessed it, the Appalachian Mountains, mostly of North Carolina (3,000 feet, or 914 m). But a stray encounter with one under the bleachers could spell the end of your belief in anything good.

MOUNTAIN HEMLOCK (*Tsuga mertensiana*)
aka black hemlock, alpine hemlock
"The Wannabe Bad Boy"

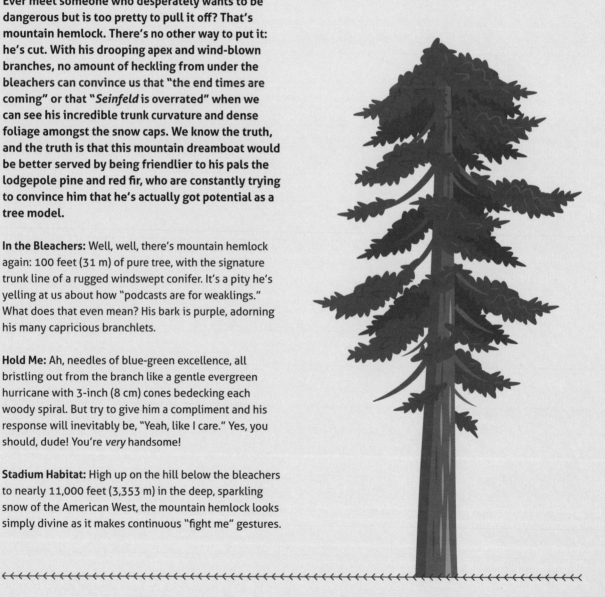

Ever meet someone who desperately wants to be dangerous but is too pretty to pull it off? That's mountain hemlock. There's no other way to put it: he's cut. With his drooping apex and wind-blown branches, no amount of heckling from under the bleachers can convince us that "the end times are coming" or that "*Seinfeld* is overrated" when we can see his incredible trunk curvature and dense foliage amongst the snow caps. We know the truth, and the truth is that this mountain dreamboat would be better served by being friendlier to his pals the lodgepole pine and red fir, who are constantly trying to convince him that he's actually got potential as a tree model.

In the Bleachers: Well, well, there's mountain hemlock again: 100 feet (31 m) of pure tree, with the signature trunk line of a rugged windswept conifer. It's a pity he's yelling at us about how "podcasts are for weaklings." What does that even mean? His bark is purple, adorning his many capricious branchlets.

Hold Me: Ah, needles of blue-green excellence, all bristling out from the branch like a gentle evergreen hurricane with 3-inch (8 cm) cones bedecking each woody spiral. But try to give him a compliment and his response will inevitably be, "Yeah, like I care." Yes, you should, dude! You're *very* handsome!

Stadium Habitat: High up on the hill below the bleachers to nearly 11,000 feet (3,353 m) in the deep, sparkling snow of the American West, the mountain hemlock looks simply divine as it makes continuous "fight me" gestures.

The Firs (genus *Abies*)

Within the Pinaceae family, no other genus of conifers flaunts their wealth quite as conspicuously as the firs. Several factors differentiate them from the slightly more varied spruces, including their blunt, flat needles, larger size, and more rigid branching. But everyone knows that the true distinguishing characteristic of this close-knit clan of conifers—other than their sunglasses-clad security detail—is the upright cones that they keep high in their crowns where no one can touch them.

So paranoid are they of losing such a reproductive goldmine of tree embryos that they curve their needles upwards on the branches that bear them. Any hungry tree rodent must brave this particular adaptation. Additionally, the firs are rather greedy: the cones disintegrate before they hit the forest floor, meaning: if the firs can't have them, neither can anyone else.

22

WHITE FIR (*Abies concolor*)
aka Colorado fir, Sierra white fir, concolor fir
"The Spy Kid"

White fir was, for a long time, just a good-looking rich kid that enjoyed his mountain home and kept his head down. Until he was recruited by the Tree-IA due to his social connections, charm, and ability to disappear into any coniferous forest. Then he began to realize that he loved his fellow trees more than his family's wealth, and now travels across the US under a variety of pseudonyms and subspecies—Colorado white fir, California white fir, Sierra white fir, concolor fir—doing a variety of clandestine operations and returning home in time to finish his transpiration homework.

In the Bleachers: As the truly platonic fir with stiff branches rising to a conical spire, White Fir can get in, foil an encroaching mistletoe invasion in an out-of-state forest, and get out without being noticed. He can grow anywhere from 75 to 250 feet (23 to 76 m). The tree Houdini.

Hold Me: The stiff yet soft needles (1 inch, or 2.5 cm) of white fir are where he demonstrates his quality. The two-ranked needles on fertile branches curve up to show a bit of backbone. But beware if you crush them in your hand: you may fall into a lemon-pine spell that will make you vulnerable to interrogation. Meanwhile, his upright cones (3½ inches, or 9 cm) can range from purple to brown-green, frustrating any attempts by the Mistletoe cartel to pin him down.

Stadium Habitat: The white fir has as many spots in the stands as James Bond does passports. Up at 8,000 feet (2,438 m) in the Sierra Nevada he consorts with Jeffrey pine to get the dirt, but down at 3,000 feet (914 m) in Oregon, he pops a few rainwaters with Douglas-fir—one of the only trees that knows the *true* white fir.

SUBALPINE FIR (*Abies lasiocarpa*)
aka alpine fir, Rocky Mountain fir
"The Growth Spurt Fir"

It's a little awkward for subalpine fir to do most anything these days: fit into a swimsuit at Jeffrey pine's pool party, predict the inseam for a new pair of jeggings, talk to another tree via mycorrhizal communication. Everyone still wants to hang out with her because of the prospect watching the redwood scene in *Return of the Jedi* on the fir family projector in their Rocky Mountain estate, but it's clear that subalpine is moderately uncomfortable during every hang, since her recent growth spurt has left her rather tall and wildly narrow, like being stretched out by a toffee machine. It's a good thing her most devoted pals—Pacific silver fir and Engelmann spruce—are always there to dance with her and ensure that she has a good time whenever Timbaland comes on during the Homecoming Dance.

In the Bleachers: Subalpine fir's unmistakably narrow profile (up to 150 feet, or 46 m) is the reason that incense-cedar has taken to calling her "pencil-trunk" in the halls of Tree High. This is especially rich coming from him—he literally supplies wood for pencils!

Hold Me: All the way up to her spire, subalpine fir has marvelous foliage (1 inch, or 2.5 cm)—perhaps the densest and most vivid blue-green needles of any fir, while her purple fir cones are dotted with resin.

Stadium Habitat: While she loves hanging out in the stands at 10,000 feet (3,048 m) in her southern range, she states that "sometimes it's actually really fun to go down to sea level and watch redwood throw a few completions. Events can be fun, I guess!"

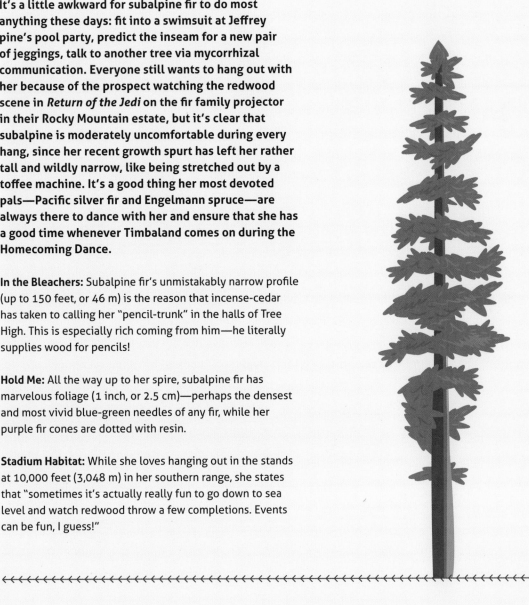

24

GRAND FIR *(Abies grandis)*
aka lowland fir, giant fir
"The Hesitant Scion"

Tree paparazzi recently nabbed this quote from grand fir in the Tree High hallway: "No, I have not watched the latest episode of *Succession*, nor do I plan to." Grand fir is conscious of the fact that every tree at Tree High knows that he'll one day be the pa-tree-arch of a large fortune, and, frankly, he doesn't care for it. He looks the part, sure: large and sturdy, symmetrical and glossy in his foliage. His inheritance is even present in his name: grand. But what he doesn't have the cones to do is tell the world what he'd really like: a nice, quiet life in the northwest with a decent view of the sunset.

In the Bleachers: A grand old fir, for sure. Be-suited with a designer spire and a rounded crown, he's every inch a forest king, down to his arrow-straight branched glory and excellently kingful red-brown bark. "If they only knew the truth . . . " he says.

Hold Me: Glossy. Shiny. Well-kempt. These needles are the stuff of pedigree legend. But there's something hidden here—a cry for help, perhaps? And his 2-inch (5 cm), pale-green cones give a subtle hint at his modest wishes for a life brimming with others' expectations.

Stadium Habitat: Grand fir has a friendly relationship with white fir when he's in town around 5,000 feet (1,524 m) in the Rockies. They pretend to watch the game, but really it's just a lot of high-pressure unloading from grand fir while white fir lends a patient ear.

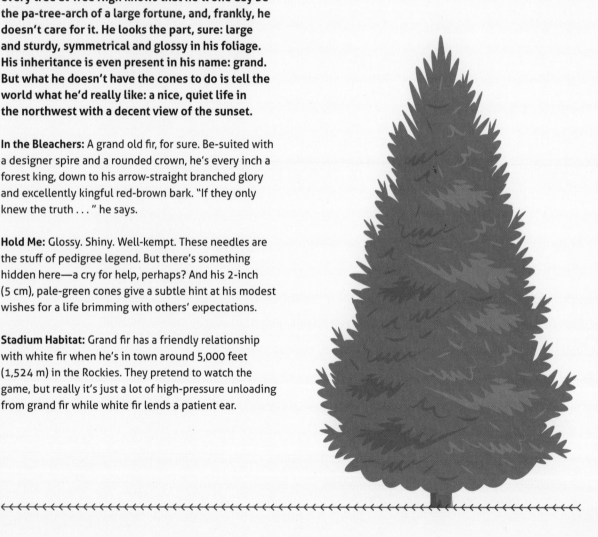

25

NOBLE FIR (*Abies procera*)
aka red fir, feathercone fir
"The Faramir"

In Tolkien's *The Lord of the Rings* (by far the most popular fantasy series at Tree High), the character Faramir is looked upon by his father as the lesser of two brothers, when in reality he is truly the more gifted in character and even metaphysical prowess. So it is with the noble fir, who may not be tapped to lead a wealthy empire yet displays her virtues all the same. Her enormity is unsurpassed among firs, but it is her care for and attention to the ecological domain of the Northwest that make her a true star. If you travel behind her from fifth period to sixth, you'll hear hushed whispers of "Faramir! Faramir!" from the student body. Will she one day rise to take her rightful place in tree-dom?

In the Bleachers: Like a stone-set Númenórean, the impressive height of the noble fir (up to nearly 300 feet, or 91 m) accompanies an incredible conical taper to her crown. Read that word again: crown. And even her most aged bark refuses to become ridged and furrowed—it stays scaly and gray, full of the resin blisters of youth!

Hold Me: The blue-green needles below could fool you that this is just another case of excellent fir foliage. But no: up above on the more fertile branches, the needles are four-sided, thick, and royal. And the cones, don't get me started on the cones: nearly 7 inches (18 cm), purple, green, or red, with lovely fine hairs accompanying each scale. Your Majesty!

Stadium Habitat: The noble fir is simply too busy watching over the wellbeing of the Northwest rainforest at around 4,000 to 5,000 feet (1,219 to 1,524 m) in order to pay attention to the game. But a visit in the stands from California red fir, her most dependable emissary, is welcome in times of great disturbance.

26

BALSAM FIR (*Abies balsamea*)
aka Canada balsam, eastern fir
"The Materialist"

Balsam fir enjoys its comforts. Perhaps that's why it prefers to spend its winters indoors as one of the most popular Christmas trees in America. There are few luxuries that balsam, along with its southern cousin Fraser fir, is not attracted to, including the pampered life of a nursery, the drinking of tap water over the holidays, and being bejeweled with an inordinate amount of rounded glass balls. Who cares if your life is relatively short for a tree when there are so many perks to relish?

In the Bleachers: Small (40 to 50 feet, or 12 to 15 m) and compact, the balsam fir is the very picture of holiday consumerism—a little too symmetrical, conical, and spired to be considered trustworthy.

Hold Me: The balsam has delightful purple cones (3 inches, or 8 cm) that it loves to brag about nonchalantly for hours. A bit of gloss on the dark-green needles. "But you haven't looked underneath them! I have two white lines running parallel! That's my best feature!"

Stadium Habitat: While balsam fir adores Nova Scotia for a bit of midwinter heli-skiing and salmon sashimi, you'll often find it rubbing shoulders with red fir or eastern white pine around sea level for the Big Game. "Please don't touch my foliage—I just got it pruned."

27

DOUGLAS-FIR (*Pseudotsuga menziesii*)
aka Douglas-spruce, Oregon-pine
"The Opposing QB"

Everyone at Tree High loves to get behind redwood. He's a great quarterback, he's the tallest tree in the world, and, well, he's a really, really good guy. But Douglas-fir is a close second. While he's not a true fir (hence the hyphen), he has a mythos of his own: back in the day, there were rumors of Douglas-firs being taller than redwoods (up to 400 feet, or 122 m)! This gives the guy some major heart, and he knowingly puts this storied history (along with the knowledge that he's North America's #1 timber tree) into every completion.

In the Bleachers: In the dense, wet forest of the Northwest, Douglas-fir towers nearly 150 feet (46 m) on average, with drooping branches building up to a pointed apex. This tree knows what he's here to do: tree out.

Hold Me: And just in case you thought this epic tree was all business and no pleasure, I'm here to inform you that his needles are soft and light green, traveling all the way around the twig like a spruce. But, of course, he's not a spruce. He's big Dougie! And his trove of adorable cones (3 inches, or 8 cm) have bracts that poke out like little mice. (Note: I've heard this myth many times but I still have no idea how the bracts are supposed to resemble mouse tails.) All in all, this guy's got a playful side.

Stadium Habitat: Right where he belongs, sweating sap on the field. After the game, especially if it's a loss, you can find him crawl up to 3,000 or 4,000 feet (914 or 1,219 m) to say hi to his devoted pal, grand fir.

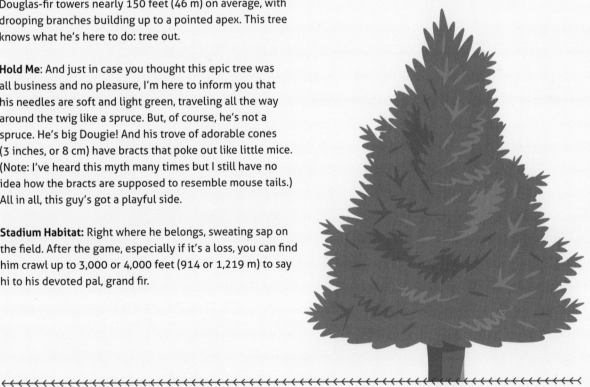

28

BIGCONE DOUGLAS-FIR (*Pseudotsuga macrocarpa*)

aka bigcone spruce

"The Screwup Younger Brother"

<<<<<<<<<<<<<<<<<<<<<<<<<<<<<<<<<<<<<<<<<<<<<<<<<<<<<<<<<<<<<<<<<<<

Families aren't simple. Bigcone Douglas-fir knows this. He's tried changing his name to bigcone "spruce," which many Californians still call him. But this guy's awkwardly large cones make his genus rather obvious due to their papery bracts. He's no athlete, topping out around 140 feet (43 m) and rarely growing higher than 70 feet (21 m). A lot of the time, he'll grow as wide as he is tall, making him the object of ridicule in the hallways. Mostly, he'd prefer to be invisible rather than be seen as Douglas-fir's screwup younger brother. But when it's just him and bigleaf maple hanging out, you get a feeling that these two really understand what it is to be weird.

In the Bleachers: Bigcone Douglas-fir's seemingly endless branches sometimes stick out from his trunk at right angles, like a busted-down old Spanish galleon.

Hold Me: Uh-oh, here it comes: this guy's cones are huge (6 to 8 inches, 15 to 20 cm), with the same papery bracts as his perfect older brother. But while awkward, they reveal a hidden talent: uh . . . the talent of bigcones, I guess? Similar to his older brother, his foliage (1 inch, or 2.5 cm) is soft and spiraled around his twigs, but perhaps a bit sharper. Can't win 'em all!

Stadium Habitat: Bigcone Douglas-fir prefers a decent view of the game (3,000 to 6,000 feet, or 914 to 1,829 m) in the Southern California mountains, where he can take an illicit puff of concentrated carbon dioxide with Jeffrey pine and not be noticed.

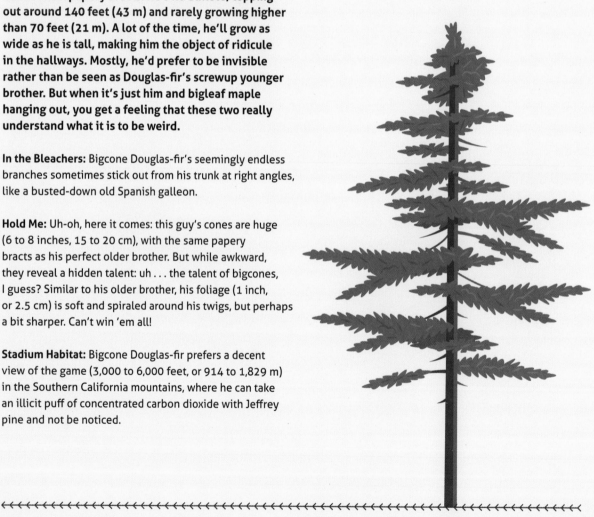

29

ATLAS CEDAR (*Cedrus atlantica*)
aka Atlas Mountain cedar
"The Gorgeous Foreign Exchange Student"

It's a well-known fact that the Atlas Mountains are not technically in North America. They're in Morocco. So why is the incomparable Atlas cedar—one of the "true cedars" of the world, meaning its genus is *Cedrus*—even *at* the Big Game? Well, first off, there's a lot of visiting trees here and plenty I haven't named. But the Atlas cedar is special . . . for me! I owned a beautiful example of it in bonsai form until its untimely death a few months ago, and it's important for me to relate to you the following fact: the Atlas cedar may not be native to North America, but it is the most breathtaking foreign exchange student I have ever laid eyes on.

In the Bleachers: Slight in stature, rarely reaching 70 feet (21 m), the Atlas cedar's pyramidal crown is sometimes open and bushy, and sometimes cascading and ethereal. And, oh yeah, this tree is *blue*.

Hold Me: The needles of this tree, arranged in what are referred to as "rosettes" or "spurs," meaning bursts of needles (1 inch, or 2.5 cm), are sometimes greenish-silver, but are often bright blue because of our obsession with cultivating this magnificent quality in the Atlas. Go us. True cedars like the Atlas bear upright cones (2 inches, or 5 cm) similar to the firs that stay on the tree, maturing for a year before they disintegrate.

Stadium Habitat: You can find the Atlas cedar near the bottom of the stands, as it enjoys a moist, temperate environment after being displaced from its native mountain range. Players on both teams will typically get distracted and botch plays because of its beauty.

30

WESTERN LARCH (*Larix occidentalis*)
aka western tamarack, hackmatack (seriously)
"The Poet-Tree"

Genus *Larix*, represented by three native larches in North America, is simply built different. It's the only genus in the great old family of pinaceae that is deciduous. And that, my friends, takes spiritual bravery. Enter the western larch—who resists the temptation to retain her needles during the winter in order to demonstrate the rewards of being a nonconformist. When all the pines are staying in their deep green lane, larch gives us a golden autumnal explosion of color. When photosynthesis slows down in the winter for the firs, the western larch hibernates, baring her soul to us in all its skeletal glory.

In the Bleachers: In the fall, you can find western larch at the Big Game by seeking out the only conical conifer with needles of gold, often rising above the fray (up to 200 feet, or 61 m). What a breathtaking, if fragile, offering for any lucky enough to look upon't! The bark of older western larches is red-brown and plated, as if nature herself set out to draw a contrast of scarlet and gold—the most vital and coveted colors.

Hold Me: The golden rosette foliage—like Frost said—simply cannot stay, while the cones of the western larch are like a cross between Douglas-fir and hemlock: tiny (1 inch, or 2.5 cm), flexible, and with slight bracts extending from each scale.

Stadium Habitat: The Northwest mountains between 3,000 and 6,000 feet (914 to 1,829 m) give a beautiful central location in the stands to this sublime conifer: "Until the time we meet in twain/The Big Game stays my golden rain!" Bless her.

TAMARACK (*Larix laricina*)
aka hackmatack (yes, again), American larch, eastern larch
"The Free Spirit"

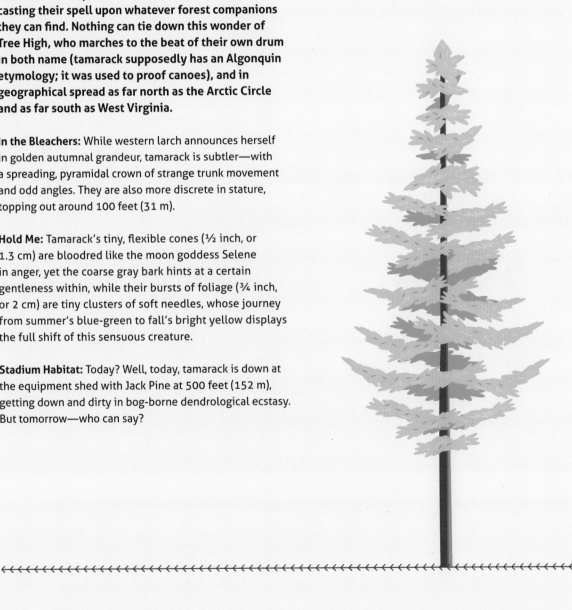

The tamarack reps *Larix* on the Eastern continent, casting their spell upon whatever forest companions they can find. Nothing can tie down this wonder of Tree High, who marches to the beat of their own drum in both name (tamarack supposedly has an Algonquin etymology; it was used to proof canoes), and in geographical spread as far north as the Arctic Circle and as far south as West Virginia.

In the Bleachers: While western larch announces herself in golden autumnal grandeur, tamarack is subtler—with a spreading, pyramidal crown of strange trunk movement and odd angles. They are also more discrete in stature, topping out around 100 feet (31 m).

Hold Me: Tamarack's tiny, flexible cones (½ inch, or 1.3 cm) are bloodred like the moon goddess Selene in anger, yet the coarse gray bark hints at a certain gentleness within, while their bursts of foliage (¾ inch, or 2 cm) are tiny clusters of soft needles, whose journey from summer's blue-green to fall's bright yellow displays the full shift of this sensuous creature.

Stadium Habitat: Today? Well, today, tamarack is down at the equipment shed with Jack Pine at 500 feet (152 m), getting down and dirty in bog-borne dendrological ecstasy. But tomorrow—who can say?

The Yews (genus *Taxus*)

In North America, the yews (family Taxaceae, genus *Taxus*) are a family without a home. Their particular physical characteristics—evergreen but not conifers (they produce an annual, berry-like seed) and soft, flat, alternately-arranged needles—make them outcasts among the gymnosperms. As opposed to overseas, and most particularly in the UK, where many members of their family are known as illustrious Receivers of Memory (they love *The Giver*) at over two thousand years old, the yews feel out of place at the Big Game in North America. They do well enough in class, sure, but few here at Tree High understand their significance abroad.

32

PACIFIC YEW (*Taxus brevifolia*)

aka western yew

"The Volunteer"

Honestly, Pacific yew doesn't give a rip about his family's lack of appreciation at Tree High, because he's too busy being a model citizen tree. Yes, yes, if you eat his seeds and foliage you could die, but he's also a giver of life: the chemotherapy drug Paclitaxel is derived from his bark, which is a critical weapon against breast and ovarian cancer. In fact, it's the best-selling cancer drug ever manufactured. Pacific yew: a study in tree-citizenship!

In the Bleachers: Well, to be honest, Pacific yew isn't what we might refer to as "studly." Coming in at 30 to 40 feet (9 to 12 m), with a messy crown wrought by a goofy, twisted trunk, his most valuable features aren't necessarily visible to the naked eye.

Hold Me: On the male trees, teeny-tiny cones appear, and, on the females, a tiny brown seed (¼ inch, or 0.63 cm) is encased by tiny red fruit (⅜ inch, or 0.95 cm). The seeds are poisonous, so don't even think about it. The foliage here is well-intentioned yet unremarkable—soft, flat, and short (½ inch, or 1.3 cm).

Stadium Habitat: Wherever it can grab an empty seat in the Pacific Northwest up to 7,000 feet (2,134 m). That being said, being a good tree overcoming his evil toxicity impulses is its own reward.

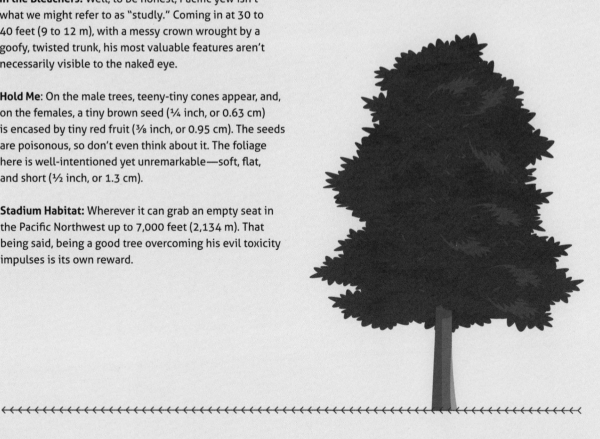

CALIFORNIA TORREYA (*Torreya californica*)
aka California nutmeg, stinking-cedar
"Smelly T"

Torreya isn't technically a yew, but he is in the yew family, which at least gives him something to cling on to with respect to social status. And that's a good thing, because this tree doesn't have much else going on. He doesn't have the usefulness of Pacific yew nor the interesting demons that he battles. His wood isn't terrible, but there isn't enough of him to make it commercially interesting. His fruit kind of resembles nutmeg, or, like, nutmeg you can't actually eat. Regardless, the thing for which everyone knows the torreya at Tree High is his stench. Crush some needles in your hand and you'll understand what I mean. I managed to overhear a white fir's reaction as torreya greeted him at the game. It was . . . cold:

In the Bleachers: "Oh. Hey, man. Yeah, I see you've got a neat rounded crown. Yeah, I see you're 40 feet (12 m) tall. Oh, uh, later on? Oh, I think I'm pretty busy, yeah, sorry."

Hold Me: "Oh, yeah I see: pollen cones on one tree, 1-inch (2.5 cm) green seeds on another. Great. Your foliage? Yeah, it's cool, I guess . . . roundish-flattish, shortish-longish (2 inches, or 5 cm). Hey, look, I'm sorry, dude, I really gotta go—"

Stadium Habitat: "Okay, listen, dude, you're being whack. You're a fine guy but why don't you go back up the bleachers to the central ranges of California where you belong? We've got nothing for you down here at sea level. Sorry. I'm just being real. Peace."

The Cypress Family (family Cupressaceae)

There's a bit of an ongoing taxonomic rumble over at Tree High; it concerns the cypress family (Cupressaceae). The question is whether the cypresses, who count the junipers, the cypresses proper, the false-cypresses, the incense-cedar, and arborvitae amongst their squad, should also lay claim to the members of the baldcypresses (contested family Taxodiaceae, which includes the giant sequoia and the coast redwood).

While the two groups are biologically similar in their wood—fortifying themselves with a great deal of rot-resistant chemicals—their presentation differs immensely: the stereotypical cypress look features flat or clumped sprays of scaly branchlets with small or berry-like cones, while the members of Taxodiaceae have pinnate needles similar to hemlock but often softer. Giant sequoia doesn't, but it's unique enough in its enormity that it feels much more at home with the Taxodiaceae titans. While botanists and dendrologists debate this in the hallowed halls of academia, these two families debate this their own way in the halls of Tree High: through the interpretive power of dance. At the Big Game, however, everyone tries to keep their rivalries in check so as not to scare the saplings.

34

ARIZONA CYPRESS *(Cupressus arizonica)*

aka Cuyamaca cypress, Paiute cypress

"The Tree That Is Always Embarrassed by His Parents"

If there's one student who's easily frustrated at Tree High, it's this splendid example of a western North America-style cypress, whose explosions of scaly foliage hint at the punk persona within. He pop-and-locks his way through Tree High under his pseudonym, "Cuyamaca," which, he insists, is "an expression of my true self." But at the Big Game, he's often accompanied by his father, *Mister* Arizona Cypress, who frequently humiliates him by letting everyone know his *real* species name: "'Cuyamaca?!' Why go by that when you have the splendid surname of "*arizonica?!*'" Cue Cuyamaca's crown in hands.

In the Bleachers: Though he can reach heights of 60 to 70 feet (18 to 21 m), he's often limited to 40 feet (12 m). His growth habit is conical and peaked. While "Cuyamaca" might try to make a play for his unique artistry in his name alone, he often misses the creative nature of his own bark, which flakes off in red, blue, and green peels.

Hold Me: Again, why doesn't "Cuyamaca" just look at his own foliage—blue-green (glaucous) and lovely—for proof that he's special? And what about his marvelous pyriscent cones (1 inch, 2.5 cm) that wait for fire to release their ammo? And look, I think "Arizona Cypress" is a *fine* name!

Stadium Habitat: While he dots the dry Southwest between 3,000 and 5,000 feet (914 and 1,524 m), you can often spot "Cuyamaca" having a showdown with his dad at the rainwater refreshment area: "Dad, I just wanna dance!"

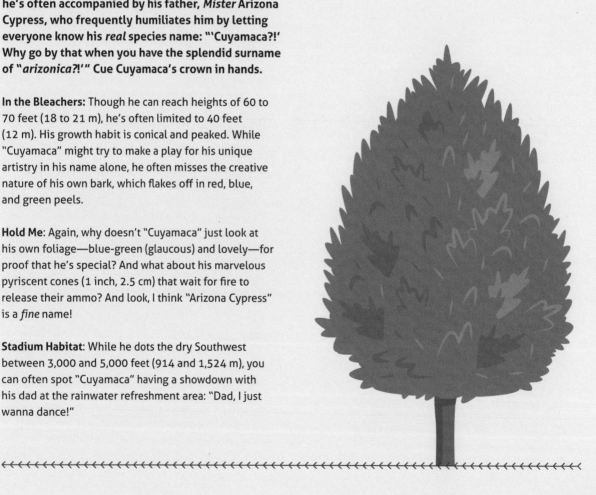

35

MONTEREY CYPRESS (*Cupressus macrocarpa*)
"The Beach Bum"

While many confuse the Arizona cypress for a variety of others found in the American West—McNab cypress, Santa Cruz cypress, Gowen cypress, just to name a few—ain't no one mistaking the Monterey cypress. One of the most dramatic trees in North America, the Monterey cypress spends her days soaking up the sun, wind, and saltwater air of the Pacific Coast then contorts herself to suit her surroundings. She may not live past two or three hundred years in a family where living past a thousand is commonplace, but, to quote the Monterey cypress: "Why would I want live on an icky-wicky mountain forever when I could catch some rays and ride some waves and just pollinate for days on end in beautiful Point Lobos State Reserve?" Point taken.

In the Bleachers: Who is that 60-foot (18 m) *queen* with flat, dense, spreading sheets of foliage twisting their ways toward the blue Pacific and looks like she's about to cliff dive? It's the rare Monterey cypress, of course. Also, are we all seeing this fibrous, sun-bleached bark, contorted into movements reminiscent of the ancients? Wicked.

Hold Me: It takes some major cones (1½ inches, or 4 cm) to live this laid-back lifestyle and not give a riptide what anyone else thinks of you. But here's where Monterey changes her tune: while everything else about her is wild and free, her foliage is deep green, thick, and photosynthetically boss.

Stadium Habitat: Only where the waves are rough enough for a tree like her, meaning the rocky shores of the West Coast near the field. Witness opposing team QB Douglas-fir stop and stare mid-play.

The Junipers (genus *Juniperus*)

Honestly, no one builds a crew like these guys. Often looked down upon by the larger, more upright conifers for both their smaller stature and their berry-like cones, the twists and turns of each ancient limb in this family is a study in grace. While they mostly live in the dry piñon-juniper woodlands of Western North America (the junipers are far from being "dry" themselves . . . their cones are a critical ingredient in gin), their kinship is tightened by their constant performances in the halls of Tree High, wherein every flying limb is a testament to a band of buddies united by spirit and dedicated to aesthetic excellence in tree dance. Of late, the soundtrack has tended toward Golden Age of Hip-Hop stalwarts Run Tree-MC. While many of them aren't covered in this guide (apologies to Sierra, Utah, and many other homies), no one gets dizzy like a juniper.

ROCKY MOUNTAIN JUNIPER (*Juniperus scopulorum*)

aka Colorado juniper, river juniper, Rocky Mountain redcedar

"The Tree with a Cool Hobby"

Every tree guide will take a similar point of view about the Rocky Mountain juniper: good tree, works hard, cool wood. But he's got a secret: on his off-nights from dance practice with the crew, he readies his most weather-contorted forms for collection as yamadori—or a naturally-formed bonsai tree. After collection, he spends years becoming an object of bonsai perfection, showing marvelous interplays of deadwood and live, thriving foliage. That's going to be killer on college applications.

In the Bleachers: Because he's so widespread, this multi-talented student can present a variety of forms, ranging from upright (50 feet, or 15 m) and conical to stunted, twisted, and haunting. On the one hand, this tree's trunk might be that of a typical juniper: red and peeling with golden sections of aged wood. But his trunk might also twist with the chaos of hell itself.

Hold Me: The foliage here is scaly and oppositely arranged, meaning two twigs come from the same point, but his mop of pale green often presents as a cascading waterfall full of quarter-inch "berrycones" on his mountain abodes.

Stadium Habitat: This guy is most comfortable talking Top Fives with ponderosa pine on the rocky soils of the Rockies themselves in the mid-bleacher section at around 5,000 feet (1,524 m).

37

CALIFORNIA JUNIPER (*Juniperus californica*)

aka desert white cedar

"The Hot but Secretly Deep Tree"

<<<<<<<<<<<<<<<<<<<<<<<<<<<<<<<<<<<<<<<<<<<<<<<<<<<<<<<<<<<<<<<<<<<<<<<<<<<<<<<<<<<<<<<<<<<<<<<<<<<<

There are no two ways about it, California juniper is one of the hottest trees at Tree High. This is mostly due to the fact that it prefers the climate of Joshua Tree National Park and occasionally the Mojave Desert as well, where temperatures can drift up to 130 degrees Fahrenheit (54 degrees Celsius). It's also got some extreme trunk movement to match, having evolved to withstand the pain of the most arid landscapes known to trees. But this Juniper also has a secret depth: specimens have been found that approach two thousand years in age, with radial trunk thickness of only 18 inches (46 cm). This means that for every inch of growth, there are a hundred growth rings.

In the Bleachers: There's not all that much that delineates the California juniper from the Rocky Mountain juniper at first blush—short and scrubby (maximum 25 feet, or 8 m) with an irregular crown and perhaps some mighty fine deadwood properties.

Hold Me: The foliage on this sucker makes it another favorite for yamadori bonsai collectors, and its bursts of bright yellow-green scales are a geometric wonder. The prominent displays of thick, white-blue berrycones are sure to grab a spectator's attention.

Stadium Habitat: The high desert (3,000 to 5,000 feet, or 914 to 1,524 m) is the prime location for this juniper. A perfect place for an obviously hot tree to see the game and evaluate each team's strengths and weaknesses based on the empirical properties of their modal wood density. Wouldn't guess it from such a hottie, huh?

<<<<<<<<<<<<<<<<<<<<<<<<<<<<<<<<<<<<<<<<<<<<<<<<<<<<<<<<<<<<<<<<<<<<<<<<<<<<<<<<<<<<<<<<<<<<<<<<<<<<

38

ALLIGATOR JUNIPER (*Juniperus deppeana*)
aka checkerbark juniper, mountain cedar

"A Tree of Culture"

Alligator juniper isn't satisfied with the typical, shedding juniper bark that he says makes his compatriots "look like they require a shave quite, um, badly." That's why he's brought back the latest fashion from Oaxaca, in which he occasionally spends time at the southern end of his range. He'll groove with the other dance crew members, sure, but what he's really interested in is letting folks know about his remarkable bark, which is almost unnaturally grid-like. "It's quite the fashion in Wah-HA-Ca."

In the Bleachers: Alligator juniper manages to top 50 to 60 feet (15 to 18 m) on rare occasions, making his irregular crown all the more capricious and esoteric. The real showstopper here, of course, is the bark, which, though dull gray, is quite intense in its cracked alligatority—almost like you're in a conversation with someone who can't stop using the word "alligatority," which is not a word.

Hold Me: The foliage here is also a little pricklier than the previous junipers, with sharp scales protruding from the branchlets below the softer scales above.

Stadium Habitat: Though he insists that he "doesn't enjoy games of brutality," you can still spot the Alligator juniper chilling with piñon and ponderosa in the desert mountains up to 8,000 feet (2,438 m).

39

EASTERN REDCEDAR (*Juniperus virginiana*)

aka pencil cedar, red juniper

"The Tree with No Beat"

Look, it's really embarrassing when your own dance crew votes to make you the "equipment manager" instead of actually, you know, a dancer. But that's what happened to eastern redcedar, who, despite her widespread presence in the eastern half of the United States, grows just about as straight and boring as a pencil, for which she was previously sourced in the nineteenth century. But the eastern redcedar takes this diss in stride, refashioning herself with a "juniper"-less name in order not to distract from the talent of her fellow crew members. Quite the stand-up tree.

In the Bleachers: There's a good chance that you've seen the eastern redcedar if you've spent more than two minutes outside on the East Coast: somewhat conical, though broader with age (up to 60 feet, or 18 m). Dreadfully uncool, but a terribly sweet lady.

Hold Me: So the foliage is green and . . . dark and . . . kind of ratty, I guess? I don't know, I mean every time I hug an Eastern Redcedar I immediately regret it. And the small, glaucous berrycones are, um, toxic. So, no gin. Bummer.

Stadium Habitat: She's happy wherever she doesn't get brutally mocked for her kindness, decency, and amenability. Usually helping the older tree folks find a seat. And even *they* give her a tough time on occasion. "I can take it," she says, "I'm thick-barked."

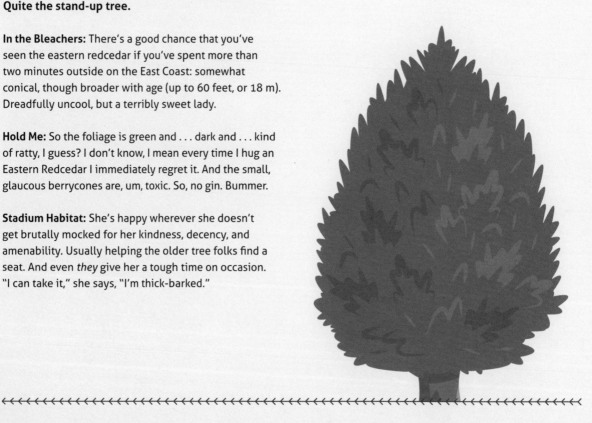

40

INCENSE-CEDAR (*Calocedrus decurrens*)

"The Tree with a Chip on His Shoulder"

It's rare to find incense-cedar in a good mood. Perhaps that's because he's so accustomed to people thinking he's "just a small giant sequoia," or that the only thing he has to offer is lumber for the production of pencils. The incense-cedar doesn't belong to a major group of trees except for the "false-cedars," which isn't even much of a botanical grouping. Because of all of this, this tree takes its frustrations out on others, which might be why incense-cedar is the closest thing that Tree High has to a bully. There's plenty that commends the incense-cedar— beautiful deep-fissured bark, lovely aroma, grand and picturesque depictions of age—but if we're told over and over that we're worthless, sometimes we start to believe it.

In the Bleachers: Yes, it's true: the conical form of this mountain tree gives him the impression of a young sequoia. Despite the fact that he can grow up to more than 200 feet (61 m) high and 12 feet (4 m) wide, incense-cedar dwells on this unfortunate fact the most. The similarity is mostly in the bark, which is simply stunning—the dark brown adorned with deep fissures make it look like a recently broken bar of chocolate.

Hold Me: Honestly, this guy could use a hug. So, if you spot his flattened sprays of cypress needles, clutch a few and hold him tight until he turns into a blubbering mess in your arms, then hold him some more. You may also just find yourself a couple of adorable, tiny (½ inch, or 1.3 cm) cones hanging from the end of his branches.

Stadium Habitat: Mixing with sugar pine and ponderosa around 5,000 feet (1,524 m) in the California mountains, incense-cedar loves a good heckle. But what he needs are a few tree fans to tell him that he's perfect just the way he is.

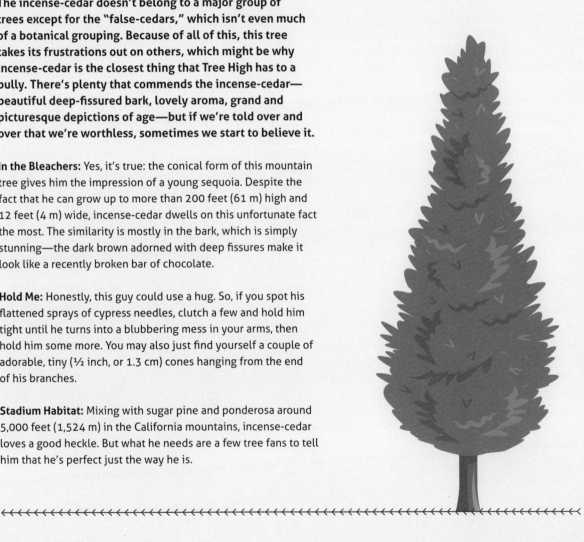

41

WHITE-CEDAR (*Thuja occidentalis*)

aka northern white cedar, American arborvitae

"The Imposter"

Wouldn't it be frightening if, one day, over coffee, your significant other turned to you and said, "By the way, I'm not who you think I am?" Well, there's a similar situation going on with the white-cedar, who attempts to elide the crucial hyphen that separates all true cedars (like the atlas cedar), from all false-cedars (like the cruel but misunderstood incense-cedar) by going as "white cedar" in several tree guides. Perhaps this is because the white-cedar has a storied medicinal history of helping early Western explorers avoid scurvy, and he's grown too big for his birches now. Regardless, if he tries to introduce himself to you at the Big Game as "Mr. White Cedar," look him straight in the bark and tell him plainly, "Nice to meet you, Mr. white-cedar." That'll put him in his place!

In the Bleachers: Supremely common on the East Coast of the United States, this dense and conical member of the arborvitae family (a favorite for hedges) will boast of heights greater than 100 feet (31 m), but don't let him fool you—he typically hangs around 40 feet (12 m). Like juniper bark, the red-brown trunk's shedding habit is a splinterphobe's worst nightmare.

Hold Me: To be fair, the foliage here is rather attractive: sprays of dark green, small-angled cypress scales resemble those of his brother, the handsome western redcedar, but the teeny-tiny fleshy cones (⅜ inch, or 0.95 cm) are a dead giveaway that this is no true cedar.

Stadium Habitat: The Northeastern US into Canada is fertile land for this moisture-loving faker, whose xenophobia makes him relish the idea of kicking out the introduced true cedars. Um, I guess someone didn't get the memo that the Big Game is supposed to be . . . fun and inclusive?

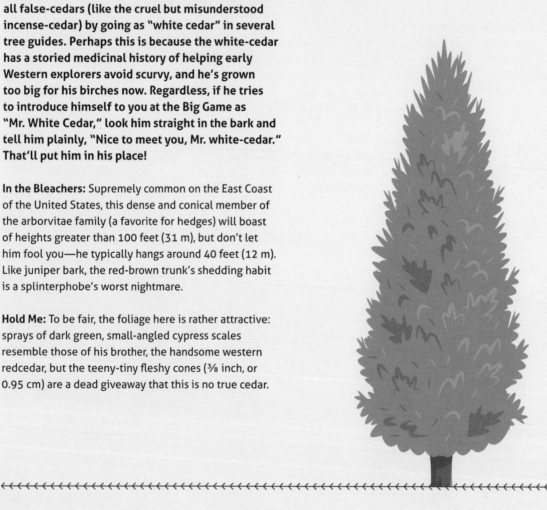

42

WESTERN REDCEDAR (*Thuja plicata*)
aka giant arborvitae, canoe-cedar
"The Protector"

<<<<<<<<<<<<<<<<<<<<<<<<<<<<<<<<<<<<<<<<<<<<<<<<<<<<<<<<<<<<<<<<<<<<<<<

The western redcedar and its monumental importance in Indigenous peoples' households, totem poles, canoes, and a wealth of other uses in the Pacific Northwest, have always made this tree a highly respected member of the Tree High community. But when old-growth forests were logged extensively for the use of Cedar shingles after European colonization, the redcedar's importance became that much greater in the eyes of its peers. Suddenly, not only was the Redcedar the critical ingredient in the roofs above our heads, but its dwindling numbers established every living, aged tree a surviving miracle in itself. But redcedar shrugs off these tribulations: "Just trying to keep my baby brother (white-cedar) out of trouble."

In the Bleachers: While sighting a young redcedar is a lovely if forgettable experience, the experience of seeing a millennium-old, battle-scarred warrior is not: 12 feet (4 m) wide and 250 feet (76 m) high, its multiple apexes reach for the heavens while tufts of drooping limbs work their shady magic below. The pairing of a buttressed trunk and fibrous bark make it clear that this tree has seen some shit.

Hold Me: The foliage is similar to that of its brother, white-cedar: flattened green sprays. But on the western redcedar, there is also purpose, self-possession, and a quiet strength. It also doesn't waste too much time on its cones (½ inch or 1.3 cm), which are brown and plentiful in the fall.

Stadium Habitat: Wherever you need it in the vicinity of sea level to 6,000 feet (1,828 m) along the Pacific Coast. As long as there is rain, the redcedar will see you through.

<<<<<<<<<<<<<<<<<<<<<<<<<<<<<<<<<<<<<<<<<<<<<<<<<<<<<<<<<<<<<<<<<<<<<<<

43

ALASKA-CEDAR (*Callitropsis nootkatensis*)
aka yellow cypress, Nootka cypress
"The Perpetually Confused Tree"

<<<<<<<<<<<<<<<<<<<<<<<<<<<<<<<<<<<<<<<<<<<<<<<<<<<<<<<<<<<<<<<<<<<<<<<<<<<<<<<<

Alaska-cedar is not a dumb tree. In fact, it's a pretty smart tree. And resourceful! It was and is a critical tree for the Nuu-chah-nulth Indigenous peoples of Canada, who tell an origin legend that the Alaska-cedar originated as three women who escaped into the forest, only to be transformed into trees—hence the soft, silky bark that comes off in fibrous sheets. In fact, the Alaska-cedar receives its scientific name from the Nuu-chah-nulth peoples, formerly known to European invaders as the Nootka people. The Alaska-cedar has also been at the center of taxonomic disputes for nearly two centuries now, caught between being grouped with the "false-cypresses" (genus *Chamaecyparis*) and its own genus closer to the true cypresses (*Callitropsis*). Recent data has shown it to be more of the latter, but just keep your comments to yourself and let the tree have a break for gosh sakes.

In the Bleachers: Some Alaska-cedars approach 200 feet (61 m), with a narrow crown and drooping branches, but most are much shorter.

Hold Me: Honestly, buddy, there's no two ways to put this—the Alaska-cedar's got some confusing foliage. Drooping, spreading, and scaly, this bright green (bordering on yellow) foliage spotted with dots of resin hints at every group in the cypress family. And bunches of its round, 1-inch (2.5 cm), quite-cypressy cones on the floor of the Pacific Temperate Rainforest don't clear things up, either.

Stadium Habitat: In order to get some clarity, Alaska-cedar sets up shop at the game next to the extremely not-confused western redcedar around 2,000 feet (610 m) in the Pacific Northwest.

<<<<<<<<<<<<<<<<<<<<<<<<<<<<<<<<<<<<<<<<<<<<<<<<<<<<<<<<<<<<<<<<<<<<

The Baldcypresses (family Taxodiaceae)

From a taxonomist's standpoint, this grouping of trees will always be missing something: the coast redwood might belong more fittingly to the Sequoioidae family sub-group (which also contains both the giant sequoia and the dawn redwood, native to Asia), the giant sequoia has foliage that hews more closely to cypresses than the others in this family, and the baldcypress has little in common with these other species aside from her pinnate needles. But if you bring all this up at Tree High, eyes will glaze over before you can say the phrase "subtle nuances." Why? Three Words: biggest, tallest, burliest. Except for the baldcypress herself, but even that tree is superlative in its ability to party. Without further ado:

44

BALDCYPRESS *(Taxodium distichum)*

aka deciduous cypress, swamp cypress

"The Spring Break Tree"

I hope you've got your older sister's ID ready, because baldcypress has invited us all down to the Gulf Coast for the craziest vacation imaginable! Aside from her unique haunts—she grows wonderfully in the swampier areas of the world—there's little about this wild tree that doesn't scream "complete and utter party gymnosperm." She can go for days (read: multiple centuries), change outfits without missing a beat (read: appear as separate subspecies "Pondcypress"), and still strike a pose at 3am at the Big Cypress National Preserve in Naples, Florida (literally!). Add to all of this the most interesting thing about her: she's a deciduous conifer, surprising us with a gold gown at closing dinner before the vacay's over. Utter legend.

In the Bleachers: Um, whoa. Do you guys see that tree down there? The one with the wide base and the tapering trunk all leading up to a flattened mass of foliage at the top (120 feet, or 36 m), like her hands are in the air, waving around as if they just don't care?!

Hold Me: I mean, baldcypress cannot be contained! Her waves of golden foliage in the fall reveal themselves to be feathery needles in two ranks along her stems, flat and soft. In the autumn, her 1-inch (2.5 cm) cones, round and pale green, fall into the watery depths, ready to pass on the party to a new generation.

Stadium Habitat: By the time the baldcypress makes it back from the Gulf in time for the Big Game, she just needs a break. Spot her with a pair of sunglasses and a 32-ounce (946 ml) Evian water bottle napping on the shoulder of loblolly pine.

45

GIANT SEQUOIA (*Sequoiadendron giganteum*)
aka big tree, Sierra redwood, giant redwood
"The Big Guy with a Heart of Gold"

Say the words "giant sequoia." What comes to mind? Tiny babies smiling inside an endless expanse of cavernous wood? He's enormous, we know. Like 55,000 cubic feet (1,557 m³) enormous (in General Sherman's case—the largest tree by volume in the world). But here's the thing: you think you know, but you have no idea: giant sequoia is actually a big softy. You can find him enjoying the game in the stands with a host of pals—sugar pine, ponderosa pine, black oak, and others—because he's a giving tree who might not have all that much time left on this earth because of, well, "how things are going." So he'd much prefer to spend it with the ones he loves most by his side (and maybe a little brown-bag rainwater).

In the Bleachers: Well, folks, he's easy to spot. Whether young (less than three hundred years) and beautifully conical, or old (approaching twenty-five hundred years) and bearing masses of 7-foot-thick (2 m), twisting limbs traveling up and down his trunk (which remains 10 feet [3 m] thick even at his 150-foot, or 46 m mark) and adorned with bunches of abstract foliage, this fella is nothing if not special.

Hold Me: While his characteristic cypress foliage in strands of spiky scales might hint at some sort of aggressive posturing, the giant sequoia knows how to disarm anyone in the vicinity and get a laugh while he's at it: puff the scaly cords out in a million directions like a cypress explosion up and down his branches. Never fails to rile up his buddies. Meanwhile, his tough-as-nails cones (2½ inches, or 6.5 cm) can't wait for the next low-intensity forest fire to release his seeds.

Stadium Habitat: A peaceful, good-spirited enclave in the dry Sierra Mountains at 7,000 feet (2,133 m) with warmth (read: healthy fires), pals (trees), and gratitude (active photosynthesis).

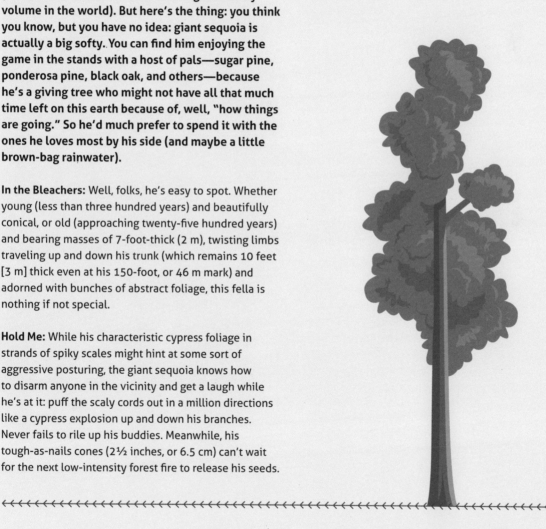

46

COAST REDWOOD (*Sequoia sempervirens*)

aka redwood, California redwood

"The Class President/Tree with Most Varsity Letters"

The coast redwood's renown as the QB on the home team at the Big Game this evening is only an infinitesimal part of his seemingly endless appeal at Tree High. During the day, he's easily spotted in the halls, as he's the world's tallest tree and second-largest by volume (although at one point prior to its extensive logging, there were redwoods even larger than General Sherman). But he also helps out every other tree with their genetic adaptation homework, because the coast redwood has six sets of chromosomes and nearly ten times more base pairs of DNA than *human beings*. He supplies lumber of the most enviable kind—strong and light and beautiful (though its history of logging is quite tragic). He also gives the best advice, since many of his kind have been around for more than two thousand years to accumulate the most marvelous tree wisdom. He does all of this and performs like a divine species on field at the Big Game, where his unsurpassed athletic grace and beauty gives hope to even the meanest of trees.

In the Bleachers: Tall (the highest recorded tree, Hyperion, stands at 379 feet, or 116 m). Limbs splayed outwards and gently curving upwards toward a pointed crown. Tall. It's clear that this bark was forged by something unearthly—dark brown, furrowed, soft, and moist—more like living flesh than the bark of any other tree. Does that gross you out? It shouldn't, because it's incredible. Giant burls (benign growths) on the trunk can grow 6 to 7 feet (1.8 to 2.1 m) across on a 20-foot (6 m) diameter beast.

Hold Me: Each redwood branchlet, with its dark-green, pinnate needles (1 inch, or 2.5 cm) searching for another piece of sky, is a small marvel in itself. Break one for the scent of the primordial forest, untouched by the hands of man. The cones that decorate the end of each branch (1 inch, or 2.5 cm) look like a tasty, crunchy snack.

Stadium Habitat: Where he was born to be. In the middle of the action on the field (sea level), throwing completion after completion against his worthy but inferior competitor Douglas-fir in the moist forests of Northern California and the Pacific Northwest.

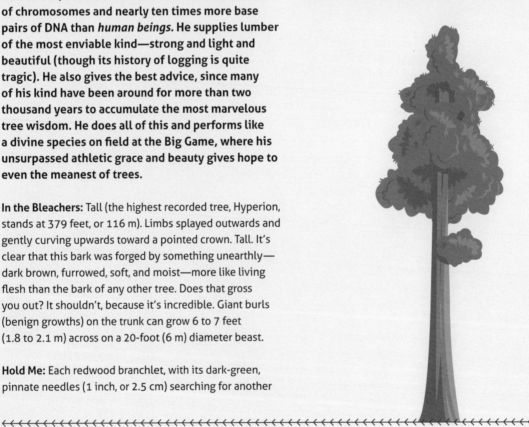

Gingkophyta (single extant species *Gingko biloba*)

As the only living member of an entire phylum, the gingko tree has borne witness to every geologic period since the Permian period, more than 250 million years ago. Let's pay our respects.

47

GINKGO (*Ginkgo biloba*)
aka maidenhair tree
"The Mascot"

‹‹

No one quite knows how to deal with ginkgo, who, as the most ancient tree at Tree High North America and every Tree High at nearly three hundred million years, is supposedly a gymnosperm because of his naked seeds. He's also a stinky fellow due to his vomit-inducing pulp, he's nearly indestructible in terms of health and his evolutionary line, and he's always excited. So Tree High made a cold calculation: they tossed him in a gigantic mushroom suit (fungi are alternatively wonderful and terrifying for trees) and let him do his thing as the uninhibited mascot at every Big Game. No smell, no worries about him getting hurt, and no shortage of chanting!

In the Bleachers: The ginkgo's compact crown with straight branches (50 feet, or 15 m) is pyramidal when young and sometimes multi-stemmed, and his scaly silver bark seems almost prehistoric itself.

Hold Me: His stinky seeds are, say it with me now, "G-R-O, O-S-S, they're GROSS! They're GROSS! They're GROSS!" The distinctive fan shape of the Ginkgo's leaves have themselves a unique vein-pattern, radiating from a single point at the leafstalk. They turn a beautiful yellow in the autumn.

Stadium Habitat: While the ginkgo is said to be native to Asia, where he has been cultivated for thousands of years, he will happily grow anywhere, bounding back and forth in his fungi suit between all coasts and elevations . . . anything to get those trees hyped!

‹‹

Chapter 12

Angiosperms

The angiosperms are widely recognizable by their broad leaves and flowers, though these aren't necessarily prominent on all species. We can assume that they mostly evolved later than the gymnosperms, since they tend to rely on insects and animals for pollination as opposed to wind.

What does this mean for the angiosperm students of Tree High North America? Well, you might notice a slight difference in attitude from their be-needled counterparts: the gymnosperms can be moodier in general in their colder climates, while the angiosperms are naturally adapted towards higher rates of respiration, light, and warmth. Ergo, they're sunnier in general.

The Magnolias (family Magnoliaceae)

No trees better represent this sunny nature than the grand inheritors of the family title Magnoliaceae. In addition to being among the most ancient angiosperms, having evolved amongst conifers and ferns prior to the advent of bees and butterflies (which is why they prefer pollination by beetle), the magnolias are widespread around the globe comprising roughly two hundred species, of which eleven are native to North America. Most people will be familiar with their enormous flowers (reaching a foot, or 30 cm, in diameter), fruits that grow in clusters, and big, goofy leaves.

SOUTHERN MAGNOLIA (*Magnolia grandiflora*)

aka evergreen magnolia, bull-bay

"The Play Place Tree"

With its smooth, spreading branches that always seem to be optimally placed for a good handhold, the ubiquitous southern magnolia is ground zero for the blooming arborophile in the spring. Perhaps I'm biased, as my own climbing tree as a child was indeed a southern magnolia cross, whose wide leaves gave remarkable shade as I recorded my own skyward trajectory by which branch I could reach. But you'd be hard-pressed to find a tree who isn't more friendly to the young person and more encouraging of daydreams.

In the Bleachers: Unlike the gymnosperms, angiosperms don't prize height in their growth habits. They're less personally ambitious and more attuned to character development. The southern magnolia is exhibit A in this regard, topping out at 60 or 70 feet (18 to 21 m), but whose pyramidal assortment of branches conjure images of vernally-induced fancy and forgotten freedoms of whoopie pies and sunflower seeds. Whoa, sorry, I just blacked out. Coming back now: in general, angiosperm trunks have a great deal more spread at their base, as is the case here, with some peeling scales on the gray bark.

Hold Me: The main attraction of the southern magnolia is its enormous, white, powerfully scented flowers (8 inches, or 20 cm), shaped like a cup. Red fruits appear later in a hairy cone-arrangement (3 inches, or 8 cm). Southern magnolia's ovular, dark, smooth-edged and leathery leaves grow to 8 inches (20 cm), with distinct brown underside.

Stadium Habitat: Native to the American South, the southern magnolia is the "S" in the word "TREES" spelled out by a few shirtless silly hearts in the bottom row of the bleachers near the field (sea-level).

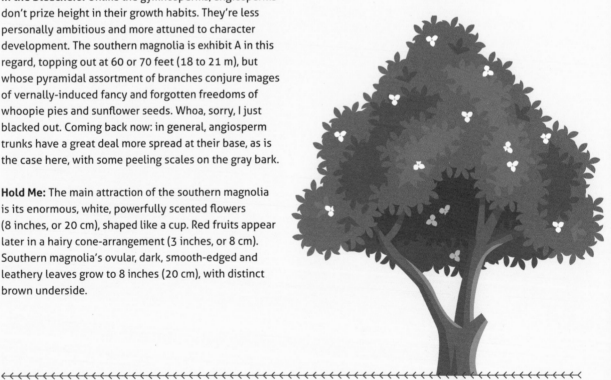

49

BIGLEAF MAGNOLIA (*Magnolia macrophylla*)
aka silverleaf magnolia, umbrella-tree
"The Homecoming Royal"

The co-winner of "Homecoming Royalty" along with ponderosa pine, was bigleaf magnolia, whose leaves—the largest in North America measuring more than 3 feet (0.91 m) in length—make them incredibly popular and willing to give helpful photosynthesis tips to anyone who will listen, which is everybody. Sure, engaging in sports is tough because of the tendency of their enormous leaves to shred mid-tackle, but their personality more than makes up for it.

In the Bleachers: Honestly, can't miss them. They don't often grow taller than 30 feet (9 m), and their rounded crown with heaps of cookie-sheet-sized leaves makes them appear like a restaurant server balancing too many plates.

Hold Me: The enormous white flowers (10 inches, or 25 cm) are often obscured from below by the leaves. Hairy bundles of red fruits and seeds adorn the branches as well. But what are they like, these comical, enormous leaves? Bright yellow-green, 8 inches (20 cm) wide and typically 20 to 30 inches (51 to 76 cm) long. They have a rather interesting shape, as the widest area is nearer to the blunt-pointed end than the leaf's bottom, which has a shape like a butt. Not toothed, but wavy. Not smooth underneath, but hairy. True wonders of the world!

Stadium Habitat: While ponderosa pine, the Homecoming Quing, is bounding up and down in elevation, shaking hands and trading winks, the Royal is more localized, growing in the valleys of Alabama and Mississippi. In other words, sometimes it's easier to have everyone come to you. And they do, my friends, they do.

50

SWEETBAY (*Magnolia virginiana*)
aka swampbay, laurel magnolia, sweetbay magnolia
"The Tree That Only Goes by One Name"

<<<<<<<<<<<<<<<<<<<<<<<<<<<<<<<<<<<<<<<<<<<<<<<<<<<<<<<<<<<<<<<<<<<<

Although it's technically a magnolia, somewhere along the line the sweetbay dropped that designation in its common name, preferring to go by the pop-star worthy "Sweetbay." Although some trees have speculated that the otherwise-not-terribly-remarkable sweetbay has done this in a punnish attempt to be known as a "Sweet Bae," the tree takes issue with this: "My boldness simply makes others uncomfortable. And I'm okay with that."

In the Bleachers: Only growing about 30 feet (9 m) on average, the sweetbay's modest crown belies its wild confidence.

Hold Me: Sweetbay's lovely small flowers (2 inches, or 5 cm) give off the aroma of a tree that is aware of its own arboreal influence. And while the 4-inch (10 cm) leaves, ovular and pointed, are nothing to write home about, a swift crush of fruit, leaves, and flowers gives off the olfactory excellence of a sweet, sweet bae.

Stadium Habitat: The moist soils of the American South make a perfect statement for the sweetbay, who can be spotted at the fence of the 20-yard line dancing to "Purple Rain."

<<<<<<<<<<<<<<<<<<<<<<<<<<<<<<<<<<<<<<<<<<<<<<<<<<<<<<<<<<<<<<<<<<<<

51

TULIP TREE (*Liriodendron tulipifera*)
aka yellow poplar, white-poplar, tulip-poplar
"The Sensitive Dreamboat"

Tulip tree is *so* sensitive, but sensitive in that 1990s Ethan Hawke way: "Hey. You. You look like you're in need of a good leaf. Here, take one of mine. It's shaped like a tulip, see?" This tree, despite being rather colorless when it comes to personality and distinguishing features—other than its tulip-shaped everything—always has your best emotional interests in mind. Quoth the tree: "I have prime diameter for optimal huggery. And after you're done, I'll be around if you need me. All up and down the East Coast."

In the Bleachers: You can spot this guy by his icy-gray profile. He can certainly be striking (up to 200 feet, or 61 m), but it's also satisfying to take a load off at his base, while digging into some Mary Oliver.

Hold Me: The only deal breaker here is that he's a little too eager to tell you one particular thing about himself: "Wow, that's really kind of you to hold my four-lobed leaves, which look like a tulip. Oh, these old things? Those are just my green and orange flowers (2 inches, or 5 cm), also resembling a tulip. And yeah, those are my fruits. Almost like little tulips."

Stadium Habitat: "I mean, wow, I'm so flattered you asked. I'm not particular—anywhere on the East Coast in low forest where we can be chilly and hold each other tight during the 3rd Quarter. With my tulip-shaped leaves."

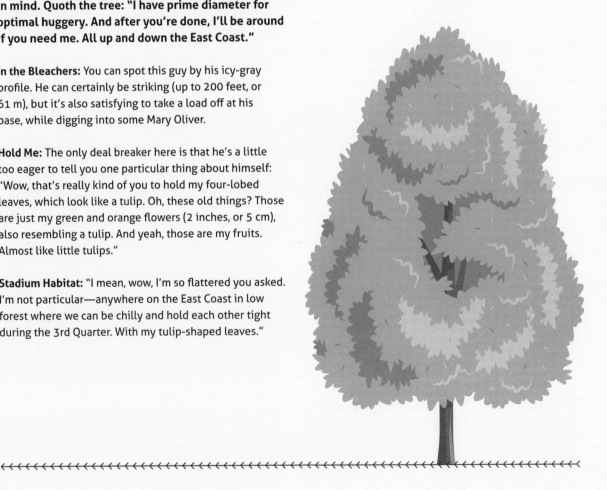

The Oaks (genus *Quercus*)

It's a crime only to discuss six members of the nearly one hundred species of oak tree that grow in North America, but it would be insane to name every member of this enormous band. Yes, they are a band. And the fact is, they're quite good! Some covers here and there, sure, but the oaks—consisting of three groups: the white oaks, the red oaks, and the golden cup oaks—are so musically advanced for their age that a world tour with their European counterparts is now on the table for next summer.

The line-up is, of course, constantly changing, but there are a few things all oaks have in common: the presence of acorns (this is the biggie), clustered buds leading to sprawling limbs, and wind pollination. But the groups? Well: the white oaks have soft-lobed leaves and drop their acorns in a single calendar year, the red oaks have pointy-lobed leaves and drop them after two, and the golden cup oaks are somewhere between the two. But when they're together playing a house party at Hickory's, every variation is complementary. Here's the current lineup.

52

AMERICAN BEECH (*Fagus grandifolia*)
aka North American beech
"The Unflappable Manager Tree"

Every collection of tree egos needs one amazing visionary tree to understand what each one needs and to help that tree make the best decision for every tree involved. That's why the praiseworthy American beech—who isn't an oak but is a member of the family—manages to keep her bark smooth and gray while young, but also smooth and gray as she ages. Nothing can ruffle this stalwart. A lot of trees have even taken to calling this tree the unofficial seventh member of the band.

In the Bleachers: American beech keeps it marvelously buttoned-down in public, a mere 60 feet (18 m) tall with a widely spreading crown. She can get droopy on occasion, sure, but this tree is a masterclass in commanding authority. The luscious silver of her bark made her a favorite of J.R.R. Tolkien and also every couple who ever wanted to declare their love on a tree trunk and had a Swiss Army knife handy. But bless her, the tree takes it and doesn't complain.

Hold Me: The simple, toothed leaves of the American beech (4 inches, or 10 cm) can flash an alarming yellow in the autumn before they fall, but most of the time they're a steady bright green, even in times of crisis.

Stadium Habitat: Popping up to 6,000 feet (1,829 m) to shake hands with the big-wigs all over the East Coast of the US, then retreating to invisible haunts during the half-time performance, the American beech is everywhere and nowhere.

NORTHERN RED OAK (*Quercus rubra*)
aka eastern red oak, gray oak
"The John Lennon Tree"

When most people think of oak trees, they probably think of the northern red oak, the foremost ambassador of the red oaks and the band member most akin to the Smart Beatle. Like John, this tree is formative in its contributions to culture, except while John's was lyrical and rhythm-guitar-based, this tree's is mostly construction materials-based. That doesn't mean that it can't write a rhyming couplet while jamming until daybreak, however. You should have heard it croon "You've Got to Hide Your Nuts Away" at the Homecoming Parade concert.

In the Bleachers: Eminently recognizable, handsome, upright, occasionally rounded, and tall (frequenting 100 feet, or 31 m). Gray-ridged bark.

Hold Me: It's the leaf of your youth: 6 inches (15 cm), with seven to eleven pointed lobes that turn dark red in the fall. Each deep-brown acorn has its own mop-top.

Stadium Habitat: The international fame of this tree is based on its widespread presence in the Eastern United States, but when the speakers are on during half-time in the stadium, it's like it's everywhere.

54

WILLOW OAK (*Quercus phellos*)

aka pin oak, peach oak

"The Sam Cooke Tree"

The often-overlooked contributions of the willow oak (another of the red oak group) to the music of the oaks-at-large can readily be described as "not great." But the truth is that the willow oak—with his thin, pointed leaves that don't conform to our regular ideas of a multiple-lobed oak leaf—probably has a better sense of who he is and what music he likes to play than any other tree in the band. Like his idol, Sam Cooke, the willow oak is a native to the American South, where his leaf dissimilarity to the other oaks have led to many delusional hecklers decrying his place in the band. Nope, try again.

In the Bleachers: The willow oak stands shoulder-to-shoulder with the red oak (100 feet, or 31 m) and is just as spreading. While some might find the stripes of the willow oak's acorns his most attractive feature, it's actually the smooth, gray bark that stands in contrast to the roughness of the red oak's ridges.

Hold Me: The foliage of the willow oak is, of course, distinct from that of other red oaks. The leaves are narrow, pointed, and smooth-edged, turning orange in autumn.

Stadium Habitat: The oaks' performance from the field at halftime resonates differently with different parts of the stadium, with nightmare fungus Sudden Oak Death calling the whole operation "a bunch of deadbeats biding their time." But no one says that when willow oak opens his stomata for "Don't Know Much About Dendrology."

55

COAST LIVE OAK (*Quercus agrifolia*)

aka California live oak, encina

"The Jimi Hendrix Tree"

‹‹‹

Like Jimi Hendrix before him, the coast live oak, final representative here of the red oaks, is famous for fires. Though Hendrix preferred a guitar conflagration during Monterey Pop, the coast live oak enjoys being the center of attention during every one of the oaks' half-time performances, lightning up his tiny, toothed leaves during the wildfire season to create a spectacular inferno worthy of Hendrix himself. On occasion, his bandmates have to remind him to tone it down—there's no way a tree can burn like that for long.

In the Bleachers: Slightly scrubby in height (around 30 to 40 feet (9 to 12 m), the live oak has a nearly 13-fret spread (up to 200 feet, or 61 m). The bark is corky and weathered like the visage of a hard-rock icon.

Hold Me: The ovular, spiny leaves (2 inches, or 5 cm) are evergreen, preferring to party for two years before they fall to the sandy ground below, while the narrow, pointed acorn of the coast live oak hints at demons within.

Stadium Habitat: When not lighting up the stands at halftime, find the coast live oak on the coast of California, where deprivation of the spotlight makes it susceptible to deep valleys and depressions.

56

WHITE OAK (*Quercus alba*)
aka eastern white oak, stave oak
"The Paul McCartney Tree"

While the northern red oak is the most famous member of the red oak group, the white oaks lay claim to the white oak itself, who aspires for crowd-pleasing leaf-lobes, bright green acorns, and copious spreading of the limbs. It labels Paul McCartney, the grandmaster of melody, as its idol. While the range of the northern red oak and white oak overlap almost identically, there are hidden frictions between the two trees. They often spar over what should come first, aesthetics (white oak's position) or utility (that of the northern red oak). But they give up their differences during the celestial harmonies on "Let it Beech."

In the Bleachers: The white oak can really hit the high notes, up to nearly 200 feet (61 m), in fact. But it usually stays around 70 to 80 feet (21 to 24 m), rounding out its splendid bright-green crown with wondrously spreading limbs. The gray-ridged, almost powdery bark of the white oak chips into checkerboard pieces as it ages, adding a certain chromatic complexity.

Hold Me: The softness of each of the seven to nine lobes is easy on the eye and pleasing to the touch, while the electric-green acorns always have the crowd crying out for one more chorus of "Hey, Root."

Stadium Habitat: When not playing its Hofner Violin bass knockoff and launching into falsetto at halftime, White oak is diligently writing a new tune amongst the sea-level pines of the East Coast.

57

SOUTHERN LIVE OAK (*Quercus virginiana*)
aka live oak, Encino, Virginia live oak
"The Johnny Cash Tree"

There's little that doesn't commend this member of the white oaks, so-named because his evergreen foliage makes him appear "live" year-round. He knows that he's nearly as iconic as the "Man in Black" himself, having appeared in a variety of films that have established his internationally-known screen presence—perhaps most famously in *Forrest Gump*. But the idolization doesn't stop there for this tree. The southern live oak aims to duplicate the far-reaching genre-bending of Johnny in his branching patterns as well, which can snake along the ground and rise back up and fall again and go up yet again, just as Cash did in life. The average tree fan might go nuts for a white oak proper or a willow oak, but it's the rebellious spirit and rhythmic intensity that make the southern live oak an icon.

In the Bleachers: Just as Cash dipped into rock 'n' roll, blues, and whatever else suited him in the moment, so go the curved limbs of the southern live oak, extending a greater distance outwards (to 160 feet, or 49 m) than he could ever hope to grow upwards (usually about 50 feet, or 15 m). The Spanish moss that often adorns this tree can upstage the rough patterns of the furrowed bark.

Hold Me: To hold a precious leaf in one's hand (3 inches, or 8 cm) is to witness the fragility that this has always endeared this tree to us. Though evergreen, the leaves are lightly toothed as if to express his anger within.

Stadium Habitat: Though beset with troubles, the southern live oak aims to get through it all with the help of his frequent companion on the field level: southern magnolia.

58

CANYON LIVE OAK (*Quercus chrysolepis*)
aka goldcup oak, canyon oak

"The Stevie Nicks Tree"

While the nomenclature of the golden cup oak group is certainly evocative, there isn't a great deal to distinguish her from the rest of the red oaks and white oaks, except that she shares characteristics of both. But the canyon live oak, with her mountainous California digs and stupefying presence, takes Stevie Nicks as her inspiration. While she may not have quite the vibrato or song-writing talent of Ms. Nicks just yet, she does have the free-spirited nature of a charismatic songwriter whose travels along the interior of America's West Coast may one day bring forth a witchy greatness.

In the Bleachers: Though short of stature (30 to 40 feet, or 9 to 12 m), the canyon live oak's spreading branches make her a perfect tree to match the golden California sunset. This tree's gray bark rises to a sensational twisting of the limbs, almost requiring an iridescent scarf of some kind to accentuate her beauty.

Hold Me: Each acorn is 1 inch (2.5 cm) long, capped with a "golden-cup." Though the leaves can be smooth and narrow (2 inches, or 5 cm), they can also have sharp teeth just like the final chorus of "Rhiannon."

Stadium Habitat: While the canyon live oak loves a huge band to back her powerful vocals, some say that she's thinking of going back to her roots in the dry hills of California, at around 4,000 feet (1,219 m), to pick up where she left off. But those are only . . . rumors.

The Birch Family (family Betulaceae)

At Tree High, the birch family is well known for the seriousness of its artistic pursuits. This is embodied in the beautiful bark of these trees, reaching its zenith in the simply stunning peeling varieties of birch. They also all have simple, toothed leaves arranged alternately on their branches and subtle flowers. The separate genuses in this family communicate their distinct passions: the birches proper (genus *Betula*) have long been associated with drama club, often vying for leading roles in Shakespearean productions, while the alders prefer fine art, and the hornbeams—who describe themselves as "art-adjacent"—prefer the path of the critic, writing endlessly on the importance of beauty in tree culture.

59

PAPER BIRCH (*Betula papyrifera*)
aka canoe birch, white birch
"The Drama Queen"

Words, words, words: that's all the paper birch concerns herself with—acting them, inspiring them, providing the material for them. Popular and in demand the world over as a leading interpreter of the great dramatists, paper birch always finds a way to assert her dominance in the field—whether that's through the spellbinding beauty of her peeling bone-white bark in the autumn against her yellow leaves, or proving once-and-for-all that no one does a better Irina from *The Seagull*.

In the Bleachers: This crown has no equal: spacious and somewhat drooping, the paper birch (50 feet, or 15 m) often appears like a welcoming ghost to the emotionally intense woods of the North. Whilst declaiming a sonnet or resting a branch over her crown in agony ("Out, out! Damned spot-disease!"), it can be difficult to take your eyes off her peeling white bark, smooth and revealing of a fiery orange on the underside.

Hold Me: The flowers and tiny cone fruit are understated and lovely, and each alternately placed leaf (3 inches, or 8 cm), shaped as a teardrop, falls only after a spectacular display of autumn yellow.

Stadium Habitat: Paper birch isn't often found at the Big Game ("Why watch pretend violence when you can perform it, instead?"), but she's a staple of the entirety of the Canadian North when raising money for this autumn's production of *Tree Sisters*.

YELLOW BIRCH (*Betula alleghaniensis*)
aka gray birch, silver birch
"The Southern Ingenue"

It would be irresponsible of me to say that yellow birch and paper birch *never* clash when vying for roles, because the truth is they do share some territory in Maine, which makes this an inevitability. But owing to yellow birch's obsession with American plays, in particular those of Tennessee Williams (Tennessee also happens to be the southern border of her natural range), yellow birch is much more interested in the sultry nature of a repressed heroine, which gives her a distinct sun-bronzed color (you should have seen her in *Catkin on a Hot Tin Roof*).

In the Bleachers: While paper birch is often mannered in her interpretations, yellow birch fills the stage with raw intensity (towering up to 100 feet, or 31 m), casting the shadow of a wide trunk and rounded crown upon her devoted admirers. The glow of the yellow-brown bark covering yellow birch's wide trunk is intensified by its peeling, as if to cast off the pain of yearning.

Hold Me: Her leaves are slightly larger than paper birch (4 to 5 inches, or 10 to 13 cm), which makes her explosive Act II finale (autumn) even more compelling in its bright-yellow exuberance.

Stadium Habitat: Yellow birch is currently dating blue spruce, which allows her fiery passion to continue off-stage, but almost never sees her paramour due to their exclusive geographic distributions. Yellow birch is often seen near sea level on the East Coast, looking vertically up and to the West with tears in her eyes.

61

RIVER BIRCH (*Betula nigra*)

aka red birch, black birch

"The Hamlet Tree"

I know a lot about this tree because I was once just like this tree. Like the river birch, I thought it would be fun if I went around my high school quoting the darkest dramatic texts I could find. ("Have you read Artaud's *Theatre of Blood*? Makes *Macbeth* look like *The Land Before Time*.") Nicknamed the red birch or black birch, this tree leans into its sullen nature, aiming to show us that the peeling red vitality of its young bark will soon fall away to reveal depressing black plates. Thanks, sweet prince, like we needed a reminder.

In the Bleachers: Of average height (60 feet, or 18 m), with upturned branches creating his signature forked appearance, one could be forgiven for wanting to steer clear of this self-conscious sulker. "My thoughts be bloody, or be nothing worth!" the river birch shouts at you as it rends its peeling gray, brown, and red bark.

Hold Me: Like a dagger waiting to be thrust, the thickly-toothed, 3-inch (8 cm) leaves of the river birch hammer home the point again that, yes, this is an intense tree.

Stadium Habitat: Find the river birch walking along the fence line at sea level in front of the field before the game, challenging southern magnolia to a duel . . . of words.

RED ALDER (*Alnus rubra*)

aka Oregon alder, western alder

"The Studio Art Tree"

Red alder recently filled up their electives card with every variation of studio art they could find—root sculpture, bud drafting, even natural-light photography. That's because this tree is obsessed with how trees process *themselves* through fine art. Often mocked for their reclusive haunts in the Northwest into Canada, the red alder is simply "on a retreat." In fact, red alder regularly improves the soil through harboring nitrogen-fixing bacteria on their roots. In doing so, they quite literally achieve a more beautiful world through fertilizing the ground they grow on.

In the Bleachers: This lovely soul of a tree forks similarly to river birch, but spreads outward to a rounded crown (80 feet, or 24 m) as they mature. The smooth, gray bark of the red alder becomes scaly as it ages. Yet, as the tree states, "let it be known that I have earned these scales."

Hold Me: The simple leaves here are slightly more rounded than birch and larger (5 inches, or 13 cm). Like other alders, they bear seeds in coned fruit, and tiny winged nutlets float down to the ground in the autumn.

Stadium Habitat: Find this isolated tree toting its easel on the Northwest side of the bleachers, where they can paint the far-off river to their heartwood's delight (red alder loves riverbanks.)

AMERICAN HORNBEAM (*Carpinus caroliniana*)

aka blue beech, ironwood

"The Tree High Newspaper Opinion Columnist"

The hornbeam, known for its wood density and strength, yet tiny stature, laments that "criticism" is known as such, since he rather aspires to highlight the *achievements* of tree artists like his closely related birches and alders. But while the hornbeam has found peace with his existence as a commentator, that doesn't mean he can't take a punch himself. When quaking aspen recently called him a "lesser sapling" after hornbeam described aspen's fall foliage as "predictable and almost hypnotically boring," hornbeam had a simple reply: "Prove me wrong."

In the Bleachers: Often found detailing the dramatic merits of the Big Game, this small tree (20 to 30 feet, or 6 to 9 m) with rounded crown and spreading branches might easily be missed in a cursory glance at the stands.

The bark, often covered with lichen the way an old writer's brow might be piled with hard-wrought wrinkles, is gray and blotchy.

Hold Me: Ovular and toothed, the hornbeam's leaves (3 inches, or 8 cm) offer no pretensions, though his writings do occasionally harbor some. His tiny fruit clusters (4 inches, or 10 cm) are ready to fall amongst the male and female catkins (1 inch, or 2.5 cm) at a moment's notice.

Stadium Habitat: Hornbeam is happiest on the East Coast, the land of its artistic forebears, or wherever there's good conversation in the stadium that isn't drowned out by cheers. Unfortunately, he's on deadline this evening—there's a good chance we won't catch him.

The Maples (genus *Acer*)

It's well-established that humanity loves trees, but what's less well known is that some trees love human beings right back. Maples go by the genus *Acer*, which means "sharp," but the key to understanding the extent of their philanthropy is in their leaves, which are referred to as palmate for their tendency to have multiple lobes extending outward from a central point. You know, like a human *hand*? This tribute is only the most explicit of a group of trees who wear their heartwood on their twigs, and who, like certain famous cartoon mermaids, have aspirations of being where the people are.

64

RED MAPLE (*Acer rubrum*)
aka scarlet maple, swamp maple

"The Philosophical Rebel"

Nothing could make the red maple happier than to be amongst the people. That's why her range is an astounding 25 degrees of latitude on the East Coast of the United States and Canada. Find this maple in cities and forests alike, where she's certain to give everyone a reason to cheer when she turns bright red in the autumn. This symbiotic relationship extends to her cultivation—she's one of the most popularly bred trees in the Northern Hemisphere. How do the other trees at Tree High feel about this affinity for people, many of whom have had such a tortured relationship with their some of their human pals? Well, Albert Camus once defined the rebel as the one who does not accept inhumanity yet simultaneously recognizes the humanity of her oppressor. And every tree loves a rebel.

In the Bleachers: Red maple, in the summer, is actually bright green, often 75 feet (23 m) with a rounded crown made of straight branches, and the ridged, gray bark of an older red maple is as familiar to you and me as the feeling of autumn itself.

Hold Me: Though the leaves (4 inches, or 10 cm) are more often than not three-lobed and toothed, they occasionally bear two extra lobes, which, when bright red in the fall, make a hand holding a leaf feel like a hand holding a hand. Furthermore, the fruit of the maple—the samaras, or "keys"—wisp down like tiny helicopters, making it clear that this tree knows what we like.

Stadium Habitat: Everywhere, wet or dry, forested or urban, from the Mississippi eastward. At the Big Game, it bears a huge painted "R" in the word "TREES."

65

SUGAR MAPLE (*Acer saccharum*)

aka hard maple, rock maple

"The Baker"

What's that saying, "The way to a man's heart is through his stomach?" Change "man" to "all of humanity" and you've got yourself the personal motto of the sugar maple: the most strategically brilliant tree when it comes to getting a person's attention. Though it takes roughly 35 gallons (132 L) of tree sap to make a gallon (4.5 L) of maple syrup, these trees are among the most beloved in all of America for their combination of confectionary brilliance, fall color, and usefulness as lumber. "Open wide, Mama's got something delicious for you!"

In the Bleachers: The density of the sugar maple's foliage, combined with the lovely upward swing of its branches (to 70 feet, or 21 m), make for a fabulous representation of the word "tree." On older trees, the bark can be quite a bit darker than the youthful light gray, and you might spot a few scars on the tree folks who have had excessive sap harvestings in the past.

Hold Me: Each leaf here is a five-lobed wonder: long-toothed and beautiful gold in the fall, while the keys are forked and almost parallel.

Stadium Habitat: The sugar maple prefers a certain chill in her metabolic efforts to produce such a mind-blowing amount of sweetness, so she stays mainly in the Northeastern stands close to where a stray human being may be in need of a delicious Vermont Maple Candy.

SILVER MAPLE (*Acer saccharinum*)

river maple, white maple

"The Tree That Tries Too Hard"

It's as if the silver maple, which shares his Eastern geographic distribution with red maple and sugar maple, looked at those trees, then said, "Wow, how do I do that, but worse?" Indeed, this tree is constantly stepping on figurative rakes in the halls of Tree High: it's one thing to want the attention of people through producing a ton of fruit and sap and branching for beautiful leaves, but it's quite another when the sap ain't good and the branches snap off too easily and the keys litter the ground like trash. Suddenly one looks quite foolish.

In the Bleachers: While the crown is typically rounded and the size is decent (up to 90 feet, or 27 m), the silver maple's long branches often droop lazily, like he's bitten off more growth hormone than he can chew. The trunk is also maple-typical, growing into furrowed gray ridges with age.

Hold Me: We can give the silver maple credit for getting this one right: the leaves (6 inches, or 15 cm) are deeply-lobed and both toothed and pointed, varying with the environment. They turn a reliable shade of yellow in the fall. But, oy, the fruit: at your feet there are just piles and piles of keys that seem like a real waste of effort.

Stadium Habitat: Oof, I'll tell ya: this fella doesn't hold a candle to sugar maple and red maple, but that doesn't stop him from anxiously asking them for tips on getting people's attention down near the fence during halftime.

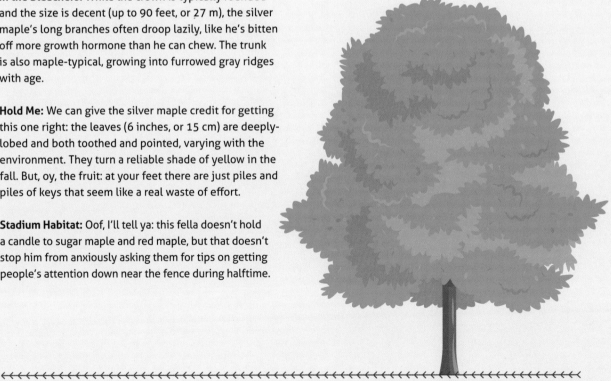

67

BIGLEAF MAPLE (*Acer macrophylla*)

aka broadleaf maple, Oregon maple

"The Tree Whose Parents Are Gone for the Weekend"

While the red maple, the silver maple, the sugar maple, and ten other species are duking it out with every single gimmick imaginable on the East Coast, the bigleaf maple has it all figured out: Pacific Northwest, big leaves, donezo. And I mean *big*: these suckers can grow up to a foot (30 cm) wide, and, with their massive stems, can approach 2 feet (61 cm)! And hey, did you hear? It's just bigleaf maple up in the Pacific Northwest this evening—no neighboring maples to tattle-tell on him, and his mother-trees are in Banff for the weekend! Let's get nuts!

In the Bleachers: Well, I mean . . . the leaves. But other than that, this tree (70 feet, or 21 m) has a delightful drooping habit and somewhat pointed crown that takes inspiration from the conifers around him. The bark opts for a more brownish tone that zags with respect to other maples.

Hold Me: The enormous leaves (up to 12 inches, or 31 cm) are as beautiful as they are sizable: the five distinct and deeply wrought lobes are almost architectural in their pointed spires and buttresses and bright gold in the autumn. Also, they are big. On the other hand, the keys are barely wide enough to rest on your forefinger.

Stadium Habitat: This loner chills with the cool kids up between 1,000 and 5,000 feet (305 and 1,524 m) on the Pacific Coast out west. Sure, he likes tourists just fine, but, dude, have you tried some of this groundwater that Sitka spruce just spiked? Wait, are those . . . sirens? Did someone call the cops?! Oh my god, you guys, I told you not to invite bitternut hickory!

68

OHIO BUCKEYE (*Aesculus glabra*)
aka fetid buckeye, American horse chestnut
"The Tree That Simply Will Not Stop Telling You Where It's From"

Did you know that the Ohio buckeye is from Ohio? Because the Ohio buckeye knew that. In fact, it won't let anyone or any tree in the vicinity *not* know that. "That's so funny, when I was growing up in *Ohio*, we didn't need to worry about powdery mildew. I'm from Ohio." Why does it feel the need to mention this so much? Well, maybe because this tree doesn't have a lot else going for it: It's somewhat stinky, its fruit is toxic, and it's not very remarkable except for a few short weeks of decent flowering. Despite all this, it somehow has an array of historically successful athletic teams named after it.

In the Bleachers: Somewhat shrubby (30 feet, or 9 m) with irregular crown. But, hey, it's from Ohio!

Hold Me: Upright yellow flowers (6 inches, or 15 cm) that smell terrible along with its nasty branches. Palmately compound leaves, meaning five ovular, pointed leaflets (5 inches, or 13 cm), bind together from a central point. Classic Ohioan.

Stadium Habitat: Within Ohio, south of Ohio, and west of Ohio. Sometimes hanging with silver maple down near the field. But mostly in Ohio.

The Loners

From here on out, the remaining angiosperms don't roll nearly as deep as some of our aforementioned famous families. There might be a few members of the impossibly varied rose family strewn about (Rosaceae), and, of course, the ash brothers (blue and green) always have each other's backs. But, for the most part, the following trees are independent-spirited and unbounded by either clique or taxonomy.

SYCAMORE (*Platanus occidentalis*)

aka American planetree, American sycamore

"The Tree That Loves Shop Class"

Sycamores are recognizable throughout the continent, as they're one of the most widely planted trees for their intimidating size and the variegated nature of their bark, which peels off in large sheets of gray and brown. But at Tree High, this tree is known to flourish in shop class, where all that crumbly dust from his bark is simply seen as part of the environment and not a reason for other trees to wear safety goggles and a mask.

In the Bleachers: Depending on the environmental factors at play, sycamores can be lazy and nearly abstract with their trunks, or extremely focused, shooting directly skyward. Regardless, the twisted limbs make for an open, spreading crown.

Hold Me: Similar to a maple leaf, the multiple lobes (3 to 5) of the sycamore leaf (4 to 8 inches, or 10 to 20 cm) are toothed and pointed. Sycamore's leaves are also markedly floppy. And the sycamore's got balls. It's true! The seeds are contained within a brown, hairy ball that litter the sidewalks of suburban United States in the late autumn.

Stadium Habitat: A moist environment is preferred, but the sycamore will sit anywhere in the lower half of the stadium in order to catch the Big Game at close range. You can find him in the East, in the West, and everywhere in between, scoping out this beautiful land.

SWEETGUM (*Liquidambar styraciflua*)

aka redgum, sapgum

"The Musical Theater Tree"

"What's that sound? / That soundy-sound! / Babe, who's that tree? / That tree is me!" These joyful musical theatre lyrics are intoned by the sweetgum every autumn. Their seemingly impossible array of purples, yellows, oranges, and reds, often on the *same branch*, are based off of their devotion to Andrew Lloyd Webber's *Joseph and the Amazing Technicolor Dreamcoat*. True story!

In the Bleachers: The sweetgum is quite intent on informing you of their presence. Just follow the trail of that catchy whisper-singing "Dizzle . . . dazzle! Dazzledizzledizzle!" and you'll find a 60-foot-tall (18 m) tree with a rounded crown awaiting your attention.

Hold Me: Ouchie! Be careful handling the seed balls of this one—they're famously spiky and make for excellent "projec-tiles! Projecky-jeck-tiles, hey!" For whatever excessive energy the sweetgum emits, they truly do have talent, and their five-lobed leaves, each pointed like a star, make for a splendiferous rainbow every fall.

Stadium: Find the sweetgum holding the microphone at sea level in the American South, ready to belt out the National Anthem and incorporate some borderline-obnoxious coloratura into the melody.

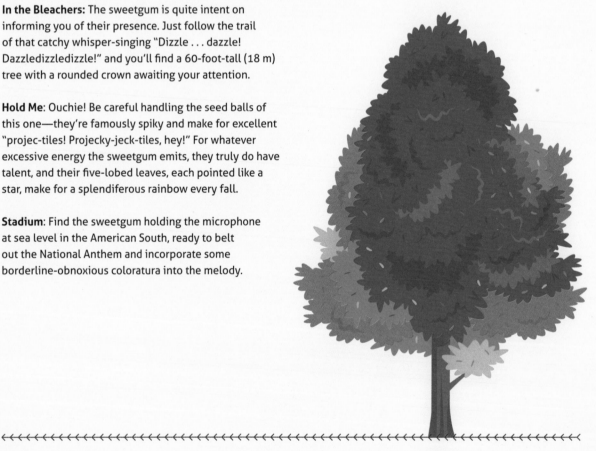

71   AMERICAN CHESTNUT (*Castanea dentata*)
"The Injured QB"

A century ago, American chestnut was still the largest deciduous tree in the United States, with a native range said to encompass nearly one quarter of the hardwood trees east of the Mississippi. It had trunk diameters approaching 12 feet (4 m). Its wood was strong and marvelously light, its fruit brought an annual agricultural windfall, and its ecological presence was nothing less than central to East Coast forests. Then the chestnut blight struck, and, by 1950, chestnuts had vanished into myth. There are still a few around but almost none grow beyond sprouts from stumps until the blight fungus takes them. You can still see American chestnut, the former starting QB, sitting on the hill by himself atop the far reaches of the Tree High pastures, waxing nostalgic over the old days.

In the Bleachers: In its times of glory? More than 100 feet (31 m) of pure tree power, with a rounded crown signifying its importance. Now? A series of weakened sprouts from trunks that have met their fungal enemy already. The trunk was gray and furrowed, resembling that of redwoods in old black-and-white photos.

Hold Me: The palmate leaves (7 to 9 inches, or 18 to 23 cm) are elliptical and narrow, pointed at the end and toothed at the sides. Few reach their full potential now. And the chestnuts, oh, the chestnuts! A spiny hide hid three sweet, carrot-flavored morsels. All gone.

Stadium Habitat: I'd say it's best not to hope that American chestnut will show up to a game, but I'm a creature of hope, and so are the many scientists, researchers, and geneticists trying to find a way to bring American chestnut back onto the field.

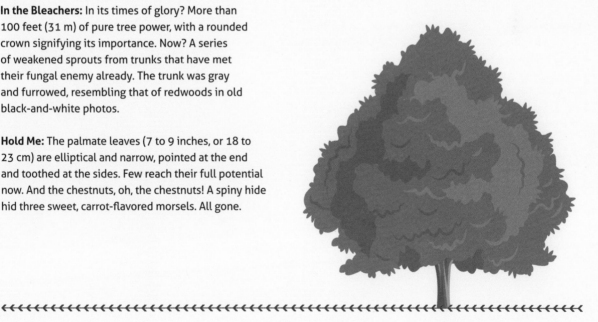

72

SASSAFRAS (*Sassafras albidum*)
aka white sassafras
"The Supplier"

Sassafras has a bit of a mixed reputation at Tree High: there's no denying her marvelous scent of freshly cut twigs, which have made for delightful historical flavoring in root beer and even some not-so-virgin liquid treats of Indigenous peoples, who combined it with molasses and allowed it to ferment. But sassafras, however storied she may be for supplying many at Tree High with a valuable flavoring for illicit rainwater, lost her party reputation when her roots were classified as carcinogenic by the Food and Drug Administration (FDA). Her reputation hasn't recovered since.

In the Bleachers: Rarely reaching 50 feet (15 m), sassafras enjoys her low profile, with twisted branches floating upwards to make a rounded crown.

Hold Me: Look, it's on you if you want to interface with this rough-barked bad girl, whose slight blue berries (⅜ inch, or 0.95 cm) and green-yellow flowers hint at the allegedly toxic being below. But it's certainly fine to snap a twig or two here, because the subsequent aromas will remind you of all your failed experiments making homemade soda. And don't neglect the leaves (4 inches, or 10 cm), featuring one to three soft lobes that turn a wide variety of colors in the fall.

Stadium Habitat: Witness the sassafras skulking along the entire eastern half of the United States up to mid-stands (5,000 feet, or 1,524 m), exchanging pollen for twigs with various deciduous buyers.

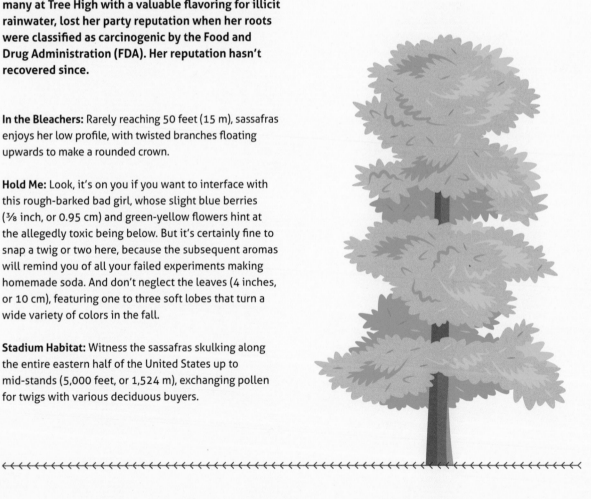

73

COMMON PAW-PAW (*Asimina triloba*)

aka false-banana

"The Sweetie"

The paw-paw is just the sweetest tree. Known for her fruit, which are like tiny, lumpy bananas in taste and size, this tree has been appreciated by everyone from the Sioux and Osage peoples to modern foragers. But paw-paw, who goes from class to class and bleacher to bleacher lighting up the moods of nearby trees with an "aw, shucks" or "it's just so nice to be a part of this," is the most adorable presence one could ask for.

In the Bleachers: As a precious tree (rarely reaching 35 feet, or 11 m) in the understory of the East Coast forests, the paw-paw cuts a subtle profile, with her floppy foliage fanning upwards on a thin trunk into a spreading crown.

Hold Me: The paw-paw fruit ripens in the fall and a skilled forager (some parts on this tree are toxic) can probably grab one for you. The paw-paw's oblong, pointed leaves (8 inches, or 20 cm) are just peachy until they're smushed. Then they smell like poo. "I like being stinky," she says with a mischievous grin.

Stadium Habitat: The paw-paw is a regular throughout the bleachers of the East Coast, popping up to Appalachia (2,600 feet, or 793 m) to sweeten the mood of all the grumpy East Coast pines. She couldn't care less about the Big Game but will happily chat with you about it.

74

EASTERN REDBUD (*Cercis canadensis*)

aka red-bud, Judas tree

"The Super Religious Tree"

The eastern redbud is a marvel. She's the native North American answer to the Japanese cherry blossom, and she shows her marvelous pink-and-white flowers every spring. But the redbud herself has a dark backstory—she's said to be related to the tree on which Judas Iscariot hanged himself. Yikes! As compensation for this rumored notoriety, she brings forth a divine display of flowers as a show of spiritual contrition. Please don't bring it up with this tree, though—she's quite sensitive about the subject.

In the Bleachers: Slight (30 feet, or 9 m), meek, and rounded, the eastern redbud prefers to cultivate modesty at most times of the year save the Holy Days (early spring).

Hold Me: Leaves heart-shaped and smooth-edged (4 inches, or 10 cm), almost enough to convince you that everything is just fine under the bark. And don't get fresh: the eastern redbud is quite happy perfecting her clusters of pink and white flowers (½ inch, or 1.3 cm) and seed pods (she is, of course, a legume) without any interference from trees with bad intentions.

Stadium Habitat: The Southern stands to 2,200 feet (671 m), where she can watch the lovely game without worrying about any *other* corrupt apostles approaching her with terrible ideas.

75

HONEY LOCUST (*Gleditsia triacanthos*)

aka sweet-locust, thorny-locust

"The Tree That Haunts Your Dreams"

Now this tree isn't a student per se, but it does haunt the dreams of every student at Tree High. Let me explain: You probably remember the 1984 classic *A Nightmare on Elm Street*, no? Well, here's a secret—the elm was the original victim. That's right—that movie was based on the goings-on at Tree High itself! And the Freddy Krueger in all of this? The honey locust, a breathtakingly nightmarish phantom of a tree whose long spines are enough to give even the stoutest Douglas-fir a season of sleepless nights. The spines evolved as a defense against the enormous megafauna (big, browsing animals) of the Pleistocene period—we can see a similar growth in silk-floss trees (genus *Ceiba*) of South America. One word of advice: if you see this tree, you do what I do and run.

In the Bleachers: All seems normal at a distance. Nice tree (80 feet, or 24 m). Open crown. Green! But things take a turn when suddenly, Ah! You've been stabbed! Stabbed by 8-inch (20 cm) wooden barbs adorning the fissured bark!

Hold Me: Quick, grab a handful of its foot-long (30 cm) pods to seal the wound! Oh, no, it's not working! Grab something else! Maybe the leaves, which are pinnately compound, with oblong leaflets! Oh gosh, it's . . . it's . . . getting dark . . .

Stadium Habitat: WHOA! You wake up in the middle of the stands at the Big Game! Was it all a dream? You can't tell, after all, the honey locust is rumored to be *everywhere the soil is moist.* Sweet dreams, tree folk.

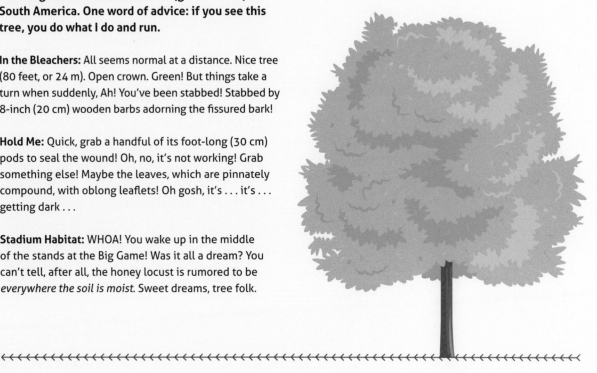

76

BLUE PALO VERDE (*Parkinsonia florida*)

aka paloverde

"The Tree with a Tanning Machine"

<<<<<<<<<<<<<<<<<<<<<<<<<<<<<<<<<<<<<<<<<<<<<<<<<<<<<<<<<<<<<<<<<<<<

If blue palo verde were a person, you'd be terrified. That's because this tree adores SPF-free tanning so much that he insisted his wealthy father buy him a luxury tanning machine. Yikes. As the state tree of Arizona, blue palo verde has developed the adaptation of tiny leaves and bright green bark, which is full of chlorophyll. As opposed to most trees, blue palo verde makes the lion share of his sugars in his bark so that he doesn't have to worry about too much transpiration drying him out through his leaves. A clever tree, clearly, but wise?

In the Bleachers: A contained fella (20 feet, or 6 m), with a bright green trunk leading to a bunch of a bare green branches.

Hold Me: When the bright yellow flowers (1 inch, or 2.5 cm) appear in spring, one could swear that this tree's admirably chromatic torso seems almost balanced. But oh, what a shame that this tree barely puts in the time with his bipinnate leaves, which appear only infrequently throughout the year.

Stadium Habitat: During the Big Game, find palo verde at 2,000 feet (671 m) in the southwest desert with a tanning box around his trunk: "Where the atmosphere is thin enough and the sun bright enough that literally nothing stands between me and UV nirvana." Sounds supremely unhealthy, but okie-dokie.

<<<<<<<<<<<<<<<<<<<<<<<<<<<<<<<<<<<<<<<<<<<<<<<<<<<<<<<<<<<<<<<<<<<<

BLACK WALNUT (*Juglans nigra*)

aka American walnut

"The Tree That's Obsessed with His Car"

"Get in, loser, we're going to Great Smoky Mountains National Park." So says the black walnut tree—the foremost representative of the walnut family that also includes the hickories and the wingnuts, whose nuts and wood are legendary for their toughness and tastiness. They know this, and that pure ego is what encourages them to act so recklessly. After wrapping his previous car around giant sequoia last month while texting shagbark hickory, black walnut got himself a '68 Chevy to cruise for trees. But while he likes to paint himself as a real ladies' tree, he's actually got a soft spot for eastern redbud. Rumor has it she might be into him too, but good luck getting her over-protective dad to put away his Roundup whenever black walnut drives by.

In the Bleachers: Upright with a spreading crown of reaching branches (up to 130 feet, or 40 m), this bad boy of broadleaves cuts a handsome, if dangerous, silhouette. Careful you don't burn your finger on one of his herbal tree ciggies, because if you aren't, you'll get a clear look at the gray fissured bark of the most coveted hardwood in America.

Hold Me: Ten-to-twenty pointed, toothed, pinnately compound leaflets make up each leaf. At your feet, the ground is littered with bright green husks, covering a thick shell and bitter seed ("Hey, you want a snack? Go across the pond to my loser cousin *English* walnut, *pfuh, pfuh, I'm soooo English!*") What a rude tree!

Stadium Habitat: If you catch black walnut at the Big Game, which is never a sure thing considering how sought-after he is, you'll spot him behind the stands, looking cool as a cucumber tree in the Eastern Forests until he goes all jelly-legged at the sight of eastern redbud.

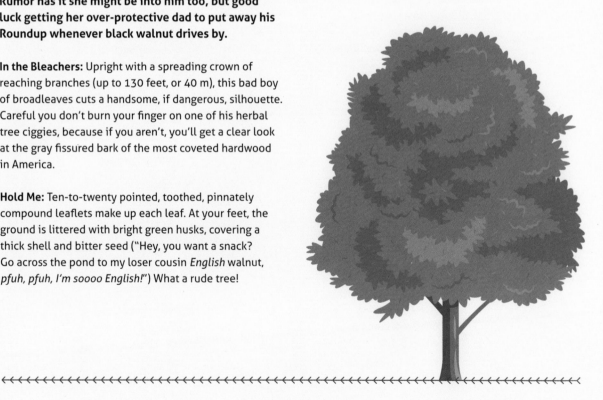

78

BUTTERNUT (*Juglans cinerea*)

aka oilnut, white walnut

"The Tree That's Always Saying the Wrong Thing"

‹‹

As a less-esteemed member of the walnut family, butternut is technically allowed to ride shotgun in black walnut's Chevy, but only because black walnut's dad, Mr. Walnut, told him that he had to. That's because butternut suffers from butternut canker, a disease that has diminished his population to around 20 percent of its normal range. But he's also not any wiser for it: it's common to hear butternut, who is known for his oil-rich nuts that factor into everything from maple-butternut candy to the ceremonies of Indigenous peoples, put his big old root in his mouth. Just yesterday he was seen cruising by a cluster of river birches and yelling, "Birch, please! Birch, please! Ha ha. No, I'm just kidding—I actually respect you guys. 'Guys', wait, no you're not guys! You're tree . . . chicks! What?

Anywho, wanna cruise in this . . . uh, car?" Black walnut, who was in the driver's seat, was seen to have his crown in his hands.

In the Bleachers: Butternut's spreading, rounded crown can be a goofy, if tragically uncommon sight (50 to 60 feet, or 15 to 18 m).

Hold Me: Butternut's pinnate, toothed leaves can measure nearly 2 feet (61 cm) in length, while the deep-brown husks (2 inches, or 5 cm) that hang in clusters house the oily nut.

Stadium Habitat: Just follow the sounds of the overenthusiastic tree yelling, "Team tree, baby! Team TREE!" over by the middle Northwest forests. But have pity on this guy, there ain't enough of him to learn.

‹‹

79

SHAGBARK HICKORY (*Carya ovata*)
aka scalybark hickory
"The Tree That Shags"

No use trying to avoid the elephant in the forest here, folks. If the black walnut is the Kenickie of the trees, shagbark Hickory is the undisputed Danny Zuko. And. This. Tree. Shags. It shags all day and all night, in fact. And I don't just say that because its bark is shaggy and sloughs off in great, gray, sensual shreds. No, sir. This tree absolutely loves to meet up with bigleaf magnolia or really any other tree that's within shagging distance. Who cares if they can't propagate? Sure, this gives him quite the reputation at Tree High, but, folks, that's just music to his root hairs.

In the Bleachers: Though not terribly impressive in height (70 to 80 feet, or 21 to 24 m), the licentious spreading and drooping crown of the shagbark Hickory is the first hint that this tree has a one-track mind. And the peeling sheets of bark from his trunk make him look positively ripped.

Hold Me: Most report that the soft, pinnate compound leaves (10 inches, or 25 cm) have a gentle caress about them, with only five to seven leaflets and a terminal leaf at the end to add some humor into the mix. The hickory nuts resemble green walnuts but are smaller (2 inches, or 5 cm).

Stadium Habitat: While Jack pine and tamarack are outside the equipment shed on the East Coast, shagbark is inside. Who's with him? Depends what day of the week it is.

80

BITTERNUT HICKORY (*Carya cordiformis*)

aka pignut

"The Humiliated Younger Sibling Tree"

It's all right there in the name, everyone. Just imagine being the younger sibling of shagbark hickory—a tree known for both the lustiness of its nuts and their tastiness. That's why bitternut hickory prefers to keep her head down, hoping that if she focuses nonstop on her squirrel avoidance homework then she won't have to hear such taunts from incense-cedar as "Hey Bitternut! Heard they had to send in a whole team of arborists into the equipment shed to clean up your Big Bro's bark this morning!" Eww!

In the Bleachers: Somewhat shorter (60 feet, or 18 m) and squatter than her big brother, bitternut would prefer that you not compare her broad crown to her brother's libidinous one.

Hold Me: Bitternut, as expected, takes no interest in anyone eating her nuts (1 inch, or 2.5 cm), so as to distinguish herself from her brother. That's why they're completely inedible. On her stems are nine compound, pinnate leaflets. No more, no less. Nothing to attract attention.

Stadium Habitat: Find bitternut hickory all across the Eastern US stands, switching positions every week. Usually with an enormous baseball cap and truly humongous sunglasses over her crown.

QUAKING ASPEN (*Populus tremuloides*)
aka trembling aspen, golden aspen, popple

"The Popular Populus"

Quaking aspen guards his reputation closely, but also has the savvy to insert himself seemingly into every aspect of life at Tree High. Mountain Club? President. East Coast Cuties? Treasurer. He even bakes a pine cone cake for old Ms. Limber Pine (who teaches Tree-ography) to up his Tree-P-A. But plenty of tree folk assert that all of this is a ruse, and that he's only interested in propagating his (admittedly intense) beauty into the world via asexual root reproduction. Take a look at who he sits with in the cafe-tree-ria: a bunch of clones who all share the same root system!

In the Bleachers: Quaking aspen (30 to 40 feet, or 9 to 12 m) always makes sure everyone can see his thin, bone-white bark and narrow profile gleaming in moonlight. And, while his bark's lack of peeling is its most distinguishing feature (do *not* confuse this tree with Paper Birch, "or else . . . ")— he also has frequent dark branching scars that gaze upon you like primordial eyeballs.

Hold Me: The bright-golden beauty of aspen in autumn is legendary. Enormous clusters of clonal groves, like Utah's famed "Pando" that boasts a fifty thousand-year-old root system, are simply breathtaking in their shuddering masses of toothed, heart-shaped leaves (2½ inches, or 6.4 cm) attached perpendicularly to a flattened stem, which makes them "tremble" in the wind.

Stadium Habitat: All over. Up to 10,000 feet (3,048 m) in the Rockies, where he consorts with limber pine and Colorado spruce, and down to the lucky backyards of Eastern Canada. Makes me tremble just to think about it.

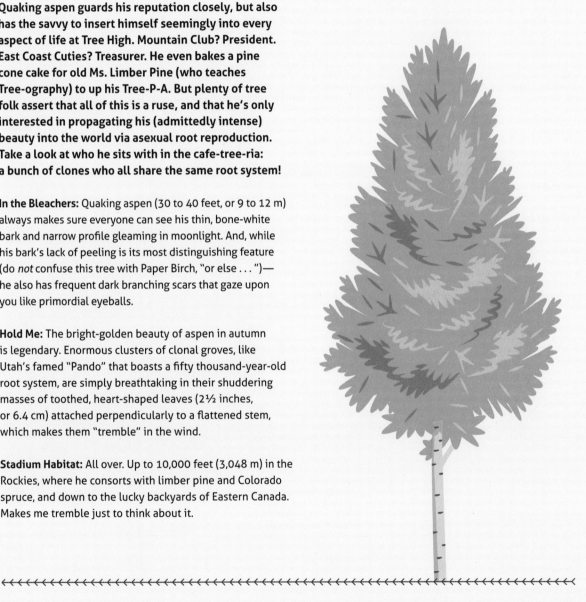

82

EASTERN COTTONWOOD (*Populus deltoides*)

aka necklace poplar, southern cottonwood

"The Tree That Loves to Party but Is Also a Pillar in the Community?"

Eastern cottonwood is baffling. Like her high-achieving sibling quaking aspen, she's a member of the genus *Populus*, but unlike quaking aspen, eastern cottonwood seems much more driven by sheer confidence than ego. This tree is often broken into three subspecies that reveal this wild compartmentalization: as the ordinary *eastern* cottonwood, this fast-growing tree can attain nearly 5 feet (1.5 m) of new growth in a year. As the *plains* cottonwood, this tree is a critical marvel in the Great Plains, creating shelter and food for untold species. And then, as the *Rio Grande* cottonwood, this tree simply *requires* a crazy flood of rainwater just to sprout! How does she do it *all*?

In the Bleachers: Approaching 100 feet (31 m), the cottonwood's wide and spreading branches might make her seem like an oak, but she makes sure to have more forking in her architecture to preempt this identification mistake. Smart! And the deeply-furrowed, graying bark of old trees lets you know that this tree means business.

Hold Me: The pearl- and cotton-like seeds on her catkins signal a tree that also knows how to rage! Large leaves (5 to 6 inches, or 13 to 15 cm), triangular with flattened base and toothed edges, say it all: Cottonwood knows how to prioritize photosynthesis above all else.

Stadium Habitat: As a "pioneer tree" that is often the first to grow after flood or fire, look for eastern cottonwood getting an early seat at sea level across the great plains. Be sure to say "hi"—this tree is great.

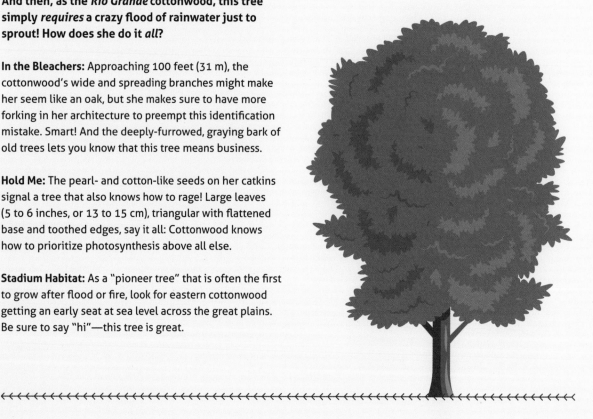

83

BLACK WILLOW (*Salix nigra*)

aka swamp willow

"The Bark-Care Genius"

No one is going to call any of the genus willow (*Salix*) the most beautiful trees that they've ever seen. They're often multi-stemmed and shrubby, with leaves that resemble rotting field sickles. But here's the thing: they know how to take care of their bark, and that makes them one of the most sought-after wellness sages at Tree High. Black willow herself is a source of salicin, which converts to salicylic acid, which is just, oh I don't know, *the most popular skin care chemical on the planet.* Got a spot? Ask black willow! 824k on TikTok!

In the Bleachers: From a distance, she's multi-stemmed and irregular (around 50 feet, or 15 m). But beauty lies within when it comes to this tree (on the inner bark at least, because that's where the manufacture of the chemicals occurs). The bud arrangement on the twigs, which alternate pleasingly, is where black willow puts most of her tree-care know-how (the bark itself is dark-brown and ridged).

Hold Me: The narrow, curved leaves (4 to 6 inches, or 10 to 15 cm), have tiny teeth along the edges.

Stadium Habitat: Anywhere there's a tree that needs tips on dealing with a bothersome outbreak of lichen. But usually the moist areas of the Eastern United States, and typically the wet areas of the South with an unobstructed view of the field.

84

WEEPING WILLOW (*Salix babylonica*)

"The . . . Um . . . Well, the Tree That's Really Sad"

The weeping willow has gained international fame for his inability to take a joke. And I use international quite literally here. The weeping willow is an introduced species from Asia, but he's so commonly interbred with other willows to form his trademark "weeping foliage" that he doesn't really know *where* he's from these days. Perhaps that is one of the reasons that he simply cannot stop the tears. That, and the fact that he can't get over Paper Birch despite the fact that it's been millions of years since their evolutionary divergence.

In the Bleachers: Can't miss these waterworks. While the trunk and the tree in general are short (35 feet, or 11 m), the weeping willow has a seemingly endless network of cascading branches. Like other willows, the bark here is nothing to write home about—gray and ridged—but the drooping branches bear long green-yellow twigs, giving the tree a youthful appearance year-round.

Hold Me: The distinctive sickle-shaped willow leaves (4 inches, or 10 cm) turn into graceful masses of golden-yellow in the fall, lending some brightness to this sappy guy.

Stadium Habitat: "Oh, just plant me anywhere. Everywhere sucks," willow says. And we do. At least along the East Coast bleachers. Weeping willow is often incorrigibly depressed during the game itself, but when the oaks strike up a sad ballad during halftime, well . . . he'll weep even harder.

85

RED MULBERRY (*Morus rubra*)

aka purple mulberry, moral

"The Tree That's Completely Uninterested"

‹‹

"Oh, I'm a tree? Wow. Look at that," croaks the mulberry tree when you remark upon her varying leaf structure, which sometimes has three lobes, sometimes two, and sometimes none. This tree's peers have been trying and trying to get her to care about having some consistency in her leaf shape, especially since she has so many other wonderful features such as delicious berries and useful wood, but she just can't be brought to care. Of late, bigleaf magnolia has made it their personal mission to help red mulberry realize her potential. Reports are that it's not going great.

In the Bleachers: Mulberry's irregular crown and short trunk make her rather inconspicuous (50 feet, or 15 m), but "honestly, I really don't care if anyone notices me. Life isn't just a popularity contest."

Hold Me: "Everyone is on my case about this. Yeah, sometimes my leaves have three toothed, rounded lobes, sometimes none. Doesn't seem like that big of a deal."

Stadium Habitat: Typically, she's apathetic as to where she gets a seat as long as it's not "too, too cold, ugh." Lately she's been having to listen to bigleaf magnolia say stuff like, "Reach for the crown. Even if you miss, you fall among the branches!"

AMERICAN PLUM (*Prunus americana*)

aka red plum

"The 'Regular' Tree"

The American plum knows that he's a common target of zingers from the other students at Tree High. But he doesn't care. This proud member of the genus *Prunus* knows the value of a good prune, and that's why he insists that every member of Tree High have a transpiration movement at exactly 10 a.m. each morning, just when foliage starts to heat up from the sun. You can bet that *he'll* be there.

In the Bleachers: This short tree (25 feet, or 8 m) is a spectacle of flowers in early spring, but his often-thorny presence never detracts from his main mission: xylem health.

Hold Me: The American plum's bunches of five-petaled flowers (1 inch, or 2.5 cm) are characteristic of the rose family, of which it is a part, and the scaly brown bark on older trees offsets the dark red plums (1 inch, or 2.5 cm) for which it is famous. The plum is happy to let you examine its 3-inch (8 cm), elliptical, pointed leaves, which grow oppositely and have sharp teeth, while he's sitting down for his daily movement, if that doesn't gross you out.

Stadium Habitat: A satisfied smile adorns the face of this self-described "prince of digestion" as he watches the Big Game from the Northeast and Midwest, and anywhere that's nice and moist.

87

BLACK CHERRY (*Prunus serotina*)
aka wild black cherry, rum cherry
"The Mall Goth Tree"

The black cherry has a bunch of cherry cousins, all of whom are more frequently used for domestication of the fruit in question. But while black cherry has no problem lending her name to certain candies to lend a little pizzazz, she revels in it when it comes to her personality: find this tree at Hot Topic trying on a new pair of Caffeines and picking out a spiked chain to tie around her trunk. "What other tree hath fruit so dark, so fair and all-consuming? But all you sheep, bite not my pits, for the taste of cyanide dwells within!" Amazing.

In the Bleachers: As the largest tree in genus *Prunus*, the black cherry is commonly 70 to 80 feet (21 to 24 m) tall, with a bulky, asymmetrical crown that tapers below. "Hast thou seen my scaly bark, gray like old men sick with lusty impotence?" Um.

Hold Me: "What say you to my bunches of fruit (½ inch, or 1.3 cm) so night-black as to conjure visions of Lothar?" Just . . . so intense. Leaves are toothed (4 inches, or 10 cm) and turn gorgeous shades of gold and red in the autumn: "Ah, autumn: the season that lies." Very well.

Stadium Habitat: When black cherry finishes spouting nonsense, she's busy finding a new seat anywhere in the Eastern United States so that she can continue harping upon "the fickle and debased games of trees" to any uncomfortable neighbor.

BLACK IRONWOOD (*Krugiodendron ferreum*)
aka leadwood

"The Densest Tree"

<<<<<<<<<<<<<<<<<<<<<<<<<<<<<<<<<<<<<<<<<<<<<<<<<<<<<<<<<<<<<<<<<<<<<<<<

"Small but mighty" might be the best way to describe the black ironwood, a tropical tree relegated to Florida and the Keys that never grows above 30 feet (9.1 m). But this little-known arboreal wonder makes for one of the most critical blocking trees on the field during the Big Game. How? Well, what if I told you that the wood of this tree has a specific gravity of 1.35, indicating that it is the densest, heaviest wood in North America (and, some say, the world)? Watch how a charging Brazilian Balsa tree promptly shatters when faced with the prospect of black ironwood holding its ground!

In the Bleachers: Slim gray trunk, and spare, mild-mannered crown be damned: this tree is unmovable as stone.

Hold Me: Furthermore, simple and toothless leaves (2 inches, or 5 cm) give any adversary a false sense of confidence. Wait until black ironwood lets them know its wood sinks in water.

Stadium Habitat: Front and center at the 20-yard line on the Caribbean coastline. Pound for pound, this tree is three times as strong as redwood himself.

HAWTHORN (Genus *Crataegus*)
aka mayhaw, hog-apple
"The Out of Control Tree"

Trying to get a handle on the many species of hawthorn is a little like trying to climb one after being doused in petroleum jelly: you'll always wind up on your ass. That's because this tree cannot be contained, cannot be categorized, cannot be described as anything other than a genus, largely due to its unparalleled adaptive abilities in North America. "Leave it to the dendronerds to try to pin me down," it's been known to say, "I like to keep Tree High walking on eggshells."

In the Bleachers: Hawthorns range from shrubby little suckers (15 feet , or 5 m) to more than 50-foot (15 m) trees with spreading crowns and curving trunks.

Hold Me: Hawthorn's leaves are usually their most distinguishing characteristic, with multiple, toothed lobes sometimes mimicking oak or sycamore, and turning brilliant red or orange depending on the location. The bunches of white flowers that adorn most hawthorns make for fabulous displays in the spring, with the exception being the One-flowered hawthorn, for whom you may replace the word "bunches" with "one-ches."

Stadium Habitat: Oh, gosh, I mean—everywhere it isn't too hot, too dry, or too windy. During the Big Game, you can see hawthorn bugging all sorts of trees for attention: magnolia, loblolly pine, red oak: "Get out of here, you FUNGUS!" "What are you, some kind of *vine*?!" "No, hawthorn, I know for a fact that sugar maple does not want to go out with you. Now please give me my birdhouse back."

APPLE (*Malus sylvestris*)
aka common apple, domestic apple
"The Transfer Student Tree"

Everyone at Tree High is sure to greet apple with a high-stem or bud-bump in the hallway. He's sweet, kind, and all-around dependable as a source of good will and chill vibes at coast live oak's end-of-semester bashes. But there's the thing: he wasn't always a student at Tree High. Sometime in the early American Colonial period, the common apple was introduced to North America and gained wild popularity, especially after Sir Johnny (who has an entire trophy case dedicated to him outside the gym) chose the Appleseed as his conversation-starter. But no one cares. The trees at Tree High can't remember a time without him. Except for the crab apples. Common apple isn't too popular with them. And, while the common apple himself is probably an ancient hybrid, his many varieties are one of the world's great agricultural wonders, be it Granny Smith or Red Delicious.

In the Bleachers: The rough and tough appearance of an apple tree can be spotted from afar, as his often-leaning, grizzled trunk is overshadowed by a tangle of spreading branches (30 feet, or 1 m). The crusty gray bark of apples makes for excellent climbing grip, but they also rank high on Mitnick's Skinned Knee Index (MSKI).

Hold Me: Apple leaves are as simple as they are familiar: ovular, toothed, and pointed.

Stadium Habitat: Though you'll often find him with his orchard crew down near the field across the Eastern United States, occasionally the apple likes to go it alone, picking a new, rainy spot to share a tall tale or two with oaky neighbors during the third quarter.

GREEN ASH (*Fraxinus pennsylvanica*)

aka red ash, swap ash

"The Duty-Bound Tree"

91

‹‹‹

"I'm not here to show off my flowers. I'm not here to grow higher than the clouds or something. I'm just trying to be a good tree." Thus spoke one of the most conscientious trees at Tree High, the green ash. There isn't much to comment on in terms of superlatives for this tree: great wood, decent bark, tough. But he doesn't really care: he does his job the best he can, photosynthesizing for himself, bestowing anti-erosion properties on his plot of soil, and being one of the most widespread hardwoods in the United States. All this despite the emerald ash borer's commitment to kill every ash tree it possibly can.

In the Bleachers: A round crown (60 feet, or 18 m). A thick trunk (3 feet, or 0.91 m). A good tree. The green ash has a bark pattern that seems at once noble and unremarkable: gray and ridged, like a red oak without the braggadocio.

Hold Me: Green ash foliage is pinnately compound, meaning two rows of oppositely arranged leaflets forming one full leaf, with a single ovate leaflet capping it at its terminus. The "key" fruit of the ash float down and litter his base.

Stadium Habitat: The green ash, spirited and purposeful, is a remarkable wide receiver—zooming all the way from the East Coast to the Rockies in moist and wet soils. Good hustle, green ash, good hustle.

‹‹‹

92

BLUE ASH (*Fraxinus quadrangulata*)

aka winged ash

"The Architecturally Inclined Tree"

If you see a tree in the hallway using his twigs in angular gestures to estimate the height and width of a doorway, that's probably the blue ash. He's not the most famous of trees, but the blue ash has an excellent sense of the monumental, using his square stems and capabilities for the production of blue dye in his twigs to make astonishingly life-like models of his favorite craggy mountains in winter. Rumor has it that the blue ash will be taking courses at Rhode Island School of Design (RISD) next semester, and plans to propose a 1:100 scale diorama of Yellowstone National Park for the new cafeteria next year.

In the Bleachers: Though he's usually around 60 feet (18 m) tall, the blue ash can pop up to 140 feet (43 m) or more, sporting a lanky, ovular crown that has eastern cottonwood all aflush. The most distinguishing characteristic of the blue ash is in its scientific name *quadrangulata*, meaning four-angled, and referring to its twigs that are square in cross section. And unlike the neat, tight bark of the green ash, the blue ash has a peeling habit.

Hold Me: While the other trees find blue ash and his nerdiness just adorable in general, they also suspect that he has a bad boy side, judging from his narrow, sharp leaflets upon his pinnately compound leaves.

Stadium Habitat: Find blue ash firmly ensconced around sea level in the Midwestern United States, not so much watching the game but admiring the modernist take on the announcer's box where American elm does his thing.

AMERICAN ELM (*Ulmus americana*)
aka soft elm
"Running Back Emeritus"

The introduction of Dutch elm disease in the first half of the twentieth century is a notorious episode at Tree High, as it took down one of the iconic North American players in the Big Game: the American elm. Now relegated to the announcer's box until he can regain his strength as a result of new hybrids, American elm still gives it all he's got on the PA system, rousing the crowd with his mellifluous calls and hilarious banter. Occasionally, he'll ask American chestnut to join him, where the two reflect on their glory days with a clandestine fifth of rainwater.

In the Bleachers: With his handsome, rounded crown and tendency to fork into a vase-shape up to his apex (100 feet, or 31 m), the American elm's beauty doesn't seem to hint that his career is currently on ice. The gray, ridged bark is similar to that of ash or red oak.

Hold Me: Oval and pointed, with regular teeth adorning each side, the leaves (3 to 5 inches, or 8 to 13 cm) of the American elm bear a pleasing set of parallel veins, evidence of the tree's extant strength amidst a career cut short. Ask anyone over seventy: the one-seeded "keys" were once familiar sights floating through the air in every suburb in the Eastern United States.

Stadium Habitat: The American elm prefers its protected haunts in the announcer's box, where he can avoid the dreaded Dutch elm fungus but also let other tree folk know he's still got it.

94

POISON SUMAC (*Toxicodendron vernix*)

aka poison-dogwood

"The Tree with Repulsive Ideology"

<<<<<<<<<<<<<<<<<<<<<<<<<<<<<<<<<<<<<<<<<<<<<<<<<<<<<<<<<<<<<<<<<<<<<<<<<<<<<<<<

In every pollination class, poison sumac—which is such an outcast among sumacs (genus *Rhus*) that he's been relegated to a genus meaning "poison tree"—will raise a twig and answer a question with an inevitably poisonous response, usually something along the lines of, "You know, everyone, it would be much easier if there were no human beings at all." Typically admonished by philanthropic trees like the maples, the poison sumac takes his ugliness home with him—sparing any animals or birds his noxious irritations and toxic vapors but making damn sure that any person unlucky enough to come into contact with his clear sap will feel his poisonous wrath.

In the Bleachers: Never getting above 25 feet (8 m), this shrubby, thin tree (6 inches, or 15 cm) lures in his human prey with lovely autumn foliage. The thin gray bark is not notable, but the whitish berries signal trouble.

Hold Me: Well, that would be an error. When exposed to air, the sap of the poison sumac becomes black as night as if to signal his intent, so stay away (unless you think handling pinnate foliage with ovular leaves is worth a persistent burning rash indicative of this tree's unparalleled malice).

Stadium Habitat: The swamps of the North and South on the East Coast near sea level, where it conspires with poison oak and poison ivy for the next attack, their scheming muffled by the proximate noise of the field.

<<<<<<<<<<<<<<<<<<<<<<<<<<<<<<<<<<<<<<<<<<<<<<<<<<<<<<<<<<<<<<<<<<<<<<<<<<<<<<<<

95 FLOWERING DOGWOOD (*Cornus florida*)
"The Love Child"

Flowering dogwood evolved during a time of great change (as did all trees, but stay with me here). This was when "the moon was as often as not in cancer, and Jupiter was in retrograde." As to whether that's even possible, I'm not sure. But this love child of the Eastern Forests wears her flowers in her crown prominently. This makes her an attractive ornamental for human beings but also beloved by the tree community for the air of beauty and slightly judgy kindness she brings to the table. As the state tree of Virginia, she's never slow to remind anyone that she, as well, is for lovers.

In the Bleachers: Small in stature (30 to 35 feet, or 9 to 11 m) yet round and open in aspect, the flowering dogwood wants to remind you that even the humblest trees can be truly far out.

Hold Me: The dogwood's bursts of spring flowers are yellow and green (4 inches, or 10 cm), adorning her twigs above a crackling brown bark like a groovy happening. But her elliptical, pointed leaves (4 inches, or 10 cm) that prove scarcer than in most trees demonstrate that this tree might not have her photosynthetic priorities in order.

Stadium Habitat: Find the flowering dogwood dancing to her own rhythm on the small hill next to the snack tent on the Eastern Coastline, occasionally distracting trees of every stripe on the field and off.

96

SOUTHERN CATALPA (*Catalpa bignonioides*)

aka catawba, cigar tree

"The Tree That Is Living Her Best Life"

Once upon a time, the southern catalpa, like her Northern cousin, only grew in a narrow band in Georgia and Mississippi. This tree has few uses as a resource, but, due to her bright white blooms, she was soon planted across the continent by both Indigenous peoples and Europeans. And what was once a shy, self-deprecating recluse who would brush her roots in the dirt at her, uh, roots, suddenly became a mainstay of continental beauty: batting her petals with confidence, jumping high in the air on the beach at sunset, and relaxing in an XXXXXL bathrobe with a rainwater spritzer.

In the Bleachers: On the shorter side, with a twisted trunk (40 feet, or 12 m) but featuring a lovely spreading crown, the southern catalpa is all about that "grab-any-branch-and-pretend-it's-a-microphone" life.

Hold Me: Oh, hey, girl! Is that a new set of flowers (2 inches, or 5 cm, white and trumpeted)? And my dear, those fruit pods (10 inches, or 25 cm) are just To. Die. For! But however much southern catalpa wants us to believe that her life might be 'gram-worthy, she's betrayed by her leaves (8 inches, or 20 cm), each one a pointed heart reminiscent of the bursting soul she is on the inside. Trees are complicated!

Stadium Habitat: While southern catalpa would love us to believe that she's down by the southern fence line to cheer on the players, she's actually down there to catch a glimpse of willow oak at halftime (just because you're living your best life doesn't mean the past is gone).

97

AMERICAN HOLLY (*Ilex opaca*)

aka white holly

"The Tree That Hates the Holidays"

Things started out so simple: a few leaves here and there for European Pagan rituals, some branches saved as fertility symbols, etc. But then came the English Christmas carols of the nineteenth century and American holly didn't stand a chance to define itself on its own terms against that tsunami of holiday spirit. From the end of Thanksgiving until the beginning of January, find this tree in a cynical stupor. "Personally, I can't turn up my earbuds loud enough to drown out the calls of 'The Holly and the Ivy.' And, ugh, they start earlier every year!"

In the Bleachers: Holly can grow to 100 feet (31 m), but it typically stays under 50 feet (15 m), displaying a conical evergreen crown more typical of gymnosperms than angiosperms.

Hold Me: Ouchie, friend! These spiny leaves (3 inches, or 8 cm) are of course a Christmas mainstay. The bright red berries make the female trees of this species well-known for their holiday spirit. Or, rather, their *compulsory* holiday spirit. The less-desirable males often succeed in sneaking off to riparian keggers, the jerks.

Stadium Habitat: In the American South, just in front of the fence line, American holly commonly hangs out with other misunderstood trees trying to live out their own dreams despite external expectations. "Go on, tell me: Am I a clown? Would you like me to dance? Maybe pour you a glass of friggin' eggnog? IS THAT WHAT YOU WANT?"

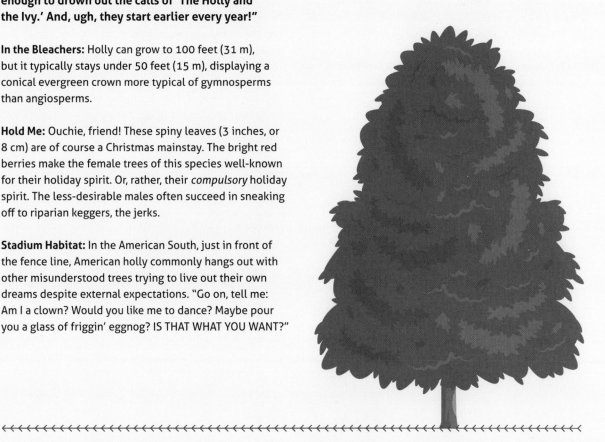

98

CURL-LEAF MOUNTAIN MAHOGANY (*Cercocarpus ledifolius*)
aka curlleaf cercocarpus, desert cercocarpus
"The Fonzie Tree"

There are a million different types of "cool" these days. There are cool geeks, there are cool slackers, and there are even "the cool kids" at large. But tell me, do any of these cool individuals compare to this stylish, high-altitude desert angiosperm, who twists his trunk according to the winds of winter and is always down for a jukebox elbow fix so that he can party with Jeffrey pine before he sets off for his next street race? Sure, he may not be an authentic "mahogany" as defined by the genus *Swietenia*, but I still give this rugged tree two very Fonzie thumbs up for his genuine class and confidence.

In the Bleachers: Look for guy's short, twisted frame (up to 20 feet, or 6 m) and chipping brown bark

and deadwood along any high mountain trail in the American West.

Hold Me: His scrubby leaves (1 inch, or 2.5 cm) almost seem like olive leaves at first blush, but then one hears them flutter in the mountain wind, which sounds curiously like "Eyyyy!" The late-summer flowers are a reminder of the kind of warmth one can have, even if he's the very definition of cool.

Stadium Habitat: Mountain mahogany brushes shoulders with the high mountain pines near 10,000 feet (3,048 m) at every Big Game on the Western slopes, willing to dispense advice accumulated throughout his six attempts at completing senior year of high school.

99

KENTUCKY COFFEETREE (*Gymnocladus dioicus*)
aka coffee-nut tree, stump tree
"The Tree with a Thermos"

The Kentucky coffeetree works hard, and he wants you to know it. "Oh, this?" he says as he fills up another steaming hot tin cup from his Thermos, "This is my own personal blend. Some might say it's 'toxic' for people to drink, but luckily I'm not a person. I'm a tree . . . hold up, got to pound another cup if I'm going to get through this fourth-period squirrel avoidance exam." He isn't a common sight in the wild, but you can catch his enormous, bipinnately compound leaves jittering around from classroom to classroom.

In the Bleachers: The coffeetree sticks around 50 feet (15 m), with scaly brown bark and an open crown that turns a blazing yellow in the fall.

Hold Me: While the pods (5 inches, or 13 cm, toxic) and spring flowers of this tree are typical of the non-showy legumes, you can't say the same for his ostentatious leaves (30 inches, or 76 cm), which he waves around like he wants the whole school to know he's wired.

Stadium Habitat: Located solidly in the Midwest, the Kentucky coffeetree often consorts with ash-y friends who understand his ambitious goals of city living. Catch him throwing back his Thermos at field level, then screaming in primal, chemical-induced support of any subsequent play.

100

PALM TREES
"The Tree That Does Not Go to Tree High"

[Palms are not trees. Please see next section.]

Chapter 13

UNPOPULAR TREE OPINION:
These Two Beloved Trees Are Not Trees

Let me expand upon the preceding blank section on page 203 that I decided to include in a spell of vituperativeness. I'm not normally a vindictive person, but I have three exceptions: when a person insults my family, when a mosquito bites my butt (yes, they love to do this for some reason), and when something that is absolutely *not* a tree decides to *imitate* a tree.

Now that you've been introduced to life at Tree High North America, you've become familiar with the textured reality of the life of trees beyond the normal scope of botany: who these trees are, what they want, what they do. You bore witness to the well-rounded goofballs, the incorrigible scallywags, and the wizened nuncles that populate our wide world. Wasn't it a fun ride? Wasn't it a thrill to understand that, despite their outward appearances, they all have a few things in common: stature, woodiness, and the most important characteristic: institutional memory by way of their rings?

Because, folks, that is the most important piece of the puzzle for me. In a world where trees have no real botanical definition—some say they're any woody growth over 10 feet (3 m), some say over 20 feet (6 m), some say they're anything with woody growth—it's important that I take my own stand on this issue. I'm drawing a line in the sand.

And the place that I'm drawing it, is at the concept of memory. The ability to say, "This is how it was wheretohenceforthwithall, when our world was young, and you were perhaps not even living." Aside from its practical applications in climate science and history, tree ring dating and analysis (dendrochronology) is such a cozy, sweet, human thing; if I give a tree a hug so tight that I accidentally brush my hand against an exposed spot of its cambium, that scratch will stay with it until death, perhaps after my own. Therefore, when cranky old-timers get out their abacuses and their arbitrary definitions of a tree, you can clap back with a simple *quality*. Sure, it's true that under this definition snails might qualify as trees and that Harry Styles with his ever-expanding ring wardrobe may be a tree as well. But it's also really fun to jazz arrogant people about silly stuff that frustrates them, so you should run with it.

Here are the two main offenders who would presume to call themselves trees, when in reality they're no more than a bunch of unknowing, unthinking automatons hell-bent on capitalizing on the good will and emotional closeness we give to the trees to whom it is rightfully owed.

Palm "Trees"

Truthbomb: All palm "trees," henceforth palm *plants*, are mere collections of vertical fibers who only exhibit age through vertical growth rather than hard-wrought ring expansion. Perhaps this is because they're more closely related to grass than anything else. But that didn't stop them from boring their way into the consciousness of even the most armchair-bound dreamer, who would rather think about these mindless schmucks swaying above a well-salted margarita than a hundred plausible and marvelous alternatives. (Hello? Monterey cypress? Ever heard of it?) Also, going forward, shade is going to be one of the most invaluable resources we can hope for. Under a palm plant? Not much.

Joshua "Trees"

I came in hot but I'm going to slow it down right now, because I'm sure a lot of you are in shock, like I was when I learned about this epoch-making deception many years ago. Perhaps, like me, you have a fondness for U2's first decade of work, and the crowning achievement thereof. How, then, could his majesty Bono lie to your face by calling the album *The Joshua Tree*?! But, like me, you will have to pull your head gently out of your nether-area, because Joshua trees are simply big yucca plants with similar fibrous arrangements to palm plants. And you know what I say: no memory, no tree. But also, soon, perhaps no Joshua, as nearly all of their native range will be eliminated due to climate change. Again, probably a shock for you. Here's my advice, if this is all news for you: Take the emotional hit, observe a mourning period, and read up on the trees that actually work overtime to cool us down. Those are my guys.

An Imagined Dialogue Between Myself and a Magnolia Tree

Setting: *My childhood farmhouse, Mohnton, Pennsylvania. Dawn, the year 2087.*

(Lights up on a solitary, broken magnolia tree, close to 150 years old but closer to death. Its limbs are splintered, its fungal infections numerous, its flowers nearly nonexistent on this spring day.)

<‹‹<

 MAGNOLIA: Come, sun. Come and undo my limbs. Take my rotten trunk and return me to the soil. Make me as the earth from whence I came.

 TOBIN'S FRAIL VOICE: Not if I have anything to say about it!

(The magnolia glances to the side, where Tobin Mitnick, 100, and leaning on a redwood staff, has shuffled in from the East. The magnolia lights up.)

 MAGNOLIA: You old . . .

 TOBIN: No, you old . . .

 MAGNOLIA: No, you old . . .

(They laugh, and Tobin collapses onto the magnolia's fragile trunk.)

 MAGNOLIA: Whoa, watch it with those lanky things, don't you know I'm dying?

 TOBIN: Wouldn't think it with how much you've got to say!

(They laugh for a beat. It fades.)

 TOBIN: How they treating you here?

MAGNOLIA: Not like they used to. Who do I have to "accidentally" let fall around here to get a little fertilizer?

 TOBIN: Ah, don't eat that stuff. It'll—

 MAGNOLIA: . . . kill me?

(They laugh.)

 MAGNOLIA: Nah, I'm fine. Going out the way I came in. Quietly. With a great view.

(They both glance up at the farmhouse up the hill)

 TOBIN: You know what I was thinking on the way over here?

 MAGNOLIA: "I should turn around?"

 TOBIN: *(laughs)* No. Was wondering if you still got the tatt.

(Magnolia smiles, satisfied, and lifts up his crumbled south branch to reveal a calloused-but-still-perceivable carving on his primary limb: "1987")

 TOBIN: The year we met.

 MAGNOLIA: The year you were born.

(Tobin looks off in the distance, lost in thought.)

TOBIN: You know, I used to go in search of adventure, to see all those ancient sequoias and redwoods and bristlecone pines—

 MAGNOLIA: . . . like Methuselah?

 TOBIN: . . . yeah, like Methuselah. Because I remember thinking that the way I would want to go, when my time came, would be under a very old, very good tree like them. But you know what?

 MAGNOLIA: What?

 TOBIN: I never had to go far to find a very, very good tree.

(The last of the magnolia's flower petals fall to the ground. They sit in silent reverie.)

 MAGNOLIA: You know these branches aren't as brittle as they seem.

 TOBIN: (*smiling*) One last go?

(The magnolia straightens up the best he can.)

 MAGNOLIA: Careful on the slippery limb, will ya? You've never been the most ginger climber.

 TOBIN: What was that I heard you say? 'Return me to the soil? Make me as the earth from whence I came?'

❮❮❮

(A moment of understanding. Tobin drops his redwood cane and painstakingly rolls up his sleeves as the lights fade to black.)

Glossary

Acorn: The seed of an oak tree, which has developed a reputation as readymade artillery amongst our more aggressive youths.

Albedo: A measurement of reflected solar radiation. This comes into play in the field of climate science, which uses albedo in relationship to the coloring of the earth.

Alternately arranged: When leaves take turns appearing on a twig.

Angiosperm: This term is often used interchangeably with "deciduous," but that's hardly accurate, as it merely describes trees that bear flowers with their seeds encased in a fruit. Pardon me while I audibly scoff!

Bark: Hi, doggie! No, but seriously this is the outermost layer on a tree, consisting of dead tissue that protects the cambium (growth layer).

Bark beetle: Any one of the many species of beetle who feast on cambium and lay their eggs there, eventually girdling and killing the tree in cases of severe infestation. Also, the vessels of many a tree plague (Dutch elm disease, most famously.)

Biome: An ecosystem particular to a shared regional climate. Could be as exciting as a rainforest or as depressing as the tundra.

Bipinnate: A leaf made of rows of leaves made of rows of leaves (there's also **tripinnate**, meaning a leaf made of rows of leaves made of rows of leaves made of rows of leaves.)

Bract: A specialized leaf below a flower that can itself look like a flower, as in bougainvillea.

Broadleaf: Don't make me spell it out for you. Okay, you got me: a broad, flat leaf. What can I say, I'm a pushover.

Bud: An immature leaf or flower, ready to show the world what it's got.

Cambium: A tree's growth layer under the bark. It's really, really gooey, and really fun to touch. Please don't touch it.

Canopy: The uppermost layer of foliage in a tree, or the wider layer formed by many trees in a forest.

Carbon sink: A large storage area for solidified carbon on Earth. The Canadian Boreal Forest and the Amazon are two of the biggest examples of this.

Chlorophyll: The magical, sunlight-to-sugar converting pigment found in chloroplasts. It ranks just below the word "frenching" on "Mitnick's Infamous List of Trauma-Inducing Middle School Words and Phrases." It's contained within the **chloroplasts** of a plant cell, which are the sites of photosynthesis.

Compound leaf: A leaf made of leaves.

Cone: The "fruit" (I am obliged to use this word because all definitions include it) of a conifer, wherein the seeds exist on scales.

Conifer: My preferred tree; one that bears cones, and usually—*usually*—is evergreen.

Crown: Tree top, pretty simple. Let's not complicate this.

Cultivar: A portmanteau of "cultivated" and "variety," indicating a tree purposely bred to exhibit characteristics of multiple trees and therefore be more sophisticated. Sort of like people who use the word "portmanteau."

Deciduous: A big ol' leaf-droppin' daddy.

Dioecious: When trees have male and female parts on separate plants. "Parts," lol.

Dicot: An angiosperm (a tree that flowers and bears fruit) with two embryonic leaves, as opposed to only one embryonic leaf (monocots). Monocots, like palm trees, do not have growth rings. Therefore, I don't count them as trees. And I hold a grudge against any tree that calls itself tree that is not, in fact, a tree.

Family: A collection of genuses.

Fascicle: A bundle of leaves, most often used to refer to the groupings of needles on a pine tree. Also sounds quite dirty. Fun word!

Flower: The name for the entire structure of a plant's reproductive, um, area.

Genus: A collection of related species.

Geode: A hollow, crystal-filled rock. *The* cornerstone product of 1990s shopping mall staple "World of Science."

Ginkophyta: The division, or phylum, that contains only a single living tree: the ginkgo.

Girth: Used to describe a tree's circumference at breast-height. It is also the horniest tree word, i.e. "I had plans to conquer the neighborhood Elm. Alas, 'twas too girthy."

Glaucous: A term for the bluish-grayish-greenish-whitish color often found on certain trees (like the Colorado blue spruce) or plants (certain agave). The waxy color often signals a tough coating meant to protect the leaf from drying out.

Gymnosperm: Had a lot of gross jokes planned for this one, but I'll just be real: it's a tree that doesn't have a fruit protecting its seeds. It usually refers to conifers.

Heartwood: The structural wood at the center of the trunk that no longer carries water or sap.

Hybrid: A plant that displays characteristics of two parent plants.

Krummholz: A short, stunted incarnation of a tree made so by winds and weather at high altitudes.

Leaf: Come on.

Leaflet: A leaf's rap name, but also occasionally refers to a leaf within a leaf.

Leafstalk: No secrets here—a stalk that attaches a leaf to a stem. Also known as a "petiole."

Lignin: The woody stuff in cell walls.

Lobed: The rounded or pointed section of each leaf's borders. Grandma used to tell me these were made with "God's cookie-cutter." I feel like Grandma lied a lot.

Loping: Large cuts of living tree branches. If performed poorly, this can make a tree supremely unhealthy and appear completely hideous.

Magnoliophyta: A slightly archaic term for the angiosperms. It would be like if someone referred to a "Boomer" as a "Baby Boomer."

Monoecious: When trees have both, uh . . . "parts," lol . . . on the same plant.

Mycorrhizal fungi: Fungi which grow on a tree's roots, developing a symbiotic relationship with the tree through an exchange of nutrients. **Mycelia** are the threads of fungal growth that establish networks between forest trees.

Node: Where a leaf attaches to a stem. I still think my use of "leaf butt" is appropriate, however.

Nurse Log: A downed trunk, which subsequently functions as a forest buffet and incubator for sundry types of life from fungi to full-blown trees.

Nut: You. I'm kidding. It's a seed encased in a hard shell, functioning as the "fruit." You can put down the monkey wrench now.

Old-growth: Forest that has never been cleared by human beings, also known as "virgin" forest.

Ovary: The area that produces the ovules, or eggs, in a flower.

Oppositely arranged: When leaves appear in pairs on a twig.

Palmate: Leaflets arranged like your fingers around your palm, which is to say, palmately.

Phloem: "Phloem? I barely even know 'em!" Love that old botanists' joke. Phloem is important stuff, folks: it's the structural cells and tubes that transport carbohydrates made in photosynthesis from the leaves down to the roots.

Photosynthesis: Another word on "Mitnick's Infamous List of Trauma-inducing Middle School Words and Phrases": photosynthesis is the single most important biological process that takes place on planet Earth. It's a simple equation, at least how it's understood in trees: Sunlight, water, and carbon dioxide go in, and carbohydrates in the form of sugars and starches, and oxygen (*ever heard of it*?) come out. The carbohydrates travel down the phloem from the leaves and into the roots of the tree. It allows the tree to grow, nutrients to return to the soil, and you and I to smoke the finest ganja I mean take a breath of Earth's wonderful air.

Phytotoxic: Anything that is poisonous to plants. And for the purposes of this book, trees.

Pinnate: A leaf made of rows of leaves.

Pinophyta: This is the division, or phylum, to which conifers belong.

Pith: Hamlet's chosen word for "importance" (III.i.94). But for the purposes of this book, the sometimes spongy center of a tree's trunk, populated by water transporting xylem cells.

Pollen cone: The male cone in conifers, which is a fragile, fragile collection of sacs that release pollen and go to pieces at the smallest challenge to their structural nature. Typical male.

Pyriscence: the tendency of seed cones to release their seeds when exposed to the heat of a fire.

Ray: The element of a tree's trunk that transports materials inwards toward the pith.

Resin: Hardened, concentrated sap that is icky, sticky, and maybe even "zlicky" (if you don't know, don't ask). Often used interchangeably with "pitch."

Roots: A combination of water- and nutrient-absorbing "root hairs" and subterranean structural wood that keep a tree upright and hydrated.

Sap: Mineral-filled fluid that travels throughout a plant. Similar to Smartwater, but often even smarter.

Sapwood: The material surrounding the heartwood, made up of living tissue that produces a softer wood. It contains the xylem and phloem structures for transporting water and sap. Also, the loser in the name war versus "heartwood."

Serotinous: When trees retain their seeds, only to be dispersed at a later time by fire (pyriscence) or another external event. An easy "twenty-something kid that still lives at home" analogy is available to you here.

Shrub: A small, woody plant.

Simple leaf: A leaf appearing singly on a leafstalk.

Stamen: The male reproductive organ in a flower, where the "anther" produces pollen cells, which contain sperm cells.

Stomata: Gas-exchanging pores on leaves.

Terminus: The growth occurring at the end of a stem or leafstalk.

Toothed: A leaf with serrations. Yes, sir, you'll find these bread knives of nature on trees from elm to birch and back again!

Transpiration: The flow of water from the roots, up the trunk, and out of the leaves.

Variegated: A word that sounds like I just made it up. I did not. It means "a leaf green in some areas and not in others."

Witches' brooms: The common name for the nightmarish balls of dense, spiky growth within a tree's branches that can be caused by any number of pathogens.

Xylem: The cells that transport water and nutrients. Also, the obvious choice for a tree-centered nightclub name.

References and Further Reading

Much of this book was a product of reflection on years of accumulated knowledge. This was attained primarily through books, which are still my favorite resources on the natural world, but there are a few websites that I've found indispensable for the tree identification necessary in part three, such as the *Gymnosperm Database*. While my primary sources for part three were *The Sibley Guide to Trees, Identifying Trees of the East*, *A Californian's Guide to the Trees Among Us*, *Conifers of California*, and *Audubon's Trees of North America*, many other works came into play for the purposes of further exploration. I've included below all books and websites cracked open even once for the composition of this book, and to show that I'm a very serious person.

Adams, Peter. *Bonsai with Japanese Maples.* Timber Press, 2006.

A Gallery of Trees: Living Art of the Pacific Bonsai Museum. Pacific Bonsai Museum, 2020.

Anderson, John Wesley. *Native American Prayer Trees of Colorado.* Circle Star Publishing, 2018.

Burnie, David. *Eyewitness: Tree.* Penguin Random House, 1988.

Chan, Peter. *The Bonsai Beginner's Bible.* Hachette Book Group, 2018.

Chekhov, Anton. *The Works of Chekhov.* Edited by Walter J. Black. Black's Readers Service Company, 1929.

Chekhov, Anton. *The Plays of Anton Chekhov.* Translated by Paul Schmidt. HarperPerennial, 1999.

Chekhov, Anton. *Fifty-Two Stories.* Translated by Richard Pevar and Larissa Volokhonsky. Vintage Books, 2020.

Chester, Tom and Jane Strong. "Plants of Southern California: *Pinus jeffreyi* and *P. ponderosa var. pacifica*". 3 August 2022, http://http://tchester.org/plants/analysis/pinus/jeffreyi_ponderosa.html.

Cirigliano, Jim, ed. *National Audubon Society, Trees of North America.* Alfred A. Knopf, 2021.

Cook, Diane and Len Jenshel. *Wise Trees.* Abrams, 2017.

Darwin, Charles. *Charles Darwin's Beagle Diary (1831–1836).* EZ Reads, 2009.

Dickinson, Emily. *The Complete Poems of Emily Dickinson.* Edited by Thomas H. Johnson. Little, Brown and Company, 1955.

Dupuich, Jonas. *The Little Book of Bonsai: An Easy Guide to Caring for Your Bonsai Tree.* Ten Speed Press, 2020.

Earle, Christopher J. *The Gymnosperm Database,* 3 August 2022, https://www.conifers.org.

Ennos, Roland. *The Age of Wood.* Scribner, 2020.

Freinkel, Susan. *American Chestnut: The Life, Death, and Rebirth of a Perfect Tree.* University Of California Press, 2007.

Hagedorn, Michael. *Bonsai Heresy.* Crataegus Books, 2020.

Hiltz, Will. *Gnarly Branches, Ancient Trees: The Life and Works of Dan Robinson – Bonsai Pioneer.* Nara Press, 2010.

Keats, John. *Complete Poems and Selected Letters of John Keats.* The Modern Library, 2001.

Kellerhals, Jerome and Mariannjely Marval. *Freestyle Bonsai.* The Quarto Group, 2022.

"Krugiodendron ferreum." *Atlas of Florida Plants,* 3 August 2022, https://florida.plantatlas.usf.edu/plant.aspx?id=3386.

"Krugiodendron ferreum." *Florida Native Plant Society,* 3 August 2022, https://www.fnps.org/plant/krugiodendron-ferreum.

Kurlansky, Mark. *Paper.* W.W. Norton & Company, 2016.

Lanner, Ronald M. *The Bristlecone Book: A Natural History of the World's Oldest Trees.* Mountain Press Publishing Company, 2007.

Lanner, Ronald M. *Conifers of California.* Cachuma Press, 1999.

Lanner, Ronald M. *The Piñon Pine: A Natural and Cultural History*. University of Nevada Press, 1981.

Lanner, Ronald M. *Trees of the Great Basin: A Natural History*. University of Nevada Press, 1984.

Leonardi, Cesare and Franca Stagi. *The Architecture of Trees*. Princeton Architectural Press, 2019.

Little, Elbert L. *National Audubon Society Field Guide to North American Trees, Eastern Edition*. 1980. Alfred A. Knopf, 2020.

Little, Elbert L. *National Audubon Society Field Guide to North American Trees, Western Edition*. 1980. Alfred A. Knopf, 2020.

Marshall, Bob. *Bob Marshall in the Adirondacks*. Edited by Phil Brown. Lost Pond Press, 2006.

Meier, Eric. "Black Ironwood." *The Wood Database*, 3 August 2022, https://www.wood-database.com/black-ironwood/.

Miller, Lulu. *Why Fish Don't Exist*. Simon and Schuster Paperbacks, 2020.

Mills, James Edward. *The Adventure Gap: Changing the Face of the Outdoors*. Mountaineers Books, 2014.

Moon, Beth. *Ancient Trees: Portraits of Time*. Abbeville Press, 2014.

Naka, John Yoshio. *Bonsai Techniques*. Dennis Landman Publishers, 1973.

Nisbet, Jack. *The Collector: David Douglas and the Natural History of the Northwest*. Sasquatch Books, 2009.

Norman, Ken. *The Complete Practical Encyclopedia of Bonsai*. Lorenz Books, 2019.

Qingquan, Zhao. *Penjing: The Chinese Art of Bonsai*. Better Link Press, 2012.

Orlean, Susan. "The Tallest Known Tree in New York Falls in the Forest." *The New Yorker,* 18 January 2022. https://www.newyorker.com/news/afterword/the-tallest-known-tree-in-new-york-falls-in-the-forest.

Oliver, Mary. *New and Selected Poems*. Beacon Press, 1992.

Pearce, Fred. *A Trillion Trees*. Greystone Books, 2021.

Petroski, Henry. *The Toothpick: Technology and Culture*. Vintage Books, 2007.

Petroski, Henry. *The Pencil: A History of Design and Circumstance*. Alfred A. Knopf, 2020.

"Pinus oocarpa." *American Conifer Society,* 3 August 2022, https://conifersociety.org/conifers/pinus-oocarpa/.

Powers, Richard. *The Overstory*. W.W. Norton & Company, 2018.

Ritter, Matt. *A Californian's Guide to the Trees Among Us*. Heyday, 2011.

Shelley, Mary. *Frankenstein,* 1818. Bantam Books, 1981.

Sibley, David Allen. *The Sibley Guide to Trees*. Alfred A. Knopf, 2009.

Simard, Suzanne. *Finding the Mother Tree*. Alfred A. Knopf, 2021.

Sussman, Rachel. *The Oldest Living Things in the World*. The University of Chicago Press, 2014.

Tekiela, Stan. *Birds of California Field Guide*. Adventure Publications, 2003.

The Tree Book: the Stories, Science, and History of Trees. Edited by the Smithsonian Institution. Penguin Random House, 2022.

Tolkien, J.R.R. *The Fellowship of the Ring*. Houghton Mifflin Company, 1987.

Tolkien, J.R.R. *The Silmarillion*. Edited by Christopher Tolkien. Houghton Mifflin Harcourt, 2001.

Tomlinson, Harry. *The Complete Book of Bonsai*. Abbeville Press, 1990.

Tudge, Colin. *The Tree*. Three Rivers Press, 2005.

White, Fred D., ed. *Essential Muir: A Selection of John Muir's Best (and Worst) Writings*. Heyday, 2021.

Williams, Michael D. *Identifying Trees of the East*. Stackpole Books, 2017.

Wohlleben, Peter. *The Hidden Life of Trees: The Illustrated Edition*. Translated by Jane Billinghurst. Greystone Books, 2018.

Acknowledgments

This silly book about trees was a remarkably rapid labor of love, and I never would have thought it possible without the initial contact, encouragement, and support from Rage Kindelsperger at Quarto. Thank you also to my editor, Keyla Pizarro-Hernández, without whom this book would be like a collection of TikTok transcripts written on the back of Hershey's Bar wrappers. To everyone else at Quarto who helped shepherd this book across the finish line, Todd Conly, Laura Drew, Cara Donaldson, Evelin Kasikov— thank you. Also, thank you to Trey Conrad for his beautiful illustrations.

To my remarkable manager, Carly Hoogendyk at Artists First, whose tireless efforts in helping me to connect my dissonant dots finally appear to be paying off, thank you. You have believed in me from the start. Thank you also to Ben Sanders, who gave indispensable advice to a first-time author. And to Josh Sandler, who helped realize this book, and Rick and Alex Ferrari, Elysia Wong, and Everett Champion, thank you, thank you, thank you.

I've had a great many tree-loving friends these past few years who I've known only on the internet, but, on the rare occasion that I meet one in person, I'm reminded that real life is where the magic happens. So many of them have helped foster ideas for this book: Casey Clapp, Alex Crowson, Justin Davies, No'a Bat Miri, Philissa Cramer, Max Falkowitz, Shelly Svoboda, and countless others. Thank you to the innumerable inspiring dendrologists and tree-lovers whose work I have devoured and loudly regurgitated these past few years.

And to my regular friends, none of whom are regular but are each wonderful and special for a thousand reasons, the very least of which is their support for my interests and this book: Jeff Schwartz, Sarah Dooley, Tace Joelle Loeb, Miriam Goldblum, Michael Snyder (for your coining of "proof"), Phil Primason, Grace Parra, among so many others. And to Lesly Kahn and the members of her Monday night class who once said, "Tobin, you should just talk about trees online," and I said, "Okay," and it worked.

Thank you to my entire family, who know that my human functionality is contingent upon active pursuit of my passions, and especially to Carver Karaszewski, who told me to put my "tree series" on TikTok, and to Flora Sahlman, who helped me crack the concept for part three. To Ethan, Ali, Delaney, Johnny, Ellen, Eben, Martine, Heath, Oren, Asa, Emery, Sue, Laura, Kit, Evelyn, Henry, Carla, Larry, Emily, Jack, Elizabeth, Ella, Olivia, Peter, Will, Adrienne, Oliver, Sebastian, Reed, Xavier, and McFly. You are the core of who I am, and not a day goes by that I don't learn something new from each of you.

Teachers come in many forms. I need to acknowledge these special people from the earliest days of nursery school, through middle-school life science, through college neuroscience, through now, where I regularly consume their brilliance through the magic of the internet. Special thanks to Master Roy Nagatoshi at Fuji Bonsai Nursery and Frank Sager, whose passion for teaching the beauty of all living things helped me to understand at an early age the meaning of mitzvot.

Thanks to Eli Grober and Tom Suberman, who helped me get my head on straight enough to write at all.

Thank you to the followers of @jewslovetrees, which I am proud to say is a tiny bright spot on the internet made up of those who love laughing while learning about stuff and delighting in weirdness. I have learned so much from each of you, and you all remind me that a tiny observation in a far-off place can change someone's entire world.

To Maria Suyapa Banegas, whose kindness lives through my daughter.

To Michael Molina, my fellow conqueror of mountains and valleys and fellow lamenter of "mean bees."

To my father, Paul Mitnick, whose every pursuit, from pine cone to woodwork, lets me know where I come from. And to my mother, Gail Delfin, whose every word serves to unleash the potential magic in her children's lives. I love you both.

Amanda and Lucy: it is the greatest thrill of my life to have words fail me at every turn.

About the Author

Tobin Mitnick is a writer and actor. He created the social media account @jewslovetrees in order to combine his love of comedy and trees. Currently, @jewslovetrees has nearly half a million followers across all platforms and has appeared on WIRED's list of the Best TikToks of 2020 along with receiving an honorable mention in the Webby Award's "Weird" category. He hosts the annual TREEMY awards for trees in film and television. Mitnick has also appeared in film, television, and on stage and has written and performed in solo shows and sketch comedy pilots. He is an avid runner, bonsai artist, and husband to Amanda and father to Lucy. He lives in Los Angeles.